First reading for every person who is seriously concerned over the strength and quality of public education as related to the future of our nation.

Whoever you are . . .

- a school board member, directing the schools . . .

- an administrator or teacher, operating the schools . . .

- the parent of a school child . . .

- a taxpayer and voter, supporting the schools . . .

- a community leader, seeking school improvement . . .

- a high school student, studying Local School Government as an integral part of American Government . . .

- an education student, preparing for professional service . . .

Whatever your role: This dynamic, practical, forward-looking book is for you!

Ten thousand (10,000) copies of the First Edition (1958-1963) firmly established the book's reputation as a basic source of "information, ideas, ideals, inspiration, and enlightenment." This Revised Edition should be even more helpful to you now.

Local and state boards of education occupy *key positions* in our American system of universal public education.

SCHOOL BOARD LEADERSHIP IN AMERICA will help you to choose board members wisely and to serve with distinction if you are chosen.

SCHOOL BOARD LEADERSHIP IN AMERICA

Policy Making in Public Education

by EDWARD MOWBRAY TUTTLE
First Executive Secretary of the
National School Boards Association, Inc.

Revised Edition

CHICAGO and DANVILLE, ILLINOIS

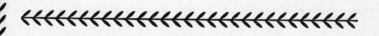

Manufactured in the United States of America
by THE INTERSTATE Printers and Publishers, Danville, Ill.

DEDICATED TO

those countless thousands of

public spirited men and women who voluntarily

have served,

are at present serving,

and will serve in years to come

on the school boards of American communities.

They it is who must inspire

the American people to keep our public schools

free and strong

so that

our beloved Nation may be kept strong and free!

A Child

A child am I, yet in me lies
   Part of the future of the race;
A child, in whom the good and ill
   Of ages past have left their trace.

* * *

Protect me now, that I may keep
   The Flag of Freedom floating high;
Protect me, that the altar fires
   Of Truth and Justice may not die.

* * *

Protect me, ye of larger growth,
   Hear my appeal; please take my hand
And lead me safely through the days
   Of childhood into Grown-up Land.

— OLIVE G. BROWN

CONTENTS

PART I – WITH THE LOCAL SCHOOL BOARD

PART II – AMONG SCHOOL BOARDS ASSOCIATIONS

CONTENTS (continued)

IDEALS TO LIVE BY

Interspersed between the chapters of this book are brief statements of ideals, based on famous quotations, as follows:

PROFESSIONAL RESPONSIBILITY

"Every man owes some of his time to the upbuilding of the profession to which he belongs."

—THEODORE ROOSEVELT

We may think of "Teddy" Roosevelt's use of the word "profession" to mean any honorable calling, occupation, vocation, or avocation to which a person devotes himself. Each such profession has a status or stature of its own resulting from the accumulated contributions of those who have followed it through the years. By his efforts, each follower of the profession consciously or unconsciously builds it up a little or tears it down a little. If he does nothing deliberately to build it up, the chances are that his participation will be self-centered and his contribution negative. It is challenging to think of school board membership as a profession whose stature in the public eye is a direct reflection of the altruism of its practitioners. State and national associations give board members opportunities to devote some of their time to advancing the standards of school boards service throughout the length and breadth of our land. — E. M. T.

INTRODUCTION
to the Revised Edition

It is exactly five years since I wrote the Introduction to the First Edition of SCHOOL BOARD LEADERSHIP IN AMERICA with high hopes that the book would "prove its usefulness as a contribution to the advancement of public education in America."

Those hopes have been fulfilled. Ten thousand (10,000) copies are in use in some 3,500 school districts throughout the country, and over 500 of these districts provide personal copies for the individual members of their boards to "keep handy" for study and reference.

Board members, school administrators, and educational leaders in institutions and organizations testify that SCHOOL BOARD LEADERSHIP IN AMERICA provides them with "information, ideas, ideals, inspiration, and enlightenment." "The philosophy, concepts, and policies outlined in the book" offer "the basis for understanding the statesmanlike role of school board membership." It is "most valuable in the orientation of new board members," helping each one "to get off on the right foot" and "to keep him on the beam."

So much for a good beginning! Now my hope is that SCHOOL BOARD LEADERSHIP IN AMERICA may render enduring service in an ever increasing number of school communities for years beyond my own lifetime. To that end, I have made numerous changes in this Revised Edition, all designed to strengthen the book's permanent appeal and usefulness.

To Part I, I have added two new chapters on "Some Principles of School Board Status, Organization, and Procedure" and on "School Crises—Reasons and Remedies." The chapter on "School Boards and School Finance" has been completely revamped, and changes have been made in other chapters, especially a new section on *"Board Relations with Teachers Organizations"* in the chapter on "School Boards and School Teachers."

In Part II, the chapters on the growth, financing, staffing, services, legislative relationships, and work-type meetings of State School Boards Associations should, if anything, be more useful than ever as the movement continues to grow in strength and influence. I have condensed the chapters on the National School Boards Association about one-third in order to make room for the new material in Parts I and III. Much of this text in the First Edition was of an historical and statistical character, no longer of such immediate significance. Those readers who, for any reason, wish to refer to the early N.S.B.A. story will, undoubtedly, be able to locate one of the 10,000 copies which went into service in school districts, colleges, universities, and libraries.

To Part III, I have added a chapter on "The Challenge to Local Control of Public Education" in the hope that the suggestions offered may help to provide an effective antidote to further efforts to nationalize the control of public education in America. Thoughtful readers will find in the three chapters in this final section of the book challenges of enormous importance to the continued freedom and strength of our public schools, and hence to the strength and freedom of our beloved Nation.

In the Appendices, the substitution for older material of the "Outline for a Ten-Session Workshop Study of School Board Functions and Relationships" will, I believe, prove to be one of the most useful features of the Revised Edition.

My warmest thanks go to all those users of the First Edition of SCHOOL BOARD LEADERSHIP IN AMERICA who took the time to express their appreciation and to offer comments and suggestions. Only another author can understand fully how much this has meant to me.

EDWARD MOWBRAY TUTTLE

August 1, 1963

INTRODUCTION
to the First Edition

It has been said with truth that here in America no greater honor can be conferred upon a man or woman by a community than selection as a member of the local school board.

Because that honor has come or may come to you, or to someone in close relationship to you, this book should be of interest and value. It is designed to help you to a broader outlook, to greater depth of understanding, and to added inspiration for distinguished service to American public education.

SCHOOL BOARD LEADERSHIP IN AMERICA is concerned primarily with attitudes and ideals, with principles and standards. It is not the usual type of book intended to acquaint school board members with the facts of school board functions, organization, and procedures. (For books and pamphlets of that kind, see the Bibliography, pages 283-87.)

This volume is arranged in three parts. The first seventeen chapters, in Part I, deal with various aspects of the services of the local school board. Part II is devoted to school boards associations (seven chapters on state associations and five on the national association). Nowhere else in print is this background information available. Two concluding chapters, in Part III, present the challenge we all face to strengthen our system of universal, free, public education as the safeguard of democracy.

In writing this book, I have had constantly before me you who will read it—board members of much or little experience, past, present, and future; administrators, teachers, parents, and citizens who come in contact with school boards; leaders of educational and lay groups working to improve our educational system; students everywhere who are seeking to understand better the significance of boards of education in our American way of life and the responsibilities they bear for effective service.

11

It is my earnest hope that in the chapters of this book all of you may find some help and inspiration. The ideals and standards set forth are not impossible of attainment, though I admit they are easier to write about than to carry out. But they are worth striving towards, and in proportion as they can be attained—board by board, member by member, citizen by citizen, here, there, and everywhere—will public education in America grow in strength and effectiveness to accomplish its great purpose of insuring the future of this nation and peace and prosperity throughout the world.

I am deeply indebted to the host of school board leaders and friends throughout the land who have helped and encouraged me in the writing of this book. It is impossible to name them all, but a few deserve special mention. To Mr. William C. Bruce and the Bruce Publishing Company of Milwaukee, my thanks and appreciation for permission to use any or all of my material originally published in *The American School Board Journal.* My successor as the N.S.B.A. executive, Mr. W. A. Shannon, reviewed and helped me with the manuscript. Dr. Robert R. Fosket, friend and former board member, listened to each chapter read aloud and discussed it with me most constructively. Miss Olga Evanoff, teacher and secretary, copied the entire manuscript and checked it with me point by point. And finally, it is safe to say that the book would never have been written had not my oldest and youngest sisters, Mrs. Nellie Tuttle Dehmer and Mrs. Aletta Tuttle Ramsay, both of Long Island, N. Y., supplied me for weeks with an ideal refuge where I could work without the interruptions of my usual sphere of activity.

So SCHOOL BOARD LEADERSHIP IN AMERICA has at last come into being. It must now speak for itself and prove its usefulness as a contribution to the advancement of public education in America.

EDWARD MOWBRAY TUTTLE

August 1, 1958

PART I

WITH THE
LOCAL SCHOOL BOARD

THE NATION'S STRENGTH

"A nation is as great, and only as great, as her rank and file."

— WOODROW WILSON

Leadership alone does not make a nation great. The level of intelligence, moral fiber, cultural development, and civic responsibility of the people as a whole is the determining factor. This is why the true democracies are fundamentally strong; it is why totalitarian governments are inherently weak, no matter how much temporary strength they may appear to attain. It is also the basic reason for supporting a universal system of free public education, designed to provide the opportunity for every person —young or old; rich or poor; brilliant, average, or handicapped—to reach his own highest development. In proportion as we strive toward this goal, America will grow in greatness. — E. M. T.

CHAPTER 1

School Boards and the Future of America

O ur American system of public education may be likened to a great mosaic picture made up of thousands of separate pieces.

These pieces represent the local school districts which are established under state authority.

Each district has its board of education made up of citizens from all walks of life who render their service on the school board largely on a voluntary basis.

The districts vary greatly in size from small rural schools which have only one teacher and a few pupils, to our big metropolitan centers where a single board of education establishes the policies for hundreds of schools and employs an administrative staff and thousands of teachers serving several hundred thousand pupils and various segments of the adult population as well.

Nowhere else in the world is there such a system of educational control, and it is safe to say that our public schools function as they do because their direction is the kind it is—of the people, by the people, and for the people, like our government itself!

We believe in our American plan for local and state control of public education by non-partisan, non-salaried, lay boards of education, rather than in a centralized national professional control such as exists in most other countries of the world (see Appendix B, "Boards of Education—American Plan," page 288).

We feel that our system keeps the schools close to the people and makes it possible to provide those variations in the school program which will best fit the needs of each district.

But there is no denying that such a system increases the difficulty of fitting all these pieces together so that we can obtain a clear view of our mosaic picture of public education in this country—what it is seeking to accomplish, how it is organized and operated, how it is housed and staffed and paid for, and how the people of America as a whole regard and support and defend their public schools.

The picture becomes clearer when each piece of the mosaic —each school district—is made as nearly perfect as possible in its own local setting, and when it fits properly into relationship with all the other districts that go to make up the system of American public education.

It is challenging to believe, therefore, that every member of a school board anywhere in this country bears a responsibility and shares an opportunity extending far beyond the limits of his own district's jurisdiction.

Why is this so?

Because, for one reason, our population is extremely mobile in these days of rapid transportation and communication. Ask any audience or group of people how many are at present living and working in the community where they went to school and you will have the answer.

The graduates of nearly every school system scatter to the far corners of the nation, and in turn each community adds to its citizenry those who have received their education in numerous other places.

It follows, then, that a poor or weak school system anywhere in the nation tends, over the years, to lower the level of the public welfare in many places.

Conversely, a strong, effective school system anywhere is an asset, not only to its own community, but to every community to which its graduates go and, hence, to the future of America.

Would that every school board member as he attends his local board meetings could keep this wider vision of the national interest clearly before him.

School Boards and the Future of America

True, he and his fellow board members have to consider for immediate disposal many routine details that vary only slightly from meeting to meeting.

But always there is before the board this greater challenge which is far from routine—to establish and maintain a public school system which will provide opportunity for each child, each youth, and each adult to develop his potentialities to their utmost and to become a citizen of maximum value to his community, state, and nation.

In other words, while maintaining the diversity and local adaptability of our public school system, we face the necessity of demonstrating its total impact on the states and on the nation in ways which will reveal to all our people the nature, the extent, the cost, and the accomplishments of this great instrument for perpetuating and perfecting our American way of life.

The future of America is directly dependent upon the quality of its citizenry, which, in the long run, is determined by the quality of the education they receive in the public schools for whose operation school boards are legally responsible.

Every board member who recognizes the extent of his responsibility also recognizes that he needs every possible aid to increased effectiveness.

No matter how extensive a member's experience may be in other lines, he cannot render his best service to his school board and to the community it represents without taking time to understand the purposes, practices, problems, and potentialities of the public schools as a factor of vital importance to the life and future of America.

> "Next in importance to freedom
> and justice is popular education,
> without which neither freedom nor justice
> can be permanently maintained."
> — JAMES A. GARFIELD

17

TARGET

"Make no little plans; they have no magic to stir men's blood . . . Make big plans; aim high in hope and work."
— DANIEL H. BURNHAM

The time has come when, with respect to education, we need to follow the advice given by Chicago's late great civic planner. We are not aiming high enough in our hopes or in our work for the schools. Our plans are not big enough to develop our educational program on a par with our educational needs in the difficult and dangerous times in which we live. We constantly try to make choices between one desirable objective and another, instead of lifting our sights toward the goal of a working plan which will include all the desirables and provide for every child, youth, and adult the fullest opportunity to grow and develop according to his individual capacity. Nothing less will suffice if this nation is to survive and prosper. — E. M. T.

CHAPTER 2

Board Members as

Educational Statesmen

Effective service of board members and school boards depends upon a breadth of understanding far beyond the confines of the local communities which they represent.

Only as board members have knowledge of the functioning of public education throughout the state and nation can they adopt policies wisely adapted to the needs of their own communities.

And, as we have seen in Chapter 1, only as the local school systems are built up to the highest level of effectiveness can they contribute as they should to the total impact of public education upon the future welfare of America and of the world.

It is both a challenge and a responsibility that individual board members shall possess the highest qualities of character and statesmanship.

The dictionary defines a statesman as a person "skilled in government and public affairs." But there are some persons so skilled whom we would hardly call statesmen.

Other qualities enter into what most of us have in mind when we speak of statesmanship. Among these are

> a subordination of personal ambition to the public welfare;
>
> wise judgment and sound discretion in the exercise of powers;
>
> true foresight conditioned by breadth of view;

19

unusual ability in promoting effective cooperation among all who must work together; and

a genuine faith in the people as the sovereign authority in our representative democracy.

To the above we must add, in the field of educational statesmanship, an unqualified belief in a system of universal public education which shall provide opportunity for every child, youth, and adult in the nation—wherever he may live and whoever he may be—to attain the fullest development of his individual potentiality for worthy citizenship with all that this implies.

Belief in Public Education

We have to face the fact, unbelievable as it may seem, that there are some people in this country, enjoying the full benefits of all the freedoms and opportunities of American citizenship, who do not believe in their hearts that every other citizen should have rights and privileges equal to their own.

These people think in terms of lower and higher orders of society, always including themselves, of course, in the higher classification with attendant special privileges.

These people feel it would be dangerous to give every American all the education he can profitably absorb, and the kind of education best suited to his individual needs, abilities, and aptitudes.

Least of all would these people agree that such education for all should be provided at public expense—at their expense.

Such people are living denials of the very democracy in which they dwell and which they pretend to uphold.

It is vitally important to the general welfare that persons of the kind described above do *not* become members of public school boards of education.

The presence upon a board of even one member who does not subscribe wholeheartedly to the basic tenets inherent in the American system of universal public education is an anomalous handicap to united and effective action by the board in behalf of its total community.

First of all, then, let it be certain that men and women selected to be members of school boards believe in public education for all without reservation, and are ready to work unremittingly to defend and support it in the fullest measure which their communities can be led to demand.

Devotion to the Public Interest

The first quality of statesmanship set forth above was "a subordination of personal ambition to the public welfare."

This quality applies with unmistakable clearness to the educational statesmen needed as school board members.

Each member must represent impartially *all* the people of the community.

Each must perform his service as a board member without bias of any kind in favor of his own interest or the interest of any restricted area or segment of the population.

Only when every member of a board of education approaches his task in this spirit can there be the harmony of discussion and the unity of action which are essential to effective service to the total public.

The consideration just stated is the chief reason why the control of public education should be completely divorced from the partisanship usually connected with the administration of other governmental affairs—possibly excepting the judiciary.

It is also the basic argument for the non-political selection of board members, and for the allocation to the board of complete freedom in the conduct and control of school affairs (see Chapter 5, point 6, pages 45-6).

Sound Judgment and Discretion

The educational statesman is a person not subject to whims, undue influence, or the making of snap decisions.

His mind is open on every question until the evidence is all in his possession.

He insists on facts—all the facts—and reaches his decisions

21

on the basis of the facts, not on the basis of his own or anyone else's unsupported opinions, prejudices, or guesswork.

He knows when to call upon experts for assistance, and he carefully studies their recommendations.

On the record, his decisions with regard to school board policy prove to be sound.

Boards of education, as we know, are created by the state and are first of all responsible for carrying out such requirements concerning the public schools as are embodied in state law.

Nevertheless school boards all enjoy, to a greater or lesser extent, wide discretionary powers with respect to the operation of their local schools.

Did boards not have such discretion, it would be impossible to adapt the educational program closely to the needs of individual communities which we Americans insist is one of the greatest strengths of our system of decentralized control.

It follows that the individual board member, working with his fellow board members, carries an unusual measure of responsibility in his job of policy making and needs statesmanlike qualities of discretion and good judgment in order to discharge that responsibility acceptably.

Foresight and Breadth of View

Of all the qualities which distinguish the statesman from the average man, this one of breadth and vision is the rarest and of greatest importance.

Most of us tend to be too narrow, too provincial in our outlook. Our beliefs and actions are chiefly conditioned by the little world around us.

We tend to follow rigid patterns that we have fallen into by habit. Our ability to adjust readily to change seems to be quite limited.

We are prone to be guided by the needs of the moment and to give little considered thought to the future.

But education deals in futures. It is always looking ahead. It

Board Members as Educational Statesmen

must be adapted to changing conditions and needs. Those who enjoy its benefits will be applying their added resourcefulness in time to come.

Years may pass before a determination can be made by individuals as to how well their education fitted them for living and making a living as citizens of America.

Very often it will happen that individuals of every age will feel the need for further study, and the opportunity should be open to them. This idea is at the root of all adult, or continuing, education which is more and more becoming a part of our public school program. It, too, builds for the future.

In every community there are men and women whose background is broader and whose adaptability is greater than the average described above; men and women who are able to "aim high" and to "make big plans"; men and women who are flexible in their attitude toward change.

Such people are needed on our boards of education. They qualify as educational statesmen.

Skill in Working Relationships

Boards of education, as we know, are policy-making bodies.

Properly functioning boards do not administer the schools themselves.

Board policies are put into operation by the school staff composed of the superintendent and his assistants, the teachers, and non-teaching workers of many kinds.

The board is dependent upon the competency and good will of its employees, which presupposes harmonious working relationships that the board must consistently seek to establish and maintain throughout the system.

The keys to effectiveness in these relationships are two-fold:

First, the recognition of school personnel as human beings with the hopes and aspirations, the doubts and fears, the abilities and handicaps, common to us all (see Chapters 14 and 15).

23

Second, the enlistment of school personnel participation in those phases of policy formation and policy administration with which they are directly concerned (see Chapter 6).

Board members who are educational statesmen understand the importance of welding everyone in the school system into a smooth working team with a sense of loyalty to the administrator, the board, and the community.

Faith in the People

Equal in importance to effective working relationships within the school system are the relationships between the schools and the people of the community, which the school board is in a key position to promote (see Chapter 16).

These "public relations" offer one of the most fertile fields for cultivation by the educational statesman and one that has been too often neglected.

Unfortunately there are some school boards and some school administrators who argue that it is their job to run the schools without any "interference," and that the less the public knows about school affairs the better for all concerned.

This argument is unsound, and school authorities following such a pattern of public disregard are heading for certain trouble sooner or later.

More and more, boards with a statesmanlike attitude toward their responsibilities are operating on the assumption that the community should be fully informed at all times concerning its schools.

More boards now believe that, in proportion as the people understand school problems, their advice, assistance, and support will greatly strengthen the hands of the board in discharging its responsibilities.

So, board meetings are open to the public and to the press, and representative committees of citizens are actively involved in studying school conditions and in offering recommendations for consideration by the board (see Chapter 17).

Board Members as Educational Statesmen

School Board Statesmanship on State and National Levels

As the collective voice of school boards becomes a more potent factor in educational progress in this country, there is increasing need that board members possessing those qualities of educational statesmanship described above shall occupy positions of leadership.

Associations of school boards in every state are steadily growing in strength and in service not only to their local member boards but to the development of statewide educational programs (see Chapters 20 and 21).

In the same spirit, the National School Boards Association is serving its affiliated state associations and is contributing to educational advancement in the nation as a whole (see Chapter 27).

The leaders of these associations need, in conspicuous measure, to exhibit

> that belief in public education,
> that devotion to the public interest,
> that soundness of judgment,
> that breadth of view,
> that spirit of cooperation, and
> that faith in the people

which mark the true educational statesman.

> *"One who never turned his back,*
> *but marched breast forward,*
> *Never doubted clouds would break,*
> *Never dreamed, though right were worsted,*
> *wrong would triumph;*
> *Held, we fall to rise,*
> *are baffled to fight better,*
> *sleep to wake."*
>
> — ROBERT BROWNING

ENDURING VALUES

*"The great use of life is to spend it
for something which outlasts it."*

— WILLIAM JAMES

Persons are privileged who spend their lives building
something which will endure when they have passed
on. Perhaps parents and teachers come as close to
this goal as any. They live on in the lives of those
whose growth and development they help to guide
with love and devotion. But members of school
boards during their terms of service, whether brief
or extended, have the opportunity to use that part
of their lives in building something of value which
will outlast them. There is great satisfaction in knowing that one has contributed to advance an educational program and school facilities to new levels
of effectiveness and efficiency in the service of a
community. In the long run, better schools mean
better citizens for the future. They create enduring
human values and help us to guarantee "that government of the people, by the people, for the people,
shall not perish from the earth." — E. M. T.

CHAPTER 3

Leadership Responsibilities of School Board Members

School board members are called upon to exercise those qualities of leadership which time and again have raised America to new heights of effort and accomplishment.

A school system never stays at just the same level; it is either getting better or poorer.

The school board knows before anyone else which way the schools are going, and has the obligation of keeping the people aware of educational needs and opportunities in its community.

If we cherish our country and our freedom, this is the time to advance boldly to new positions of strength and service on the school front (see Chapter 32).

It is not enough simply to mark time or just try to "hold the line." "No man ever defended anything for long," said the late General George Patton. He meant that the way to win is to take the offensive.

In every local district the school board should be the head-quarters, the directing center, of a campaign for better schools— schools that will most effectively meet the needs of young and old for educational growth and development.

Seven Qualities of Leadership

Someone has listed seven qualities which a leader or a lead-ing group like a school board must possess. There may, of course, be other qualities that could be added, but all will agree that these seven are essential, and it is difficult to say which is more essential than another.

1. *Integrity*—that quality which attracts the confidence of others; dependability; uprightness; honesty; loyalty. To have integrity is to be incorruptible, sound, unwavering in principle. "You always know where he stands."

2. *Perseverance*—that quality which persists in the face of difficulties, which never acknowledges defeat, which keeps an eye on the goal and tries again and yet again to attain it. "The harder you're thrown, why, the higher you bounce."

3. *Faith*—an unfaltering belief that something better lies ahead; confidence in the ultimate triumph of right; an inner sense that problems arise to test us, not to thwart us; an "assurance of things hoped for, a conviction of things not seen."

4. *Ability to Plan*—that quality without which good will and good intentions go for nought; knowledge of the facts; judgment as to relative importance; mastery of the job; skill in organizing to accomplish a purpose; efficiency in coordinating the work of others "without showing off or showing them up."

5. *Vision*—that quality for lack of which "the people perish"; breadth of view; ability to see ahead and to plan not just for today, but for tomorrow and for another generation.

6. *Initiative*—ability to move ahead without waiting to be shoved; get-up-and-go; a self-starting force which wastes no time in setting about whatever needs to be done; willingness to "go where there is no path" and to "leave a trail" which will be a guide to the feet of those who follow.

7. *Courage*—inner strength to face whatever lies ahead, to march "breast forward," never turning back or whimpering at defeat; a resoluteness of spirit that is unconquerable; self-discipline of the highest order; pluck. "I knew thee strong and quiet like the hills."

Areas of School Board Leadership

Throughout this book there are numerous examples and suggestions of ways in which school board members may meet their leadership responsibilities. Suffice it here simply to catalog some of the most important of these areas:

Leadership Responsibilities of School Board Members

1. Work for harmony and a "team spirit" within the board itself (see Chapter 5, point 1).

2. Make certain that board policies are established in cooperation with all concerned, are clearly and simply written, are made available to the school staff and the community at large, and are kept currently up to date (see Chapter 6).

3. Maintain the strongest possible administrative and teaching staff at all costs (see Chapters 14 and 15).

4. Work for a curriculum (*what* the schools teach) which adequately meets the needs of the children, youth, and adults of your community in this present day (see Chapter 10).

5. Move steadily toward adequate housing and facilities for the school population, present and future (see Chapter 13).

6. Stand for generous financial support of public education, based on an equitable distribution of the tax burden, and efficient use of the tax dollar (see Chapters 11 and 12).

7. Encourage cooperative relationships between the school system and the community to the end that all the people may have all the facts all the time about their schools (see Chapters 16 and 17).

8. Take an interest in the advancement of public education on all levels of policy making—local, state, and national (see Chapter 25).

9. Support the development of a strong, active school boards association in each state and its affiliation with the National School Boards Association (see Chapters in Part II).

10. Be alert to conditions and influences in the school district which have in them "seeds of controversy," and take steps to resolve them before they precipitate a crisis (see Chapter 18).

11. Work unceasingly to advance the quality and effectiveness of the local educational program as the soundest answer to those who advocate national control of public education (see Chapter 32).

PERPETUITY

"You are not required to complete the task, neither are you permitted to lay it down."

— THE TALMUD

Nothing could express more precisely the responsibility borne by boards of education. It is demanding and unending. Meeting after meeting, a succession of board members must wrestle with the task of providing the best possible education for young and old in the communities they serve. They never complete the work, but step by step contribute to the more effective functioning of the schools. Nor can they sidestep or neglect the duty which their fellow citizens have delegated to them, and which the state declares is legally theirs alone to perform —a public service of the highest order that goes on and on through the generations and the years. — E. M. T.

CHAPTER 4

Some Principles of School Board

Status, Organization, and

Procedure

School Board procedures vary considerably from state to state in accordance with state laws and court decisions, and there is abundant guidance available from state departments of education and from state school boards associations to insure compliance with the law and an appropriate calendar of action by any school board.

However, there are certain underlying principles of school board status, organization, and procedure which it seems desirable to discuss briefly in this chapter.

School Board Status

A school board, although it is selected and functions locally, is in reality a legal agency of the state, from which it derives its authority on the basis of provisions in the state constitution, statutes in the law, and court decisions relating to schools.

Within the framework of the law, the board has power to develop the policies, rules, and regulations which shall control the operation of the schools in its district.

Subject only to the restrictions of the law, the board has, also, more or less discretionary power to reach decisions on many matters of school organization, sites, financing, equipment, staffing, attendance, curriculum, extra-curricular activities, and a host of other items connected with the day-to-day conduct of the schools under its jurisdiction.

The board is a continuing body, no matter how much or how often it changes in membership, and action once taken is binding until modified or rescinded by subsequent action.

The board is a corporate body and can take official action only in a duly called regular or special meeting.

To be legal a board's action must be a matter of formal record showing the roll-call vote on a motion properly made, seconded, discussed, and called for by the presiding officer.

A contract made by the board is enforceable until its terms have been fulfilled even though the entire membership of the board should be changed in the meantime.

An individual board member has no authority outside a meeting unless he has been expressly authorized by the board to act for it in some specific capacity.

As agencies of the state, most school boards are autonomous and have complete authority within their local districts. However, in some states, legislatures have given city, county, or other local agencies limited authority over school boards, with the result that the school districts are subject to a fiscal dependence which is usually far from desirable (see Chapter 5, page 45).

School Board Organization

Depending on state law, most school boards hold an organization meeting once a year or once in two years. Usually such a meeting follows closely the election or appointment of new members to the board.

At the organization meeting, new members are welcomed and sworn in, officers are elected, committees, if any, are appointed, regular meetings are scheduled for the year, and agreement is reached on bylaws governing order of business, motions, voting, and other parliamentary procedure.

Chairman, or President. In most cases the presiding officer is elected by the board from its membership. In some instances the board president is so designated at the time of election or appointment.

Election within the board should preferably be by secret ballot to permit complete freedom of choice and the avoidance of possible embarrassment to individuals.

The term *chairman* is perhaps a little more appropriate for a board of education than the term *president,* since the former more accurately describes his responsibilities while the latter may carry some hint of executive functions which belong rather to the superintendent of schools.

Many boards practice rotating the chairmanship among the members. Even though all may not be equally skillful in the chairmanship role, this has the advantage of developing maximum interest and responsibility among the board members.

A presiding officer too long in office, no matter how superior his qualifications, may come in time either to assume greater responsibility than he should or to look upon his leadership as more or less routine and perfunctory.

The chairman of the board has many functions in addition to those of each board member. He presides at all board meetings and must exercise tact and firmness to keep the discussion moving along constructive channels and to know when the moment has come for a decision.

Between meetings, the board chairman is more likely than other members to be called upon to answer questions and to represent the board and the district in community meetings of various kinds.

Vice-Chairman. Many school boards also elect a vice-chairman (or *vice-president*) at the organization meeting. He functions in the absence or at the request of the chairman and should be equally qualified in his knowledge of parliamentary procedure, in familiarity with the bylaws and policies of the board, in skill at welcoming visitors and delegations to board meetings, in courteous yet firm control of discussion and voting, and in conducting the meetings of the board at all times with propriety and decorum.

Secretary. Every school board should have a secretary, or *clerk,* but there are wide variations, depending upon law or custom, as to who is appointed to this position.

In some cases a member of the board is elected as secretary. In many districts, the superintendent of schools is the secretary of the board of education. In larger districts, an outside person is often appointed as board secretary.

If the superintendent or a board member acts as the secretary, he should have a stenographer to take notes and transcribe them, so that he may give his undivided attention and thought to the proceedings of the board.

The secretary can be of great assistance to the chairman during the course of board meetings, especially if a good many matters have to be handled expeditiously, by keeping track of action taken and to be taken, by having quickly available any references that may be called for, and by acting as a timekeeper to hold the meeting within agreed upon limits.

The secretary is the keeper of board minutes, records, and reports of all kinds, and of official documents that belong to the district—contracts, deeds, insurance policies, and the like.

The secretary prepares copies of materials needed by board members, reads in meetings communications addressed to the board, answers correspondence in the name of the board when authorized to do so, and in general carries on the paper work that is so necessary and important to the conduct of a public legal body controlling what is often the largest single enterprise in the community.

Treasurer. Since every school district is involved in the expenditure of a great deal of public money, it is important that someone should act as treasurer for the school board.

More often than not there are provisions in the school law of the state as to whom this person shall be, how he shall be selected and bonded, how receipts and expenditures shall be handled, what records shall be kept to provide the board with monthly statements and periodical financial audits, how investments shall be made and securities safeguarded, and how any and all fiscal transactions shall be conducted under the board's direction or subject to its approval.

Committees. A recent study of some 4,000 local boards in the larger school districts of the nation revealed that almost half of them used no committees at all, the full board acting as a whole on all problems.

Slightly over half of the boards that were studied made use of committees of either or both of two types—standing and special—functioning as their names would indicate.

The standing committee system dates back to the days before the general employment of superintendents of schools as administrative officers, when boards of education often had many members and attempted to exercise administrative control over the various phases of school operation.

Of late years, there has been a steady decline in the use of standing committees and the practice is not advocated by most authorities in school administration. The reasons for this are presented in the following chapter as one of the "Stumbling Blocks to School Board Effectiveness" (see page 44).

There are occasions that arise in school districts which require more study than the board as a whole feels warranted in giving them. In such cases a small temporary, or special, committee of the board may be appointed by the chairman to secure the facts and report them to the full board as a basis for discussion and action. Such a committee is discharged when its assigned task is completed.

Not to be confused with committees of the board itself are committees of citizens organized to assist the school board by making intensive and long-range studies of district conditions and needs, and presenting their findings and recommendations to the board for consideration. Such committees are discussed in Chapter 17.

Legal Counsel. Since much of the action taken by school boards is governed by state laws that seemingly grow more and more complex, a board frequently finds itself in need of legal advice and service.

Help can usually be had on interpretation of the law from the office of the state attorney general or from the legal staff of the state department of education. But there are always legal procedures at the local level which, for the board's own protection, should be guided by a practicing attorney.

Boards in large city districts commonly employ legal counsel on a regular basis, often requiring the services of more than one individual, full time. Under such conditions, the senior counsel usually attends the meetings of the board both to keep himself informed as to current board policy and to render advice during discussions of action involving legal procedures.

Most boards employ legal counsel when and as needed on an irregular basis. It is always advantageous if attorneys so employed have acquaintance and some experience with school law.

Frequently lawyers are members of boards of education and most of them are glad to extend their legal experience to board deliberations. But it is unwise and unfair for a board to take advantage of such a situation, especially in cases where much time or study is involved in rendering the required service.

School Board Procedure

A school board is the policy-making agency for its district. As a continuing body, with changing membership, it is highly important that board policy, developed and accumulated from recurring board meetings, shall be readily available in written form, kept currently up to date. Chapter 6 is entirely devoted to the subject of "School Board Policy Making."

Meetings. Since board action to be legal must be taken in duly called regular or special meetings of the full board, the matter of preparing for, conducting, recording, and reporting school board meetings should receive most careful attention. Subject only to state law in some instances, a board may determine many of these procedures for itself.

The number of board meetings held varies from once a month in smaller districts to once a week or even oftener in some of the larger cities. Of late years, there has been a definite trend for all school boards to devote at least half of their meeting time to study and evaluation of the educational program in contrast to time given to financial and business matters (see page 43 in Chapter 5 and all of Chapter 10 on "School Board Responsibility for the Curriculum").

School Board Status, Organization, and Procedure

Too often board meetings extend to undue length. Occasionally this cannot be avoided, but as a general rule a meeting should not last over two or three hours. Thorough advance preparation and skillful guidance by the presiding officer will contribute to make each meeting a satisfying experience both to board members and to visitors in attendance.

Under the best procedure, materials which are furnished to board members at least twenty-four hours in advance of a meeting will include (1) the meeting agenda, (2) minutes of the previous meeting, which should have been supplied immediately following that meeting, (3) a financial statement showing the current condition of district funds, (4) a list of bills payable, for board authorization, and (5) any background and supporting information which will contribute to an enlightened discussion of certain topics on the agenda.

Agenda for school board meetings are commonly prepared by the secretary after consultation with the chairman of the board and the superintendent of schools if the latter is not the secretary himself. The items of the agenda should follow the order of business established in the board's bylaws and should be numbered for quick reference.

Ordinarily the board meeting should follow the agenda in sequence although, of course, the board is free to change the order or to add new items by consensus. It is extremely inadvisable, however, for any matter to be brought up in a meeting without previous warning. Should such a circumstance arise, unless in a real emergency, the part of wisdom would dictate that the matter be tabled until a subsequent meeting in order to provide time for study and reflection by members of the board. This will avoid taking too hasty or ill-considered action which might later be regretted.

Since school board meetings should be open to the public, except for occasional executive sessions which should be held to a minimum (see page 44), provision should be made in the agenda for visitors to be welcomed by the chairman and written petitions to be received for subsequent consideration by the board. Preferably, these courtesies should come early in the

37

meeting and should be definitely limited in order neither to keep visitors waiting tediously nor to consume too much board time.

To encourage visitors at board meetings, which will do much to create cordial and cooperative relations between the board and the public, the meetings should be held in adequate and attractive surroundings that will contribute to the convenience and comfort of the visitors and heighten a sense of the dignity of the board and the importance of public education in the life of the community, the state, and the nation.

Minutes of each school board meeting should be written up by the secretary within a day or two after adjournment. Copies should be mailed to each board member, should be furnished to newspapers and other communications media, and to any individuals or organizations in the district which offer valid reason for having them.

At each meeting of the board, the minutes of the preceding meeting should be approved, or approved with corrections, and an official copy, signed by the chairman, should be filed by the secretary as a matter of permanent record.

Whether required by law or not, it is extremely important to keep the minutes of meetings as a written record of all actions taken by the board as a public corporation, with dates, votes recorded, decisions reached, etc. As time goes on, board minutes form an invaluable history of educational progress in the district and, when properly kept, are accepted by courts of law as evidence in case of litigation.

Board minutes are also of special value to a new board member or to a new superintendent of schools in orienting himself to the affairs of the district and in identifying personalities and points of view that may have a bearing on future educational developments.

In short, there are numberless sound reasons for keeping on file accurate and complete minutes of all school board meetings, regular and special, and there are no good arguments for not keeping them. Boards which have neglected or slighted this aspect of procedure are running the risk of future trouble and would do well to inaugurate a change.

EDUCATIONAL ECONOMICS

*"The cheapest way of conducting a
school is to engage the best teachers
at the best price."*

— WALT WHITMAN

The "good gray poet" had some firsthand experience with school teaching in his youth, and, in
a broader sense, was a master teacher all his life.
Walt Whitman knew whereof he spoke in the sen-
tence quoted above. He understood that no matter
how much a good teacher is paid it can never be
enough, while anything paid to a poor teacher is too
much. By "cheapest" he meant obtaining the greatest return on the investment made with the least
amount of waste and worry. He saw clearly that
well-paid, top-quality teachers are the most economical "buy" for a community interested in the
growth and development of its children and in improving its social and economic status. Yet how hard
it seems to be, 100 years later, for some boards of
education to believe this and to put it into practice!
— E. M. T.

HELP OR HINDRANCE

"Am I a builder who works with care,
Measuring life by the rule and square?
Am I shaping my deeds to a well-made plan,
Patiently doing the best I can?
Or am I a wrecker who walks the town,
Content with the labor of tearing down?"

— UNKNOWN

It is always much easier to be against something than for something; to be destructive than constructive; to throw obstacles in the path of progress than to lend a helping hand. School board members have a peculiar obligation to watch themselves in this regard, because education, which is concerned with human growth and development, particularly of children and youth, is a constructive process. It needs freedom to adapt itself to changing conditions and to individual needs. It stifles and becomes fruitless when made to follow traditional paths endlessly and aimlessly. Under such restraints the paths quickly turn into ruts. Consequently, that school board is doing the best job for its community which spends most of its time and energy building up the school program in effective ways, and which reduces opposition and criticism to a minimum. The Bible has something to say about those who put obstacles in the way of little children or cause them to stumble —something about millstones and necks and the depths of the sea. — E. M. T.

CHAPTER 5

Stumbling Blocks to
School Board Effectiveness

Let it be said at the start that, by and large, the American public is ably represented and has reason to be proud of the service rendered by its 35,000* or so local boards of education.

The fact that most board members serve voluntarily and without material reward is evidence of the high regard in which public education is generally held, and the honor felt by our ablest citizens in being selected to give such service to their communities.

Notwithstanding the truth of these general observations, it is also true that many boards—too many—are not as effective as they should be and could be.

This writer's contacts with school boards and board members in every state in the Union have led to certain observations as to why some boards fail to reach their greatest possible effectiveness.

There will be differences of opinion regarding some of these "stumbling blocks," and of course there are wide variations in the degree of their limiting influence.

However, a frank consideration of these practices should be wholesome and perhaps helpful to boards which have been following any of them, whether consciously or unconsciously.

These points are not new. They are simply set down here in one list so that we may take a good look at them.

---

*Not so many years ago this figure was 120,000 school districts. Each year sees its further decline as the processes of school consolidation and district reorganization continue. Ease of transportation and communication in our modern world makes larger school districts possible, and experience has proved that, within certain limits, larger districts offer more effective educational programs and at the same time make more efficient use of the school tax dollar.

School Board Leadership in America

1. Partisanship

Individual board members are sometimes dominated by partisan instead of by public loyalties.

Whatever these partisan loyalties may be they prevent the board member from truly representing the community as a whole, and they inevitably result in a lack of harmony within the board which is fatal to effective action.

There is no place on a board of education for personal ambitions or grudges, for the selfish interests of individuals or special groups, for partisan politics, or for anything else except complete devotion to the educational needs of the community.

This is not to say that there are never to be honest differences of view or thorough discussion, pro and con, of each problem as it arises.

It is to say that before he casts his vote, each board member shall ask himself (1) "Am I voting solely on the merits of this issue as I understand them?" and (2) "Whatever the outcome, will I abide by and support the decision of the board?"

Such an attitude is not an impossible ideal or too much to ask of the members of any group charged with the operation of the public schools. Thousands of school boards throughout the length and breadth of the land exemplify this principle of non-partisan service.

Those boards which violate this principle, and allow schools and communities to be ripped asunder by controversies which could be settled by integrity and frankness, will find that their days are numbered (see Chapter 18).

2. Lack of Written Policies

A lack of written down school board policies, kept up to date, is a frequent source of inconsistent or ineffective action. (See Chapter 6, especially the section on "Why Written Policies Are Desirable.")

While nobody knows exactly, such studies and surveys as have been made would seem to indicate that not over one-third of the school boards of the nation have adopted written policies.

Confusion and misunderstanding between the board and the administration, between the board and the public, and between the administration and the public most often result when policies are not clearly set forth in written or printed form and made available to all parties concerned.

In recent years there has been a growing wave of interest in written policies, stimulated largely by the national and state associations of school boards, and the percentage of boards having such policy statements is steadily increasing.

It would appear, then, that this particular "stumbling block" should be one of the easiest to overcome.

3. Over-emphasis on Housekeeping

Too exclusive attention to the housekeeping, or business, aspects of school operation, to the neglect of the educational program itself, is a common weakness of many boards.

When a board meets simply to pass upon a budget, pay bills, confirm appointments, purchase sites, approve architects' plans and contractors' bids, arrange for insurance, work out bus routes, and otherwise take care of the business affairs of the schools, it is discharging only one phase of its responsibility to the community.

Of equal, or even greater importance is the necessity for the board to understand the values and purposes of public education, and to develop the ability to interpret, defend, and support constructive educational programs when the need arises.

The board which really fulfills its proper function of policy making devotes fully as much time to developing its own background regarding educational practices and programs as it does to taking care of school business.

There is increasing recognition of this two-fold responsibility in school board operation.

The programs of national and state school board conventions, as well as of regional meetings and workshops, more and more give major consideration to the leadership responsibilities of school boards for the school curriculum (see Chapter 10).

4. Executive Sessions

Abuse of closed, or executive, sessions is a "stumbling block" which school boards sometimes put in their own paths.

The first result of such a practice is to create an atmosphere of secrecy and intrigue which is not compatible with a public service.

It also results in failure to keep the public fully informed on school matters at all times.

Actually, legal action by the board *must be taken in an open meeting.*

The only excuses for private discussion preceding official action are in connection with items like personality problems or the contemplated purchase of building sites.

Even in such cases, the wise board which has established good press relations, enables press representatives to have the benefit of the background discussions, *off the record,* so that when the subject does break later on, the press will be in a position to publish a correct story based on all the facts.

The effective school board is one which rarely goes into executive session, which holds open meetings at convenient times and places announced well in advance, and which invites and encourages the attendance of individuals and representatives of community organizations who are sincerely interested in the advancement of public education.

5. Standing Committees

The operation of a school board through a number of standing committees is generally regarded as a "stumbling block" to greatest effectiveness.

Though there are some differences of opinion on this point, the trend is strongly toward board operation as a committee of the whole at all times, except when some special committee is organized temporarily for a particular purpose.

The greatest objection to standing committees is that in practice they tend to result in having several boards instead of one, both from the standpoint of the administrator and his staff and from the standpoint of the public. For example, one small group of board members is specifically identified with finance, another with buildings, another with personnel, another with curriculum, and so on.

When fractions of the school board specialize, so to speak, in particular areas of school operation, they soon come to look upon themselves as authorities and to infringe upon the administrative functions of the superintendent and his staff instead of confining their activities to the making of policy.

Finally, such a plan gives board members a very uneven understanding of school affairs in the district (intensive as regards their own committee, nebulous as regards the concerns of other committees) and thereby reduces the effectiveness of total board operation.

On the other hand, with agenda well planned in advance, and with efficient board procedure, there is no reason why all school matters cannot be considered by all members of the board acting together (see Chapter 4).

This is the manner in which the great majority of school boards in the nation operate. The resulting effect on the schools and on the communities involved is much more salutary than under divided responsibilities.

6. Fiscal Dependence

The fiscal dependence of a board of education upon the review, revision, or approval of its budget by some non-educational governmental agency or commission is likely to be a major "stumbling block" to educational progress.

Advocates both of fiscal dependence and of fiscal independence advance strong arguments to prove their respective claims.

Good examples and bad examples of operation under both systems can be cited, and it is doubtful that the issue can be settled on the basis of factual evidence.

The question really involves our conception of the relative importance of different social values.

Is education just one type of government service, or is it a very special service, no more like the other services than the judiciary is like the executive function?

The idea that direct determination through the school board of educational policy, including the extent of financial support, has greater social value for the community than to combine schools with other public services under a centralized fiscal management, seems to be steadily gaining ground.

It is clear to most people that school budgets are not made subject to approval by City Councils or other non-educational partisan bodies for the purpose of promoting better schools. The primary motive is to save money, usually at the expense of improved education.

Complete fiscal independence for boards of education is based on the concept that public education is a continuous, constructive, non-partisan service to all the people in which they should have a direct voice not complicated by any other consideration than the greatest possible good to children and youth.

7. Dual Administration

A dual administration which separates responsibility for business affairs from responsibility for educational affairs within a school system is a fertile source of school board ineffectiveness.

Here again there will be differences of opinion because occasionally, where personal cooperation is of the highest order, the dual system has been made to work smoothly.

Moreover, there are some districts and at least one whole state where dual control is legally required.

But in most states it has not proved satisfactory to separate financial planning from educational planning. Too often the result is disastrous for the educational program.

The best systems first determine what the schools should be doing for the community and then determine the financial support needed to carry out that program.

Experience has shown that for greatest effectiveness a school system should have just one administrator (the superintendent) directly responsible to the board, and that he should be given such assistants, including a business manager, as are needed to carry out the board's policies with regard to all aspects of school operation.

Summary

Seven practices which appear to be "stumbling blocks" to effective school board operation have been listed above: (1) partisanship; (2) lack of written policies; (3) over-emphasis on housekeeping; (4) executive sessions; (5) standing committees; (6) fiscal dependence; and (7) dual administration.

There may be other practices which, in greater or lesser degree, frustrate harmonious, constructive accomplishment by boards of education. But at least these seven have revealed their handicapping tendencies in a majority of cases.

Boards which are operating under any one or more of these conditions would be well advised to study their operation with open minds to determine whether some modification more closely related to widespread trends might not yield as rewarding results for them as for others.

"We need great souls to make great schools
   Or all our walls were laid in vain.
Youth asks for reasons, not for rules;
   There's more than Latin to make plain.
The road of life lies just ahead,
   And here is youth just at the dawn;
The road of life is here to tread —
   We need great souls to lead youth on."

—DOUGLAS MALLOCH

POLICY

"Take each man's censure,
but reserve thy judgment."

— SHAKESPEARE

As commonly used today, the word "censure" means adverse criticism or condemnation, but in Shakespeare's day it had a broader connotation to include opinion or viewpoint of every kind, approving as well as critical. In any case, the admonition given is that we hold our minds open to all points of view before committing ourselves. The advice is especially appropriate for members of boards of education who are subject to numerous pressures—often critical or self-seeking—from individuals and groups within the school district. Reserving its judgment until all the facts are in, the board can then reconcile conflicting demands into policy designed to accomplish the greatest good to the greatest number under its jurisdiction. — E. M. T.

CHAPTER 6

School Board Policy Making

In general, the function of a school board is to establish policies for the operation of the school system in the district, and the function of the administrator, or superintendent of schools, is to carry out the policies in practice.

The analogy that is sometimes made to the legislative and executive branches of government is only partially true with respect to school board-administrator relationships.

It is not always easy to distinguish between policy making and the operation of policy, and there is inevitable overlapping at many points depending on the personalities involved and the local conditions.

Interestingly, it will usually be found that the degree of detail set forth in a policy adopted by a board varies in inverse ratio to the degree of confidence existing between the board and its administrator. In other words, the greater the confidence, the less rigid the prescription, and vice versa.

Some Working Definitions

1. *Policies* are principles adopted by a board of education to chart a course of action for its administrator and to define the limits within which he shall exercise judgment and discretion.

Essentially, policies are a guide to the *what*, the *why*, and the *how much* of desired educational operation.

2. *Rules and Regulations*, as distinguished from policies, are the detailed directions necessary to put policies into effect. They are more likely to be formulated by the administrator with the

informal approval of the board than to be initiated or formally acted upon by the board itself.

Essentially, rules and regulations provide a blueprint as to the *how*, the *who*, the *when*, and the *where* of actual educational practice.

3. *Procedures* are working rules, or bylaws for the board itself as regards its organization, meetings, parliamentary practice, order of business, minutes, and the like (see Chapter 4).

How Policies Are Evolved

Except in a case like the creation of a new unit district and a new board under some plan of reorganization, a school board rarely has the opportunity to make a wholly new set of policies.

Most boards find a body of policy already established as a result of cumulative action on specific cases, and embodied in the minutes of past board meetings.

In addition to its own minutes, a school board seeking to prepare a set of written policies may sometimes secure helpful suggestions from a study of written policies of other boards of education, from a review of publications and reference literature (see Bibliography, pages 283-87), from its State Department of Education and state school boards association.

It should never be forgotten that every action taken by a board does one of the following three things with respect to policies, whether they have been collected and formulated in written form or not:

1. The board's action conforms to a policy already established.

2. The board's action modifies or reverses a policy previously adopted.

3. The board's action establishes a new policy with respect to a subject not previously covered.

Clearly, then, policies are not fixed or final, but are always subject to evaluation and improvement, so that the best policies are the result of a continuous process of growth and maturing.

Ideally, every policy should be arrived at by a process of discussion and deliberation involving representatives of all groups which will be affected by the application of policy—specifically, the school staff, professional and non-professional, the pupils and their parents, the taxpayers and the public at large.

The *motive* behind a policy is of significant importance.

A poor type of policy results from a defensive, preventive, or corrective intent. Such a policy is inward looking and restrictive. It results in establishing a status quo which is often only a fancy name for a rut.

On the other hand, a good type of policy results from an approving, encouraging, constructive intent. Such a policy is outward looking and expansive. It leads to growth and progress and a prompt adaptation to changing needs.

Why Written Policies Are Desirable

Lack of a set of policies, carefully organized, clearly written down, and kept currently up to date can be a major handicap to effective school board operation (see Chapter 5, point 2).

Conversely, such a set of policies benefits all who are related to the school system, within and without—board members, administrators, teachers, other employees, students, parents, taxpayers, community organizations, etc.

Such statements of policy help to avoid misunderstandings and confusion by defining responsibilities and lines of authority so that they can be readily interpreted at any level.

Written policies give continuity and consistency to the school board's position, and stand as a bulwark against undue pressure from self-seeking interests.

Statements of policy are valuable orientation aids to new board members and to new executive, teaching, or other personnel.

A set of written policies adds dignity to the school system, assists in the employment of personnel, prevents impulsive or reversive board decisions, saves administrative time, improves staff morale, and promotes good public relations.

What Policies Should Cover

No outline of policy content can be made applicable to all school districts. In fact, the greatest value comes from policies that are closely adapted to each local situation.

However, there are certain areas of policy making which should usually be considered:

1. *General policies* may include such subjects as the use of school property, transportation, athletics, solicitations, preparation and adoption of the school budget, purchasing and the letting of bids, public hearings, relations with the public and the press, and the like.

2. *Personnel policies* may include salary schedules, qualifications, areas of responsibility, professional growth, leaves of absence, tenure, retirement and social security, health insurance, extra-curricular activities, complaint procedure, and so on.

3. *Policies on the educational program* should set forth clearly the goals which the community is seeking through the courses of study provided by the schools. In addition, they may cover such items as starting age for pupils, standards of admission, tuition where applicable, methods of reporting, etc.

4. *Legal requirements* for the operation of the schools may either be set forth in a separate section of the policies, or be woven into the body of the policies wherever they are appropriate.

5. *Other areas* sometimes included are an outline of school board procedure; a chart of organizational relationships within the school system; a set of ethical standards for board members, executives, teachers, and other employees; and whatever else may be of particular local concern.

A Challenging Point of View

One of the finest examples of written school board policies is that developed over a period of years for the schools of Midland, Michigan.

These policies resulted from the application of many of the principles set forth in this chapter, but perhaps their most striking and thought-provoking feature is a four-point introduction, as follows:

"It is believed that in establishing and supporting a school system for all the children of all the people, society wants the school, as a public institution, to provide insofar as possible:

"1. A well-qualified and efficient corps of teachers of such character that if a child should become like any one of the teachers, the parents and others would still be proud of the child.

"2. Physical plant and equipment adequate to meet the most exacting needs of every learner, the like of which separate families could not provide.

"3. Experiences for effective learning the like of which the best home alone could not provide.

"4. An educational leadership which courageously and ably leads to continuous school improvement."

My Endeavor

To be true — first to myself — and just
and merciful.
To be kind and faithful in the little things.
To be brave with the bad; openly grateful
for the good; always moderate.
To seek the best, content with what I find,
placing principles above persons
and right above riches.
Of fear, none; of pain, enough to make my joys
stand out; of pity, some; of work, a plenty;
of faith in God and man, much; of love, all.

— LEIGH M. HODGES

APATHY

*"All that is necessary for the triumph
of evil is that good men do nothing."*

— EDMUND BURKE

Damned with faint praise is he of whom it must be said, "There is a good man, but he will never take a stand in public for or against anything." Good people are always in the majority in a community or in a state. Yet too often small but untiring forces of evil exploit and corrupt a majority which will not rouse itself in opposition. Apathy and indifference are the greatest enemies of human progress and well-being. In a government like our own, where the people rule, it is far easier to rally against some threat to our liberties from without, than it is to be at all times alert and active against the evils that strive unceasingly to undermine us from within. Worthy citizens, however, do not sit idly by and watch the triumph of wrongdoing. Individually and collectively they exercise eternal vigilance in behalf of freedom and justice for all. — E. M. T.

CHAPTER 7

Moral and Ethical Values
for School Boards

The section of the Beliefs and Policies of the National School Boards Association, Inc., dealing with "Responsibilities of Local School Boards" states that these include

> "a *moral and ethical* responsibility to function courageously and impartially to assure the greatest good to the greatest number at all times."

In recent years there has been criticism from various quarters that our public schools fail to teach children and youth those moral and ethical principles which lie at the very foundation of a sound and enduring democratic society. Others than the students may be involved, as will be seen.

In the realm of school board functioning, it is clear that the vast majority of board members are rendering voluntary service of a high order of integrity.

But every now and again there comes a report of some board that has not stood firmly for the right in the face of partisan pressures and prejudices.

As an example of the damage that may be done by failure on the part of the legally responsible school authorities to uphold moral and ethical principles, let us take a concrete instance reported several years ago in the *American School Board Journal*.

The case in question involved seniors in high school in a small community who cheated on their final examinations.

Subsequently, the school board, over the protests of the supervising principal, authorized the awarding of diplomas in disregard of the fraudulent returns.

Apparently the adults of this community, or at least enough of them to overawe and include the school board, were perfectly willing to throw their own morals and those of their children out of the window when an issue arose.

Whose Moral Values Failed?

Let's take a look at the facts as stated in the brief report:

1. A majority of the seniors cheated by gaining prior knowledge of the final examination questions in two basic courses.

For the weak, such knowledge was a temptation.

For the thoughtless, it was a lark.

For the average, it was a dare they couldn't resist taking.

But it is safe to assume that every student knew he or she was doing wrong.

(All this is beside the point, which might be open to discussion, of whether undue importance had been attached to final examinations in this school system.)

2. The supervising principal of the high school, when he learned of the fraud at the eleventh hour before Commencement, faced a difficult decision that had to be made at once.

As a teacher of youth he must uphold right moral conduct, but as a friend of his students he did not want to shame and punish them publicly.

The principal knew that among the students there were innocent as well as guilty.

He knew that the great majority of the guilty had had no real need to cheat in order to pass the examination.

So he frankly proposed to them all that they proceed with the public ceremonies on the understanding that immediately afterward they would set about correcting as best they could the wrong that had been done (presumably by a re-examination).

3. Then the parents stepped in and ruined the day.

They hauled down the moral standard and trampled on it before their children's eyes.

They condoned the cheating and insisted that no effort be made to right the wrong.

They were willing that their sons and daughters, innocent and guilty alike, should accept tainted diplomas and leave high school under a cloud of suspicion.

They threatened the school board with reprisals if it supported the supervising principal in his proposal to hold the students for redress.

4. Finally, what of the school board which clearly held the key to the situation.

Instinctively, at first, the board stood for the right.

It backed the supervising principal in his handling of the difficult circumstances.

It recognized that education must build character as well as develop understanding if it is to strengthen future generations of American citizens.

But when the going got tough, the school board forgot these fundamental moral and ethical principles.

It found no courage to fight for its convictions.

The prospect of possible defeat for reelection and the threatened loss of a few dollars in paid tuition to the district filled it with dismay.

So the board sold the community's birthright for a mess of pottage.

It overruled the supervising principal.

It legalized the fraudulent diplomas.

In short, it tried to vote a wrong into a right, something which can never be done.

5. No hint was given in the report of this incident that a single voice outside the school staff was raised in behalf of honor, integrity, and decent human relations.

Had one righteously indignant citizen, on or off the school board, risen to his feet and brought the angry, misguided parents

57

in this community to a sense of how what they were doing would look in the eyes of cold reflection, the whole picture might have been different.

Some solution might have been found that would not have compromised moral values nor left everyone concerned with feelings of regret and guilt which will linger for years.

What of the Consequences?

What effect did the action of the school board have on the pupils in the community—not alone on the seniors who graduated, but on many times that number of younger boys and girls down through the high school and elementary grades?

What lessons were learned in impressionable years from this incident—lessons much more convincing than those from any textbook?

Did the pupils in this school system learn that cheating can be indulged in with impunity?

Did they conclude that their teachers had no real authority to insist on what is right and decent because in a showdown the legally responsible school board would not back up the teachers?

Did they decide that no matter what they might do, their parents would take their part, and that citizens generally would wink at their failure to play according to the rules of the game, thinking it "smart" or "funny" when they got away with it?

Did they learn to reject such precepts as "honesty is the best policy," "a man's word is as good as his bond," and "a good name is rather to be chosen than great riches" as old fashioned, pious platitudes, not to be taken seriously by anyone who is wise to the ways of the present world in which we live?

Must we conclude that here was a community gone morally and spiritually bankrupt?

Could it be suspected that the young folks cheated in the first place because they knew what attitude their parents and the school board would take?

In similar circumstances, what would other communities do?

Is this incident typical of present-day attitudes toward moral and ethical values?

A Challenge to Complacency

The questions above have been presented in the strongest possible terms in order to challenge our widespread apathy and undermining complacency toward moral issues.

They are serious questions, and true answers to them would be a vital indication as to whether this nation is building upon sand or upon a rock.

This writer does not believe for a minute that the action taken in the community reported above represented the real convictions of a majority of its citizens, young or old.

If it did, then that community, and every other like it, would be doomed to ultimate degradation.

Let us believe, rather, that the great majority of people everywhere are earnestly and honestly trying to do their best in life and to stand for what is right.

Or, as the poet puts it, the bulk of our society is made up of

"Millions who humble and nameless
The straight, hard pathway plod."

Nevertheless, the hesitancy and unwillingness of good people to stand up promptly and be counted against the face of evil is the reason why so often it seems as though wrong triumphs and right goes down to defeat.

Conclusion

This chapter has been written around a single incident, but its implications are universal.

Every school board faces issues many times each year where moral and ethical values are at stake in greater or lesser degree.

On such occasions board members should remind themselves, individually and collectively, that one of the essential responsibilities of leadership is the possession of courage to stand firmly for what is right and best for the community as a whole, both for today and for the future.

THE PREJUDICE OF IGNORANCE

"Nothing is so firmly believed as what we least know."

— MONTAIGNE

In these ten well-chosen words, a great French philosopher four centuries ago expressed a basic human weakness which still plagues the world on every hand. We have all been victims of its exercise by others; without doubt we are ourselves guilty of its practice on occasion. Meetings of all kinds and sizes at every level of our social, economic, and political life too often take action as a result of the persuasive glibness of someone who doesn't know he doesn't know what he so positively asserts. Progress is continually sidetracked by a blind following of opinions and prejudices unsupported by facts. Actually, those who know most about any given subject are likely to be least dogmatic in expressing their beliefs. To develop in men a breadth of view, an openness of mind, a habit of forming convictions on the basis of fact, is the true task of education. What a slow process it seems to be, even under the best of circumstances! — E. M. T.

CHAPTER 8

Pressures on the School Board

There are in this country three groupings of organizations with reference to the public schools.

On the one hand, we have the organizations of professional educators (administrators, supervisors, principals, teachers, specialists in numerous fields, etc.) whose direct and primary concern is with the schools and the improvement of the educational program.

On the other hand, we have the multitude of organizations of lay citizens in every conceivable area of life (business and industrial organizations, farm groups, labor groups, professional groups, service clubs, veteran's organizations, women's groups, and a host of others) whose interest is indirect but nevertheless real when their attention is focused on the schools and public education.

Between these two groups of organizations, there are two organizations which are in a unique position to interpret the aims of the educational profession and the wishes of the lay citizens to each other, and thus to promote cooperative relationships which will strengthen the educational program in every community.

One of these is a voluntary organization—the parent-teacher association—which in recent years has grown greatly in membership, influence, and constructive endeavor.

The other in-between organization is the school board which bears legal responsibility for the conduct of the public schools, and which has to meet and resolve all the pressures for specific action that arise from within or without the school system.

Whenever one special organization or element in a community attempts to influence action by the school board without consulting others who should be equally concerned, or when movements for control are made secretly and without revealing all the factors involved, the result is almost certain to be dissatisfaction and strife within the community unless the board keeps a firm guiding hand on the situation (see Chapter 18).

A Case in Point

The following paragraphs are quoted from a letter received at the office of the National School Boards Association several years ago:

"As a member of the public school board of our county, I am concerned about the over-emphasis on high school athletics, particularly football. This condition has been sponsored in large measure by civic groups such as the Quarter Back Club, etc. who are very vocal in their demands for so-called "Big Time Football," to advertise the town.

"Our school board has been somewhat confused by thinking that the voice of these comparatively few people represents a public demand which it cannot ignore. Consequently a good deal of time, money, and effort are being devoted to a type of athletic development which, in my opinion, is detrimental to the general welfare of our school system. This unhealthy development is growing in intensity, and unless some means can be found to offset it, I am afraid it will grow into extremely undesirable proportions.

"Recently our county voted a bond issue for the purpose of supplying badly needed school facilities. In spite of the fact that we, as do many other areas of this country, find it almost impossible to supply adequate schoolrooms and other school facilities to meet the rapid increase in school population, nearly one-fifth of this bond issue was spent for a modern concrete stadium.

"Another unhealthy condition is the fact that the total cost of our athletic program is not put in the budget and is not paid for out of current school funds, but out of gate receipts from athletic games. This was one reason why some members of the school board thought it advisable to build a larger stadium. All moneys collected from gate receipts are retained by the high school principal (our system includes one high school with approximately 1,200 students), and he makes the expenditures from these funds. The school board gets a semi-annual report on the finances involved but otherwise has no control over the money. The only part of the athletic program paid from school board funds is the salaries of coaches and teachers in the physical education program.

"Mention is made of the above as phases of the hysteria we face. Simple opposition by one or more citizens or even school board members will not be enough to change the situation materially. I am wondering if you have any suggestions about a method of procedure which could secure public support and bring about some program more in line with common sense."

Undoubtedly reactions will vary regarding the situation described in this letter.

Some readers will be members of school boards which are struggling with a similar problem in greater or lesser degree.

There will be others whose boards have faced such a problem and solved it.

In some cases, boards have adopted policies which make it impossible that a situation like this should ever arise.

Far too many boards, without definite policies, go along in the hope and belief that nothing like this will happen to them.

Let's Analyze the Situation

Perhaps we should recall two or three fundamental principles as a basis for offering suggestions to the writer of the letter above, or to any board that faces pressures of any kind.

The public schools belong to the people of each community and state—to *all* the people, not to any particular segment or group of the population.

It follows, then, that whatever a majority of the people want the schools to embrace and accomplish, that thing the schools,

63

under the authority of the local board of education, should seek to undertake.

If, *after a study of all the facts*, a majority of the parents and taxpayers in a school district vote to carry out any athletic program like that described in the above letter, then it should be carried out until they change their minds.

But it is very doubtful that a majority of any American community, possessed of the complete pros and cons concerning "Big Time Football" for high school youth, would favor such an extreme policy, especially one so unrelated to the total physical education program of the school.

What apparently happened in the community where our letter writer lived was that a small group of "business leaders" decided to put their town "on the map" at the expense of its schools.

So they built up a case, overrode or ignored the good sense and judgment of the average citizen and parent, over-awed the school board with their demands, and established extra-legal channels for the conduct of the enterprise.

In short, high school athletics in this community was in a fair way to becoming a "tail that wagged the dog" instead of the legitimate "tail" belonging to a sound and healthy "dog"—a school system with a well-integrated program of physical education for all its youth, in which a certain amount of competitive contests occupied a controlled and proportionate place.

Let's give these gentlemen the benefit of the doubt, however, and say that their enthusiasm clouded their good judgment and common sense, rather than that they deliberately set out to defeat the full clear purpose of public education in their community.

A Way Out

This board of education, or any other subjected to short-sighted or one-sided pressures, might find a way out by taking the initiative in developing a committee of citizens broadly representative of the entire community and including advocates on both sides of the question at issue.

This committee would then be asked to make a careful study of the whole problem and to report to the board what the majority of the parents and citizens generally consider best for the children and for the welfare of the community.

Such a procedure would prevent the situation from degenerating into an argument not based on facts which might easily tear the community apart, leaving the children stranded in the middle (see Chapters 17 and 18).

The Spirit

It is the spirit that maketh alive.
I know that you must test, grade, measure,
counsel, guide, individualize, generalize,
nationalize, Americanize, Christianize,
humanize, intellectualize, spiritualize;
that you must classify on proper social levels,
vocational levels, intelligence levels,
maturity levels, psychological levels;
that you must adjust the misadjusted,
adjust the maladjusted, and the utterly unadjustable;
that you must not only be a teacher
but a psychologist, a physiologist, a psychiatrist,
a sociologist, a progressivist, a modernist,
a fundamentalist, and a 100 per cent Americanist —
all of this you must be, and more!
But forget it! Chuck it!
And once a day, if possible, just be the simple,
honest, loving human being that God made you,
and let the children be the human beings
that God made them, and between
the three of you — you, the child, and God —
the divine thing called teaching
will now and then get done!

— DALLAS LORE SHARP

WELCOME CRITICS

*"He has the right to criticize who
has the heart to help."*

— ABRAHAM LINCOLN

It is easy to criticize. All of us do too much of it,
usually with little real understanding of the things
we criticize, and with no intention of making any
effort ourselves to help improve matters. Such criticism does more harm than good, and Mr. Lincoln
implied that we have no right to indulge in it. On
the other hand, men's efforts never reach perfection. Those responsible for a task are too close to
it, too deeply involved in it, to be able to see its
strengths and weaknesses accurately. Competent
outside observers, motivated by "the heart to help,"
can often make constructive suggestions. Right now,
especially, those responsible for the operation of
our public schools need to encourage and welcome
this kind of criticism from citizens of good will.
— E. M. T.

CHAPTER 9

How Should School Boards
Meet Criticism?

"How can we turn community gripes into profit for the children?" asks a board member, and he continues, "The community has a responsibility for in-school education. How can the people be roused to an understanding of the need for better school education, and united in their support of such a program? It's a large order."

It is, indeed, a large order, but it is also a golden opportunity. Only when the whole community, and not merely some segment of it, becomes truly concerned about the quality of its schools, is any fundamental progress in sight.

Criticism Is a Healthy Sign

A board of education occupies a key position whenever criticism or controversy arises involving the public schools.

This is because the board has been delegated legal responsibility by the state for the maintenance and operation of the local school system.

The board has employed the administrator and the school staff, professional and non-professional, and has established the basic policies under which the schools shall be conducted (see Chapter 6).

Criticism is not necessarily an indication that schools are deteriorating. It is, rather, a healthy indication that people are taking an interest in public education.

During the 1930's and 1940's people generally paid little or no attention to the public schools, because their attention was centered on problems of a depression, a world war, and post-war adjustments.

It is natural to suppose that the educational process did not stand still while it was almost forgotten by the public.

Nothing else on the national scene stood still.

Think of the changes that have taken place since the early '30s in science and industry, in economic, social, and governmental affairs, and in practically every aspect of our daily living.

Teachers and school administrators represent a profession which is constantly seeking to advance in understanding its task and in finding more effective ways to accomplish its goals.

In these days, the public has been shocked out of its indifference to the schools because of shortages in facilities and personnel needed to provide adequate education for the rising flood of children, and because of the implied superiority of school systems in other countries, specifically in Russia.

If, at first glance, the public does not recognize the schools it used to know or feels dissatisfied with the product the schools are turning out, what is to be done?

School boards should be the first to welcome and encourage any reawakening of public interest as a natural opportunity to build increased community understanding and support (see Chapters 16 and 17).

Where boards are so short sighted as to ignore or sidestep or answer back legitimate questionings concerning school operation, they are in for certain and serious trouble (see Chapter 18).

A Specific Example

Criticism usually originates with a single individual who develops a pet peeve.

The peeve may be real or imagined, but the individual is able to gather a small group to his support, and suddenly they burst into the limelight with a blast in the press or a petition to the school board.

How Should School Boards Meet Criticism?

Not too long ago, a Chicago newspaper picked up an item from another state which it headlined "Parents Rap Modern Teaching."

The item reported that a group of 70 parents had protested to the board of education that "instead of so much attention in school curriculums to social studies, global attitudes, human relations, etc., more attention should be paid to the simple virtues—the teaching of basic subjects, respect for authority, consideration of others, modesty, and pride in individual initiative," and so on through several typewritten pages.

On the face of it, this criticism sounds like good sense. The question is, how much basis of fact did it have in the schools of this particular community?

The community in question had a population at the time of around 6,000. This meant, perhaps, 1,500 family units of which, at any given time, not more than 40 per cent (using nationwide figures) would have children in school.

Six hundred families with children of school age meant somewhere between 1,100 and 1,200 living parents, say 1,150.

The 70 parents who signed the protest to the board of education, therefore represented approximately 6 per cent of the parents of children in school and less than 1½ per cent of the adult citizens of that community.

This analysis indicates the first point to discover—the extent to which a criticism represents the feeling of the community as a whole.

Broadening the Base of Understanding

Such a protest as that just described is very likely to be based more largely upon opinions than upon facts.

What is needed, therefore, is not so much to present a counter argument as to involve those who are protesting in circumstances where they will have to discover and face the facts.

At the same time, the public attention that has been caught by the controversy should be capitalized on by the school board and school administration.

Criticisms of public education arise from two general kinds of motives—(1) those that are honest and sincere in their anxiety that the schools shall do a better job than they are now doing, and (2) those which are intended, for some selfish or subversive purpose, to stir up a school controversy in the hope that public education will ultimately be weakened.

Actually, the distinction between these two kinds of criticism is rarely clear cut, and most controversies, if at all prolonged, involve a mixture of both elements.

In any case, the solution is the same, and can best be insisted upon by a board of education which is alive to the combined dangers and opportunities inherent in the situation.

This solution is to broaden the base of inquiry until it involves the whole community and not simply particular segments or special groups, whether their motives are good or bad.

"When People Share, People Care"

In a democracy like ours, we have to believe that when the people as a whole are in possession of all the actual facts necessary to an accurate understanding of a given situation, they will come up with the right answer.

A board of education which stimulates a program of community-wide study of a controversial school issue needs to possess abundant faith, courage, and patience.

Faith in the essential soundness of the democratic process as the best method of arriving at permanent solutions!

Courage to accept the attack and counter-attack involved in the process of getting at all the facts!

Patience to give the procedure time to develop through its inevitable stages of confused groping, suspicious uncertainty, increasing understanding, growing cooperation, and ultimate agreement!

On the other hand, the rewards are great.

In every community where such a program has developed and has been accepted as a continuing plan, the people are solidly

70

behind their schools. The board and the administrator no longer have to give anxious consideration as to how the community will react to some change in the curriculum, to a request for an increase in the budget, or to a bond issue.

The school authorities in such a community know beforehand where the people stand, and their time can be spent in carrying out the expressed wishes of the majority, backed by adequate public support to accomplish the desired results.

So when any complaint in the community arises, and people begin to be agitated about their schools, the forward-looking board of education recognizes its opportunity to set in motion a program of community involvement that may ultimately result in progress beyond its fondest hopes.

Through it all, the real goal should never be lost sight of in the welter of details.

That goal is in the very best and highest development of children, youth, and adults as individuals and as citizens of the community.

In local public education, American democracy finds its greatest instrument for the perpetuation and increasing effectiveness of our cherished way of life.

*"All the troubles of the world
originate in the common man.
The selfish and greedy ways of nations
are just the ways of each individual man
multiplied a thousand fold.
When the morals of the common man drop,
so do the morals of the nations
and of the world."*

— JOHN CROWN

71

THE GOAL OF EDUCATION

"We all are blind until we see
That in the human plan,
Nothing is worth the making
If it does not make the man."

— EDWIN H. MARKHAM

In our daily preoccupation with material things, we are prone to overlook the fundamental truth so simply expressed by the noted author of "The Man with the Hoe." Democracy, as we understand it in America, is founded on the principle that each individual human being is the most important thing in the world. Members of school boards, busy with plans of organization, finance, construction, maintenance, equipment, transportation, curriculum, and personnel, should keep ever in mind the only real reason for the existence of schools, namely, to promote human growth and development—in short, to "make the man." — E. M. T.

CHAPTER 10

School Board Responsibility

for the Curriculum

When the Russians launched the first earth satellite in October of 1957, it led to a wave of criticism that American public education was falling behind in world leadership in science and engineering, if not in other respects.

During the heat of the debate, there were serious proposals in certain quarters that our whole system of local autonomy and control of the public schools should be abandoned in favor of national determination and administration of educational policy. More thoughtful leaders were quick to point out that no surer way could be found of surrendering for all time to come the democratic freedoms and integrity of individual citizens which our forefathers so painfully established and left as their legacy to us.

The President of the United States in an American Education Week address in November urged that every school board and every parent teacher association devote themselves to a scrutiny of school curriculums and standards "to see whether they meet the stern demands of the era we are entering."

To the state and national organizations of both the school boards and the P.T.A.'s this was not a new responsibility, but it came to them, then, with renewed emphasis.

Nearly a year earlier, at the convention of the National School Boards Association, a half-day's discussion of the "Leadership Responsibilities of School Board Members" resulted in a consensus that their No. 1 responsibility concerns what the schools in their respective communities shall teach. So clear was this mandate, that the entire convention program for 1958 was planned around

73

the theme of "School Boards and the Curriculum," and this subject has been given major consideration at school board association meetings—national, state, and regional—ever since.

The Larger Need

The education of the children, youth, and adult citizens of America has a much broader significance in these modern days than it had a generation or two ago.

It has always been a major objective to develop each individual in terms of his own needs and capabilities, no matter how short of such a goal we often fall. This is in keeping with our democratic ideals of personal worth and equality of opportunity.

But nowadays, with the tremendous advances in communication and transportation which have caused our people to become exceedingly mobile, the outcomes of the educational process assume far greater importance than ever before in terms of the common welfare.

All of us know more about our nation and the world at large than our forefathers knew about their own counties and states. Our abilities, individually and collectively, are assessed in terms of national as well as local requirements for a citizenry equipped to meet the demands of a rapidly expanding and changing technology in the midst of quickened perceptions of time and space.

In short, the market for each person's talent is world wide, and it becomes our duty to make more certain than ever before (1) that children and youth gain a thorough understanding of our American heritage of ideas and ideals, and (2) that every citizen, young and old, shall have opportunity to develop his personal talents to the fullest extent both for his own well-being and in service to his fellowmen.

It should be clear, therefore, that what the schools in any given community now teach must be geared not only to local conditions and needs but also to the requirements of the nation at large for educated, dedicated manpower.

Because the thought of a uniform nationwide educational program directed by order from some central authority is ab-

74

horrent to most Americans (see Chapters 1 and 32), we must find other ways of coordinating the curriculum policies of thousands of local school boards in terms of some common goals.

Whose Is the Responsibility?

In Chapter 5 it was pointed out that one of the stumbling blocks to effective school board service has been a tendency on the part of many boards to give major attention to the business side of school operation, and only a minimum of consideration to the educational program as embodied in the school curriculum.

Yet the sole reason for spending public money on school sites, school buildings, equipment and supplies, maintenance, transportation, administration, and teaching personnel is to provide an acceptable educational program.

Acceptable to whom? To the school board? To the school administrator and his staff? To the parents of the children in school? To taxpayers and the public generally? Or should the educational program be acceptable to all of these combined?

Legally, the school board is charged with responsibility for every aspect of the operation of the schools, including what is taught.

Professionally, the superintendent and teachers are expected to have the knowledge and training required to carry out any educational program in practice.

Personally, the parents are concerned with what their children learn in school and how well it is taught.

Financially, every taxpayer is interested in what the school tax dollar is buying, and wants it spent efficiently.

But, as citizens of their community, of their state, and of the nation, board members, professional educators, parents, and taxpayers alike, *all* have a responsibility for the kind and quality of education their schools provide.

How can this joint responsibility best be exercised? Where does the initiative lie? What means can be used to bring together the thinking and the desires of the various groups?

School Board Leadership in America

The Role of the School Board

Since, in the final analysis, the school board must legally adopt policies with respect to the curriculum, as well as for everything else pertaining to the school, it would seem logical that the board should take the initiative in making certain that its curriculum policies reflect the wishes of the total community to the greatest possible extent.

In view of present-day conditions, a board which neglects this aspect of its responsibilities falls short in its duty to the community not only, but to the state and nation as well.

In discharging its responsibility for curriculum policy, a school board must seek the cooperation of all who will be affected and concerned. The board's relationships with the professional school staff on the one hand, and with the community public on the other, make it logical that the board should wish to have the benefit of all points of view as a basis for decision making.

Practically speaking, every operating school system has a curriculum which it is following now. How that curriculum was developed, how recently it has been evaluated and revised, and how successfully school and community cooperate in its support are matters of almost infinite variation in the thousands of school districts throughout our land.

The time is clearly at hand for each board to concentrate its attention on the curriculum to make certain that its educational program does in fact "meet the stern demands of the era we are entering," as emphasized by the President of the United States. At the same time, it should neither be the desire nor the intention of the board to assume any professional administrative responsibility in curriculum matters.

Following are some of the ways that have been used by boards to build their own background of understanding as to what the schools shall teach, and to enlist the cooperation of both professional educators and the general public in developing and maintaining the best possible curriculum policies:

1. Schedule board meetings so as to devote at least as much time to curriculum matters as to business affairs. This may

be accomplished either by dividing the time at each meeting, or by holding alternate meetings for the two purposes.

2. Send out agenda to board members well in advance of meetings so that they may have time for study and understanding as a basis for consideration.

3. Streamline board meetings to conserve time spent on details and increase opportunities for educational discussion.

4. Request the superintendent to arrange with his staff to have various phases of the educational program presented to the board by directors of instruction, teachers, principals, and others at successive board meetings, until all of the courses of study in the curriculum are clearly understood by the board members.

5. Where feasible, hold board meetings at different schools in the system so that the members may become better acquainted with the work of all the schools.

6. Provide the means for securing on the instructional staff the best qualified and most competent teachers that can be found, as the surest way of guaranteeing that the established curriculum will be carried out effectively.

7. Make certain that the superintendent of schools is not overwhelmed with routine work that could just as well be done by business and clerical assistants to free his time for study, supervision, and evaluation of the educational program, which is his major responsibility.

8. Ask the superintendent to report frequently and exactly as to how well particular courses in the curriculum are working out in terms of the desired objectives, with recommendations for any indicated modifications of policy.

9. Look upon the evaluation and modification of curriculum policies as a continuous process of harmonious evolution, rather than as a subject for occasional study with resulting periodic upheavals.

10. Enlist the aid of community groups and committees in studies of various kinds with respect to how well certain

courses in the school program are meeting the wishes and desires of the people in the community, and what extension or curtailment of the curriculum may be indicated (see Chapter 17).

11. Support members of the teaching staff unequivocally in their presentation of facts concerning controversial issues, provided only that sincere effort is always made to present such facts objectively and impartially.

12. Agree upon a generous policy toward providing the quantity and quality of instructional materials recommended by teachers to enable them to present the established courses in the curriculum most effectively.

13. Spend as much time as possible individually reading books, periodicals, reports from the superintendent, and other materials relating to curriculum matters, to provide background for informed discussion in board meetings and in public contacts.

14. Attend district, state, regional, and national meetings of board members and other groups where school curriculum problems will be discussed and ideas exchanged.

15. Secure, whenever conditions seem to require it, the advice and counsel of professional educators and consultants from colleges, universities, and state departments of education, who will meet with the board and superintendent to explain new ideas and concepts of instruction and curriculum planning.

Provision for Pupil Guidance

Corollary to the necessity for offering in the schools courses of study which will meet the local, state, and national needs that have been discussed above, is the need to make more certain than we have heretofore that those who attend our schools follow the program of education best adapted to their individual abilities and aptitudes.

We all know that children and youths vary greatly in their potentialities. But, in the main, schools have been geared to the general average, with the result that those above average have found few incentives to excel, while those below average have often become bewildered and lost.

In recent years more effort has been made to provide in the schools for varying levels of ability. First attention was directed toward giving special assistance to handicapped and backward pupils. Then it was realized that unless challenges are provided for the exceptionally gifted pupils a great waste of talent will result at a time when leaders are desperately needed in all areas of the nation's life.

Yet, even though the curriculum makes provision for varying levels of ability, it is ineffectual unless means are also provided to insure that pupils follow courses of study best suited to their individual needs. This is the function of counseling and guidance.

In one sense, most teachers endeavor to guide their pupils as best they can. But beyond this, the need for a professionally trained guidance counselor in every school system or school of any size is recognized as perhaps the most important factor in making the most of the potentialities in our young people.

So, at the same time that school boards concentrate their attention on curriculum improvement they should insist on strengthening the program of pupil guidance.

Conclusion

If the local school boards of America will actively concern themselves in their respective communities, and collectively through their state and national associations, with questions of what American schools shall offer to insure maximum development of the talents of all our people, and will courageously undertake to secure the personnel and the facilities necessary to carry out such an educational program, then indeed we may feel confident that we have taken a fundamental step to "provide for the common defence, promote the general welfare, and secure the blessings of liberty to ourselves and our posterity."

VALUES

"We pay for schools not so much out of our purses as out of our state of mind."

— WALTER HINES PAGE

America is the richest country in the world. Our national income has never been so high as it is today. Yet schools generally are in dire need of a larger percentage of this great wealth. In recent years, their share has averaged from two to three per cent—too little to guarantee the intelligence and integrity of our future citizenry. Why is this? Is it because we hold education in too low esteem, laymen and professionals alike? Is it because we are not supremely convinced that real hope for the future lies in giving each succeeding generation superior advantages under outstanding guidance? Would the cost of education cease to be a question of major importance if we came to believe wholeheartedly in the values to be derived? When will the day come that, as a people, we defend, support, and exalt education as the greatest instrument of human progress? — E. M. T.

CHAPTER 11

School Boards and School Finance

Public schools are built and supported by public funds derived from various forms of taxation at local, intermediate, state, and federal levels.

A given school district may receive income from all of these sources in varying amounts, and its board of education is expected to account for all such receipts and for their expenditure.

Citizen taxpayers expect that public funds will be used efficiently and economically.

Our system of local control provides special opportunity for close and discriminating scrutiny of school budgets by the people.

As a result, it is safe to say that, by and large, tax money allocated to schools buys more nearly 100 cents worth for each dollar spent than is true of other kinds of public service where accountability is less direct.

Speaking to a great audience of board members from every state in the Union at a recent convention of the National School Boards Association, the executive assistant of the Michigan Manufacturers Association said:

"The dollar we laymen spend on education brings greater returns than a dollar spent in any other way. A dollar spent on education is probably used more efficiently, in the economic sense of the word, than a dollar spent by any other unit of government, local, state, or national. The tax dollar that goes to education is probably the most welcome tax burden the taxpayer has to pay. Behind the dollar that goes to education lie more of our human hopes, aspirations and convictions for the good of our children and the future of the world than with any other money we spend."

The subject of school finance is complex and difficult. Much has been written on its varied aspects at all levels. Each local board must be acquainted with the laws of its state regarding the preparation of the school budget, the assessment of property, the levying of taxes, the keeping of financial records and reports, the drafting of contracts, the issuance of bonds, the maintenance of insurance, and many other phases of fiscal management.

Information of this kind is always available from the State Department of Education (Public Instruction). In recent years, most state school boards associations have developed *Handbooks* for board members in their respective states that provide help and guidance not only on fiscal problems but on many others involved in school board operation.

In this brief chapter, three major considerations in the area of public school finance are singled out for particular emphasis. They are:

1. The need to develop in all our citizens a truer sense of values that will lead to an increase in the total expenditures for public education.

2. The question of securing a better balance between local, state, and federal support for public schools, with special attention to the role of the federal government.

3. The desirability of adopting standards for efficient school accounting at local and state levels.

Let's Get Our Values Clear

Appropriating authorities have a common habit of silencing or sidetracking requests for more adequate support of public education by vehemently demanding to be told where the money is to come from.

State legislatures are particularly prone to this habit. So are local political agencies, which have power of review over school budgets (see Chapter 5, point 6). Even fiscally independent local school boards have been known to evade a clear responsibility to their communities by raising the same "bug-a-boo."

Why not face the facts?

It cannot be said that in this country there is any shortage of money. The United States has never been so prosperous.

Here we enjoy the highest standard of living the world has ever known. The average American citizen is better housed, better clothed, and better fed than the average citizen of any other country on earth.

He has more comforts and more luxuries.

He works fewer hours for higher wages.

He has more money invested in real estate, stocks, and bonds.

He carries more life insurance.

He has more money in savings bonds and banks.

He does not hesitate to buy whatever touches his fancy, as witness the billions spent almost overnight for television sets and installations.

Young America spends more for comic books in one year than the total bill for elementary and secondary textbooks.

Adults spend more for liquor and tobacco, and more for entertainment than they spend for the education of their children and themselves.

What does all this mean to the future of America?

Obviously, we have the money to undergird our future with the finest system of public education for young and old that can be devised—*if we want to.*

How can we come to a truer sense of relative values?

Actually, the needs of public education, while they often seem to loom large locally, are a very small part of our total American economy.

We could easily double our support of public schools, as the report of the White House Conference on Education recommended that we do, without putting any strain on our purses.

And if we should spend two dollars where we now spend one, we would find that the extra dollar would be more than saved.

Why? Because the larger investment in better education for more of our people would lead to a reduction in the tremendous costs of crime, delinquency, mental cases, illness, accidents, and all the social obligations that arise from ignorance and carelessness.

Wouldn't it seem just plain common sense to use the years when our national income is reaching all-time high levels to put our public schools into first class condition as regards

—curriculums to meet the individual needs of every learner;

—professional staffs of the highest character and ability;

—buildings and grounds that make its schools the most attractive assets in the community;

—adequate equipment to insure effective teaching and learning in any subject?

Boards of education have a major responsibility to lead their communities to a better understanding of school needs and potentialities, and to work out with parents and taxpayers ways to provide necessary and generous support.

And by pooling experience and information through their associations, school boards can help immeasurably in strengthening and equalizing educational opportunities statewide and nationwide (see Part II).

Three-Way Support for Public Schools

There was a time not too long ago when, broadly speaking, 80 cents of the total American tax dollar was collected by and spent in local districts, counties, and states. The federal government accounted for the other 20 cents.

Today, as we all know, the situation is practically reversed—the federal government collects and spends nearly 80 per cent of America's tax dollar, leaving just over 20 per cent to local districts, counties, and states.

Despite this revolutionary shift in tax collection, better than nine-tenths of the cost of public elementary and secondary schools is still borne by local districts, counties, and states on the average, nationwide.

84

This tremendous imbalance between the agencies which collect our taxes and those which pay our public school bills would seem, from any sensible viewpoint, to indicate the need for a basic change in our thinking on the subject of the support of public education in America.

The question of support is always closely connected with the question of control, and there are those who honestly fear that any participation by the federal government in the support of public schools will inevitably lead to national control of educational programs.

This fear is well expressed in the following sentences quoted from past debate in the Congress: "The federal government should stay out of the local school districts. . . . Historical analysis proves that the evil leaders of each and every totalitarian state, on seizing control of that state first put their paws on the educational system of that nation. You can say that it cannot happen here and maybe it cannot. But let us not give it a chance to happen here."

Yet everyone knows that our American tradition legally vests the control of public education in the several states, and that the states in turn delegate a varying measure of this control to local school districts under local boards of education.

The majority of the American people are firmly opposed to the idea of any central (national, or federal) control of the public schools. To bring this about would require a change in the basic law of the land which, knowingly, they would not approve.

Nevertheless, there are always persons, some of them in high places, who advocate national control of public education because they are impatient with the slow processes of democracy and do not believe, as did Thomas Jefferson, that there is "no safe depository of the ultimate powers of society but the people themselves." (See Chapter 32, "The Challenge to Local Control of Public Education.")

Two major questions, therefore, present themselves in seeking a better balance between local, state, and national support of public education.

The first question is: Aside from the fact that it has most of the tax money, is there any basic reason why the federal government should appropriate more nearly a proportionate share of the tax dollar to support public schools?

The second question is: Can federal appropriation for public schools be made without subjecting the schools to federal control?

This writer believes that affirmative answers to both of these questions were provided in proposals advanced by the late Beardsley Ruml, the noted economist who first suggested the plan of income tax withholding which we now accept as a matter of course.

The Nation's Stake in Education. Mr. Ruml argued that, from the standpoint of the nation as a whole, a child in the public schools is a future American citizen wherever he may be, and that the nation has an *equal interest in every child* regardless of residence, race, social position, or economic status.

Moreover, the nation's basic concern is with the literacy of its future citizens, with their need for fundamental skill in communication and computation, or, if you please, in the 3 R's.

In other words, the nation's stake is in the foundations of learning for all its people and not in the variations and special adaptations of education for particular individuals or groups.

Such variations, in his opinion, should be left for determination and support in varying degrees by state and local authorities at state and local levels.

This point of view is the exact opposite of the course which the Congress has usually pursued in making appropriations for special phases of education instead of for the basic support of general school operation.

The "Flat-grant" Proposal. If, then, the nation has an equal interest in every public school child, it should contribute an equal amount toward the education of every such child. So argued Mr. Ruml.

Such a proposal is a very different approach from those that involve complicated formulas that attempt an equalization of educational opportunities which will satisfy everybody and at the same time avoid the federal control which is almost inherent in the application of such formulas.

When, however, federal support is extended on a so-much-per-child basis instead of on some kind of a calculated formula, it becomes simply a matter of honest accounting.

No direct or indirect control by the federal government over state and local educational programs would be involved. The allocation of federal money would be made to the State Departments of Education through the United States Office of Education, which, by law, is a service and not a policy-making agency with respect to the schools.

Each State Department of Education would expend the federal money for general school purposes, along with state and local funds, in accordance with the educational laws of its state, and would render an account to the United States Office of Education of the money so received and expended.

Actually, the flat-grant plan would result in some measure of equalization of educational opportunity among the states.

For example, states with the highest percentage of children per 1,000 of population would get more proportionately than would states with fewer children.

Again, states with the lowest incomes would be paying proportionately smaller amounts in taxes to the federal source of the grants they would receive.

Moreover, states where the expenditures per pupil are low would be receiving a higher percentage of their costs from the federal flat grant than would states spending two or three times as much per pupil.

Putting the Plan into Operation. Granted that the time may come when a majority of the American people, through action by the Congress, will adopt the principle of federal support of public schools on the flat-grant basis, Mr. Ruml suggested that it would be wise to start at a nominal figure per child per year.

After sound working procedures have been established on the basis of successful operation and proven merit of the plan, the support per child could be stepped up.

However, federal support should never extend beyond the point where the state and local communities would have the larger stake in the education of their children and the complete determination of its character, extent, and ramifications.

In brief, the concern of the federal government would be to provide an underpinning for a minimum program of public education in every state.

Reasoning Behind the Proposal. Mr. Ruml pointed out that this country is going through some major changes which will become more and more evident in the years to come, but about which it is already possible to make some reasonably certain predictions.

The first of these changes is the rapid and continuing increase in population of which we are all aware.

The second change is in the capacity of our country to produce new wealth, which is steadily rising as a result of research, new machines, and new methods—the "automation" process.

This increased capacity is known as "productivity" and is not the same as production; in fact, our productivity keeps rising even when production temporarily falls off.

The third change is in the reduction of the average working week which results in employment for more people, and at the same time gives the individual worker a greater amount of leisure time for the use and enjoyment of his income.

During recent years, due to the so-called "Cold War," a large proportion of the nation's increased income has been absorbed in the production of armament and in measures of defense, as well as in vast sums for earth satellites and explorations in outer space.

While appropriations for defense are likely to continue, they will not increase in proportion to the increase in national income unless there should be a major war.

It becomes apparent, then, that in order to maintain full employment in the years ahead there must be a tremendous increase in our demands for goods and services, among which education has a high priority.

School Boards and School Finance

The Challenge Before Us. The problem we face is to select the best basis on which to devote a larger percentage of the nation's increasing productivity to its system of public education.

Finding "the best basis" for a balanced and adequate financing of public education in this country is a problem to which we all have to address ourselves until we come up with an answer to which the majority of our citizens, nationwide, agrees. In the solution of this problem, school boards and their associations should play an increasingly important and statesmanlike role.

However necessary may be the billions of dollars which we appropriate year after year for the destructive instruments of defense, they must be counterbalanced by more nearly adequate appropriations in support of public education, the greatest *constructive* instrument we have for the preservation and perpetuation of our representative democracy.

Unless we provide such a counterbalance, the level of intelligence, moral fiber, cultural development, and civic responsibility of the American people as a whole will decline rather than advance, and the nation will inevitably deteriorate in strength and leadership.

Need for Standards in School Accounting

One of the most urgent needs in American education is for educational statistics that are comparable as among local districts within states and as among the several states.

Basic items of financial and other information need to have the same meaning for all state departments of education and for all local school districts if they are to be of real help in making policy, planning programs, estimating costs, measuring progress, keeping the public informed, drafting legislation, and numerous other activities connected with the efficient conduct of the public schools.

Until recent years, great diversity existed in accounting methods and practices relating to schools. As a result, confusion arose whenever efforts were made to compare one district or

89

one state with another, or to summarize receipts and expenditures for public education in any combined area or in the nation as a whole.

Today, great progress is being made in achieving standard definitions of educational terms, and uniform systems of records and reports. For more than a decade, no fewer than five and as many as ten national organizations, including the National School Boards Association in all instances, have been working cooperatively with the United States Office of Education on projects to develop and thoroughly test out a series of *Handbooks* supplying these basic standards for comparability in educational statistics.

Handbooks have been or will be issued dealing with *"The Common Core of State Educational Information," "Financial Accounting for Local and State School Systems," "Financial Accounting for School Activities," "Property Accounting for Local and State School Systems," "Pupil Accounting for Local and State School Systems," and "Staff Accounting for Local and State School Systems."*

In defining items or accounts to be included in these *Handbooks,* care has been exercised (1) to utilize, as much as possible, common understandings which had already developed throughout the country, and (2) to make each definition as clear cut as possible in order to allow for only one interpretation of the item. Any item, to be included, also had to meet the following criteria:

1. The item must provide information which is important to a local school district in the operation of its school system.

2. The item must be one of importance to local school districts throughout all sections of the country.

3. The item must be one on which there is a need for comparable figures among local school systems.

4. The item must be one which can be maintained as a matter of record with a reasonable degree of effort.

The National Defense Education Act included, among its other provisions, grants to the states, on a matching basis, "to assist the States in improving and strengthening (1) the adequacy

90

and reliability of educational statistics provided by State and local reports and records, and (2) the methods and techinques for collecting and processing data and disseminating information about the condition and progress of education in the States."

As a result of this stimulus, all States and Territories are using or have access to data processing equipment and have been able to add staff personnel for statistical services. It is also estimated that more than 1,000 local school systems are using automatic data processing equipment, and this number should steadily increase in the years ahead.

The United States Office of Education considers its program of developing *Handbooks for State Educational Records and Reports* one of the most important contributions it is making to American education, because this is fundamental to the establishment of improved and comparable state systems for collecting and processing educational information that is so greatly needed.

Conversion to automatic data processing, based on accepted standards, cannot be accomplished overnight. It takes time to plan, install, and operate an effective program to achieve the best results.

Local and State boards of Education, and their associations, are urged to exercise initiative in advocating the adoption and use of standards in school accounting as represented by the co-operatively developed *Handbooks* available from the United States Office of Education.

A new national organization came into being in 1962 designed to share information on progress in the area of educational data processing—local, state, and national. It is known as the Association for Educational Data Systems, Inc. and issues a monthly *AEDS Bulletin* for its members. It would be desirable for someone from the staff of every school system of any size to hold a membership in this association and keep in touch with current developments.

THE SIGN OF DEMOCRACY

*"I will accept nothing which all cannot
have their counterpart of on the same
terms."*

— WALT WHITMAN

American democracy is founded on the principle
of individual freedom and responsibility. Our government by chosen representatives is designed to
serve the whole people "with liberty and justice for
all." Ideally, every citizen shares equal opportunity
and bears equal obligation under the law. Actually,
there are too many instances in which unthinking
and uncaring persons seek selfish advantage at the
expense of their fellows. By hook or by crook they
secure preferred positions which relieve them and
overburden others. One striking example is to be
found in many of our tax assessment rolls where
great inequities exist. Were we to follow Walt Whitman's "sign of democracy," with each and every
tax payer carrying a fair and proportionate share
of the total need, much of the wrangling that goes
on over the cost of such public services as schools
would disappear. — E. M. T.

CHAPTER 12

School Board Initiative
in Adjusting Assessment Rolls

Nationwide, one of the greatest obstacles to the adequate financing of public education, as well as of all tax-supported services, is the failure of local assessment rolls to list every taxpayer at his fair and proportionate valuation and to keep the assessments currently up to date.

We have all known for a long time that inequities in the assessment of real property are a source of tremendous leakage in our tax structure at the local level.

But efforts to do something to correct the situation have, in a majority of cases, been tangled up politically and of little avail.

A few years ago, a number of school boards in northern Illinois (and perhaps elsewhere) took the initiative in ordering detailed surveys of the assessment rolls in their respective districts.

The results were surprising.

Here is the story—school boards everywhere take notice!

Reasons for the Surveys

As in so many other school districts the country over, these boards had reached the legal limit of their tax rate and still fell short of meeting the requirements of their budgets.

Where could they find new sources of revenue?

Someone suggested that perhaps a school board could authorize an independent survey of the district assessment rolls to get at the facts.

So each board contracted with a local firm of accountants and auditors to check every piece of real property in the school district against the official assessment rolls with a view to discovering vacant lots, old buildings, and new buildings which appeared to be under-assessed.

It was emphasized from the beginning that the survey was to be *completely impersonal.* The board was not interested in persons, or in knowing who paid less and who paid more, but only in equity—in making certain that every tax payer in the district was assessed at his fair and proportionate valuation.

The results were uniformly gratifying, and the cost of the survey was regained many times within the first tax collection year following.

Survey Procedure

The first step in each district was to make a large map of the district area and its boundaries, blown up from a county map.

Next, *half-section* maps were obtained from a commercial studio specializing in this sort of map for certain counties in Illinois and other midwestern states. (Difficulty may be encountered in some sections of the country in obtaining detailed maps, but something adaptable can usually be found by checking with agencies that use maps in public or private business.)

These half-section maps showed every piece of property by subdivision, lot number, and block number.

Maps in hand, the accountants went to the office of the county treasurer and requested permission to consult the *Tax Warrant Books.*

Tax rolls are, of course, open to public inspection, but ordinarily an individual is interested only in his own assessment and those of a few similar properties.

In this case, the accountants carried with them written authorization from each board of education, as a legal taxing body, that such a survey was to be made in its behalf.

From the tax warrant books, the accountants entered on the

94

half-section maps the assessed valuation of every piece of property in the school district, paying no attention to names of persons.

In some instances they found it necessary to go also to the office of the county recorder and consult the *Plat Books* on file there giving the legal descriptions of property boundaries.

These plat books also indicated properties carried on the tax warrant books as *exempt* from assessment—an important item to identify.

Physical Checkup

Next, the most arduous and time consuming step in the survey was to inspect every piece of property in the school district, block by block, lot by lot, subdivision by subdivision, and determine whether the assessment recorded for each item appeared to be in line or out of line with surrounding properties and the general assessment standards.

This was done simply by observation without talking to or disturbing any property owner which, obviously, the accountants making the survey had no right or authority to do.

As each piece of property was inspected, an appropriate indication was made on the half-section map as to its apparent status, using colored crayons.

Properties which appeared to be O.K. (and these were naturally in large majority) were left uncolored.

Tax exempt properties were colored in red.

New lot divisions found on property which was open on the map were indicated in blue.

New houses were indicated in yellow.

Homes and other properties where the assessments appeared to be old and out of line were colored in purple.

Reporting to the Board

Upon the completion of the physical checkup, the next step was to prepare a report to the board of education based on the findings of the auditors.

The report was compiled in loose-leaf form with a sheet for each block, giving the block's boundaries.

Notation was entered of the number of buildings (houses or other) found in the block.

Each piece of property was entered by lot number in one column, with its current valuation or exemption in an adjoining column, and with the accountant's memorandum, where needed, in a third column, as "property subdivided," "new house," "reassessment indicated," etc.

Multiple copies of the report were supplied to the board of education.

The board transmitted one copy of the report with a comprehensive covering letter to the township assessor explaining what had been done and why.

Another copy and letter were sent to the county assessor. (In Illinois the setup is such that the township assessor actually functions as a field man for the county assessor.)

The board indicated in its letters that it was not trying to prove the assessors derelict in their duty, but was actually trying to help them to be fair to everybody.

The board made no threats. It merely pointed to the findings resulting from a thorough, impersonal checkup of every item on the tax rolls, and left the township and county assessors to draw their own conclusions.

Outcomes and Observations

Results of these surveys were surprising and gratifying.

In every district surveyed, several hundred cases were noted of properties that either were missing from the rolls or were assessed below current valuations. These properties represented a substantial percentage of the total valuation of the district. When fairly adjusted they increased the district's total assessed valuation and provided additional tax revenue.

The surveys led to properties being put upon the tax rolls at their fair valuation at a much faster rate.

Board Initiative in Adjusting Assessment Rolls

Normally it takes a couple of years for new houses to get on the rolls after they are built. But many instances were found where houses were still not on the rolls after four or five years following occupancy.

Moreover, the surveys were so complete in checking *every* piece of property that there was no longer an excuse for any being missing from the rolls.

Finally the school boards planned to keep the surveys up to date year after year by checking new and revised assessments entered upon the tax warrant books, and new building permits issued by the municipal authorities.

Experience showed almost no complaint or objection to the making of these tax assessment surveys.

It was emphasized from the beginning that the surveys were being made for the boards of education and that the findings were to be given to the boards and to no one else.

The local press showed some interest in the surveys and commented upon them favorably.

Business interests in the area were found to be carrying their share of the tax load in practically all cases, and therefore they welcomed the idea of bringing everybody fairly into line.

Actually, the initiative taken by the board of education in having the survey made and in financing it resulted in benefits to the other taxing bodies such as the village board, the park board, the sanitary district board, and others. In a sense, then, such a project might well be entered into and supported jointly by all such taxing agencies.

However, the urgent need in many school districts of doing something to bring an immediate increase in financial support, is justification enough for school boards to take the initiative in seeking complete equity in assessments.

"The false can never grow into truth by growing in power."
—SIR RABINDRANATH TAGORE

ENVIRONMENT

"A school should be the most beauti-
ful place in every town and village."

— OSCAR WILDE

The thought expressed above is neither an idle
dream nor an unattainable goal. It is a practical
suggestion which, if accepted and followed, would
contribute not only to a more wholesome and happy
development of our children and youth but to the
economic, social, and civic prestige of the entire
community. Nor does the attainment of beauty in a
school plant, inside and out, necessarily involve any
extravagance in the use of public money. Rather, it
requires foresight, sound judgment, careful planning,
and wise supervision of capital investment in grounds,
buildings, landscaping, and equipment. With all
the school construction that is going on every year,
is it too much to hope that more and more boards of
education will recognize the opportunities they have
to develop an educational environment which will
raise standards of value and set new patterns for
community growth and achievement? — E. M. T.

98

CHAPTER 13

Capital Outlay by School Boards

In recent years a majority of the school boards of America have faced the necessity of enlarging their school plants. For many of them, capital outlay expenditures have been a new experience and have brought new problems.

The neglect of school repair and construction during the 1930's and 1940's, due to the depression and World War II, combined with the tremendous and sustained rise in the national birthrate beginning in 1946, produced a shortage in school facilities which still plagues many communities in spite of heroic efforts to meet the needs of increasing hosts of children for an adequate education.

Moreover, just as many boards were getting set to finance and build needed schools, the Korean War caused governmental restrictions on critical materials—steel, copper, aluminum, etc.—which resulted in further delaying school construction for several years in the early 1950's.

Since then, building has gone on apace but quite unevenly because of difficulties many local boards have encountered in enlisting public support, in forecasting shifts in population, in financing capital outlays, in acquiring suitable sites, in agreeing on architectural plans, and in securing bids and letting contracts.

Community Support and Long-Range Planning

No phase of school board responsibility lends itself better to citizen cooperation with school boards (see Chapter 17) than does school plant planning. A board needs to enlist the services of representative groups of parents and other taxpayers in making careful studies of such things as

1. Population trends in the district, both as a whole and in particular areas if more than one school is involved.

2. Projected school enrollments by attendance units for at least five years ahead.

3. Ability of the existing school plant to meet the projected enrollments and the educational program.

4. Indicated need for an increase in facilities, either as additions to existing buildings or as new buildings or both.

5. Suggested locations of adequate sites for new buildings, particularly in areas that are growing rapidly.

6. Landscaping possibilities which, without adding greatly to the cost of the school plant, will serve to make it a more attractive and valuable asset to the community.

7. Alternative methods of financing new capital outlay, and the relative advantages and disadvantages of each method for the community in question.

One of the most important outcomes of citizen participation in long-range planning for school facilities is the understanding of the facts of the situation that grows in the community while the studies are going on.

As a result, when the time comes that the school board must ask financial support for proposed capital outlays, a substantial percentage of the voters is already well enough informed to recognize the need and to give approval without an extended special campaign.

Contrarywise, a board which leaves its community in the dark as to school conditions and requirements until the moment it decides to hold a referendum on a tax rate or bond issue for capital outlay is facing an uphill task of suddenly informing an indifferent or even hostile public, with possible defeat at the polls. Reports are still too numerous of repeated attempts to pass school bond issues in certain districts. They indicate a lack of proper advance preparation on the part of the school boards concerned.

School Board-Architect Relationships

Because of the great increase in school construction, and the apparent fact that there must be much more such building for years to come before the need is fully met, architects have become increasingly interested in this field. Some few of them have specialized in school design, but many have had little such experience.

Architects themselves, and the school boards which employ them, should recognize that school design and construction differ in many ways from other types of building and require special knowledge and adaptability in the planning.

Boards should insist that their architects either (1) show evidence of experience in school design and construction, or (2) indicate a willingness to make a real study with the board, the school staff, and the community of the requirements peculiar to the construction that is to be undertaken.

Forward looking architects, construction executives, school administrators, school board leaders, and other interested persons are more and more consulting one another as to new approaches to school plant planning in the hope that generally better design, greater economy in construction, and more effective usefulness will be the result.

There are a good many factors, some of them deep-rooted, which retard progress toward better physical school properties. On the other hand, there are encouraging signs that progress is steadily being made in this important area of community development. (See Appendix G: "Barriers and Break-Throughs of School Architecture," page 307.)

Such organizations as the National Council on Schoolhouse Construction with headquarters at the George Peabody College for Teachers in Nashville, Tenn., the School Facilities Council of Architecture, Education, and Industry with headquarters at New York University, and the Committee on School Buildings of the American Institute of Architects have been formed to carry forward studies looking toward the improvement of school plant planning and the employment of new materials and methods which can be adapted to modern school construction.

Distinguishing Factors in School Construction

1. *A school plant should be the best the district can afford and should be adapted to the economic level of the community in which it stands.*

Since control of America's public schools is vested in local boards of education under state authorization, there will always be variations in the character and quality of school properties, ranging in every degree from the most elaborate to the most primitive. We cherish this local autonomy, but at the same time must recognize that it precludes any fixed standards of school construction nationwide, or even statewide, except such as have to do with safety factors, insurance risks, and related matters.

There are critics who condemn some boards of education for building schools which, they claim, are unnecessarily luxurious. It all depends upon the community concerned and the expressed wishes of the voters. If a board has involved the citizenry in its planning, as outlined earlier in this chapter, and if the community majority wants its schools to embody certain unusual features which it can afford to provide, that is its own business and nobody else's.

As a general principle, we ought to agree that our children, during the impressionable years that they spend in school, should be given the most attractive, comfortable, convenient, and challenging surroundings that the community can provide.

No community is justified in building a cheaper school than it can properly afford, or even afford at some sacrifice of less vital concerns. To skimp on school facilities indicates a lack of regard for the community's children and its future, and adversely influences prospective residents and business interests. Conversely, investments in good schools bring incalculable benefits to the districts that support them.

2. *Public school construction is paid for with public money which the total tax-paying community contributes on a nonpartisan basis.* In consequence, the money, whether large or small in amount, must be spent efficiently and without waste or else the

board which is responsible may expect to be called to ultimate account.

Critics of school construction are prone to emphasize the cost of a building in terms of the pupils it is designed to accommodate in a single year. The emphasis is entirely misleading. Cost should rather be calculated in terms of the total number of pupils the building will serve during its probable useful lifetime.

On such a basis, capital outlay for the school plant represents a very small per cent of the cost of a given pupil's education, and one of the best investments of a tax dollar that any community can make.

3. *A school plant, once built, will be expected to serve the community for at least a generation and probably longer.* Hundreds of school buildings in use today are more than fifty years old. Some of them are still fit for occupancy; most of them should have been replaced long since.

But the very length of anticipated service emphasizes the importance of careful planning in the beginning which will produce school plants that are not only durable but are adjustable to future changes in requirements.

A first consideration is that the school site shall provide land enough around the building for both recreational and educational purposes. Nothing in this country is more pathetic today than to find schools built years ago without adequate land, hemmed in on every side by residences, industries, and traffic filled streets. Such schools are no better than educational factories where mass production is carried on with little regard for the welfare of individual teachers or pupils. Surely children are entitled to something better, especially when we consider that it is primarily greater foresight and care in planning, and not simply more money, which makes the difference in the facilities.

4. *The school plant must be designed to meet the requirements of all the activities which are to be carried on within its walls and upon its grounds.* The professional term for this is that the design shall be "functional," but all it means is that the building and grounds shall fit the varying needs of those who use them.

School Board Leadership in America

As far as possible those responsible for designing a new school plant should consult all who will be involved in its use— the administration, the instructional staff, the maintenance staff, the parents and community public, and even the children themselves. Suggestions and recommendations, supported by the reasons for making them, should be solicited and, when received, should be given most careful consideration in formulating the plans. Time spent in such advance planning will reduce to a minimum regrets and futile wishes for something different after the school is built.

In connection with the annual conventions of the American Association of School Administrators and of the National School Boards Association there are displays of architects' plans and models of new schools from all sections of the country. Local boards and their architects, faced with construction problems, will find these School Architecture Exhibits a fertile source of ideas and practical suggestions which may be applied advantageously to their own situations.

In Conclusion

The school boards of America, facing the need for greatly expanded public school facilities to care for increases and shifts in population, have an unprecedented opportunity to make an outstanding contribution to the general welfare of their communities, their states, and the nation.

Communities which find themselves able to point with pride to their school facilities as both beautiful and efficient owe a debt of appreciation to far-sighted boards of education which assume leadership in encouraging that kind of capital outlay.

*"They that give up essential liberty
to obtain a little temporary safety,
deserve neither liberty nor safety."*

— BENJAMIN FRANKLIN

ALTERNATIVE

"Don't find fault; find a remedy."

— HENRY FORD

The critic is rarely a builder. He is content to point out the faults he sees in others, or in things that are going on, without any intention of doing his part to improve the situation or to lend some friendly assistance. The world is too full of this attitude, and Mr. Ford knew it. Hence the above admonition to his employees. Nowadays, there is a lot of fault-finding with our schools. Some of it is justified; much of it is uninformed; in certain instances it is down-right malicious. In any case, one constructive helper is worth a hundred critics, and it is help that the schools need—from parents and taxpayers, from board members, from the teaching profession, and from the children themselves whom the schools are chiefly designed to serve. — E. M. T.

RECIPE FOR PROGRESS

*"Wisdom is knowing what to do next,
skill is knowing how to do it, and
virtue is doing it."*

— DAVID STARR JORDAN

Accomplishment of lasting good in any field of endeavor depends upon the three qualities so simply stated by one of America's late, great scientists and educators. Schools today in every community are confronted with such a multitude of problems that boards of education and their professional administrators may easily become completely baffled or make serious mistakes unless they jointly possess these attributes of wisdom, skill, and virtue. All three must be exercised together, for any two without the third are inadequate to the need. Knowing what to do next and how to do it will accomplish nothing unless motivated by the virtue of action. Action combined with the wisdom to put first things first can only result in bungling inefficiency if knowledge of how to do the job is lacking; while action combined with skill in doing result in misdirected effort unless applied to the thing of first importance. — E. M. T.

CHAPTER 14

School Board-Administrator

Relationships

E very possible variation in the degree and character of the relationships between school boards and school administrators can be found to exist in these United States.

At one extreme there is the superintendent who thinks that the less his board knows about what is going on in the schools the better he will get along.

At the other extreme is the board which makes a figurehead of the superintendent by running the schools itself.

The ideal situation, of course, lies midway between these extremes, where the board, in consultation with the superintendent, and on the basis of all available facts, establishes the policies by which the schools will be operated, and where the superintendent, with the full approval of the board, exercises his professional skill in administering those policies and in reporting their effectiveness or need for modification to the board.

Most books for school boards and for school administrators contain chapters on the relationships between the two, and the 34th Yearbook of the American Association of School Administrators (1956) is devoted entirely to a very fine discussion of all aspects of this subject (see Bibliography, page 287).

Preceding chapters in the present volume have touched upon this matter more than once, particularly in Chapter 2 under "Skill in Working Relationships," page 23, under several of the "Stumbling Blocks" discussed in Chapter 5, and under the whole consideration of policy making in Chapter 6.

It seems desirable, however, to bring together in this chapter some of the underlying principles and principal factors involved in these relationships.

Some Basic Principles

The relationships between a school board and its administrator—the superintendent of schools—like most relationships in the affairs of men, are first of all a matter of human relations. This is a plain fact, but it is sometimes forgotten with unhappy consequences.

In the best interest of the children and of the total community the schools are designed to serve, it is essential that there shall be a friendly good will and mutual respect between the board and the administrator which make possible complete frankness, confidence, and understanding concerning the conduct of the schools.

There are two other important aspects of school board-administrator relationships which add somewhat to their hazards.

The first aspect is that on one side of this relationship there is a composite group of people who must act as a unit in dealing with the other side who is a single individual. As we shall see, this presents problems for both sides.

The second aspect is the fact that school affairs are public business and the school board and its administrator live in a glass house, so to speak, with all their actions and interactions in full view of the whole community. Whether their relationships are harmonious or the reverse is almost immediately apparent to everybody on the outside.

Still another principle of board-administrator relationships is that they are never static—always they are changing for better or for worse.

One reason for these changes is the frequent turnover in school board membership. It is a rare board that operates for more than a year or two without any change in its composition (see Chapter 19).

Another reason is the turnover in superintendents—every six years or so in the average community.

108

Finally, there is the basic principle that the school board *makes* policy and the administrator *executes* policy, which is by no means so clear-cut as it sounds (see Chapter 6), but which must be understood and agreed to if harmonious relationships are to exist between the two.

Variations in Pattern

It must not be supposed that every school board in America has its own school administrator.

The truth is that a majority of school districts, as at present constituted, are too small to warrant the employment of a superintendent (see Chapter 32, section on "School District Organization"). A conservative estimate is that there are in this country about 15,000 professional educational leaders who serve in the capacity of school superintendent.

Nor is every superintendent of schools an appointee of a board of education. Several thousand, including some state and many county superintendents, are elected by the people and, in consequence, feel no direct responsibility to the school boards which have jurisdiction in their areas. This is not an ideal state of affairs nor one conducive to effective working relationships.

Wide diversity is to be found in the size and character of the job of the appointed school administrator. The range is from superintendents in small districts of many kinds to city superintendents in centers of population all the way from 2,500 or fewer up to the great metropolitan centers like New York and Chicago.

In spite of all such variations, however, the relationships between a school board and its administrator differ in degree rather than in kind, and most of the observations which follow can be adapted to any local situation.

What the Board Expects of Its Administrator

Once having selected and employed its administrator, which is actually the most important task a school board must perform whenever circumstances require it (see Appendix F, "Procedures for Selecting the Superintendent of Schools"), the board should proceed to establish friendly and effective working relations with the administrator.

In its dealings with the superintendent, as in all other matters, the board must act as a unit, and the greater the harmony of agreement within the board, the greater the cordiality and strength of its relationship with the administrator is likely to be, other things being equal.

No member of the board has any legal authority to deal with the superintendent on an individual basis, and each member is obligated to abide by and uphold the adopted policies of the board whether or not he voted for their adoption.

Outside board meetings, the individual member naturally has more reason than the average citizen to be on friendly terms with the superintendent and to exchange views informally to their mutual enlightenment. But these contacts should never become unduly intimate nor are they in any way official.

From an official standpoint the board looks to its administrator for such things as

1. Attendance at all board meetings except on occasions when his own status may be under consideration.

2. Preparation in advance, after consultation with the board president or chairman, of the agenda for all regular and special board meetings.

3. Keeping the board minutes and their proper dissemination to the board, the staff, the press, and the community at large.

4. Keeping of all financial and other records of the district.

5. Advising with the board as to the adoption or modification of policy.

6. Promulgation of the rules and regulations designed to carry out policy.

7. Informing the board as to how the instructional program in the schools is being carried out, with a continuous evaluation of the success of the program.

8. Preparation of a budget, designed to support the educational program of the schools, for consideration and adoption by the board.

9. Recommendations to the board concerning all school personnel appointments, promotions, transfers, terminations, rewards, etc.

10. Working cooperatively with the board in the handling of all other regular and special activities and concerns of school operation, such as relations with parents and pupils, building programs, bond issues, the taking of bids, insurance, transportation, etc., etc.

11. Assisting the board in the preparation of an annual report of the school district.

12. Assuming joint responsibility with the board, through agreed upon procedures, for establishing and maintaining good public and press relations between the schools and the community.

What the Administrator Expects of His Board

First of all, the administrator expects the board to recognize him as a human being with the combination of hopes and fears, aspirations and doubts, abilities and faults, strengths and weaknesses that are common to us all.

The administrator must not pose as a superman; neither can he be a weakling. Granted his motives for service in the educational field are sound and worthy, and that he is conscientiously determined to do his best, he may rightfully look to his board for such things as

1. Proper recognition of his importance as a professional educator heading up the school system of the community.

2. Acknowledgment of the "team" relationship between himself and the board with its resulting
   sense of belonging,
   sharing of responsibility,
   opportunities for growth and achievement,
   credit for accomplishment.

111

3. Reasonable guarantees of his and his family's security and acceptance by the community.

4. Whole-hearted support of his application of the policies, rules, and regulations which together he and the board have agreed to follow.

5. Expectation that his functions will include all those items which have been listed above under the board's expectations of its administrator.

6. Sufficient administrative and clerical assistance so that his talents as an educational leader are not buried under a mass of mechanical detail.

7. Regard for the channeling of communications and complaints concerning the school system from the board to the staff and vice versa through the office of the superintendent to avoid confusing lines of authority.

8. Condonement of some inevitable mistakes with the understanding that the same mistake shall not be made more than once.

9. Assurance that the board will call his attention promptly to any act or failure to act of his which they do not generally approve, and will discuss with him suggestions for its correction, rather than to let such an area of criticism build up in silence until it bursts into open contention.

10. Freedom from approaches by board members seeking special or personal privilege either directly or indirectly.

11. Provision for his attendance at important educational meetings which may contribute to his professional growth and competency.

The profession of school administration, through the American Association of School Administrators, is engaged in raising its own standards and in developing an ever more qualified membership. This applies not only to those securing their initial preparation, but to superintendents in service who feel the need of retraining and advanced study to attain their maximum effectiveness in this rapidly changing world.

School Board-Administrator Relationships

Boards of education are in a position to encourage such professional advancement by arranging favorable terms for leaves of absence and return for superintendents whom they hope to retain, and by raising levels of qualification and remuneration when they have occasion to employ new administrators.

In Conclusion

Without too much repetition we might sum up the most important elements in an effective working relationship between a school board and its administrator as follows:

1. Unity and harmony within the board itself.

2. A clear agreement as to the respective functions of the board and the administrator and of their cooperative overlapping.

3. Written statements of all adopted policies, rules, and regulations.

4. A process of continuous growth in understanding by the board, the superintendent, the staff, and the community of educational programs and potentialities in their local application and statewide and nationwide significance.

5. Finally, and most important of all, a genuine liking and respect on the part of the board and the administrator each for the other. Both must reflect integrity, sincerity, and devotion to the goal of the best possible education for all the children of all the people, and for the people themselves whenever they seek added enlightenment.

"In a government like ours,
each individual must think of the welfare of all
as well as the welfare of his own family,
and therefore of the children of others
as well as his own."

— HORACE MANN

PRE-EMINENCE

"What nobler employment, or more valuable to the State, than that of the man who instructs the rising generation?"

— CICERO (106-43 B.C.)

How valuable do people generally consider the profession of teaching in America today? Do teachers themselves look upon their employment as noble in the sense that it is a rare and privileged opportunity to serve their community, state, and nation? Are the tangible as well as the imponderable rewards of teaching commensurate with this idea of its pre-eminence? If we were really efficient and foresighted, as we like to think we are, should we not be seeking the highest qualified among us to be the teachers of our children and youth? Should we not be insisting that these teacher-leaders receive the finest advance preparation for their task and every possible assistance while on the job? Should we not be placing the rewards to teachers at the very top in the scale of public service? In short, is there any evidence that we agree with the view expressed by a great Roman statesman two thousand years ago? — E. M. T.

CHAPTER 15

Teamwork Between School
Boards and School Teachers

Many recent educational meetings have featured speakers and discussion groups dealing with closer cooperation between school staffs and their boards of education as one phase of improving the quality of the educational program in the schools.

Is there any more reason for a teacher in a public school system to be on speaking terms with members of the board of education than for an employee in a large business or industrial corporation to know personally the members of the board of directors? And vice versa?

Consider the following:

The "business" with which the board of education and the teaching staff of a school system are concerned differs from other businesses in two all-important aspects:

First, the public schools belong to the entire population of the area served, not just to some specially interested segment of that population.

In the second place, public schools deal in the production (development is a better word) of human values with profit to "the general welfare" rather than in the production of goods and services with profit in dollars to individuals.

The combination of these two aspects makes the American system of public education unique among all enterprises in which mankind engages the world round.

Furthermore, the teaching staff is a fairly homogenous group composed almost entirely of men and women with a high degree

115

of educational development, well able to meet with the leading citizens of the community who are members of the school board and exchange ideas to their mutual benefit.

In consequence of these unique distinctions, there is every reason why the responsible directors of public education and its active practitioners should establish, wherever possible, much more than a formal employer-employee relationship.

Unfortunately, the formal relationship is all that is established in too many cases, and the resulting lack of mutual understanding and of personal exchange of ideas concerning aims and objectives, methods and procedures, strengths and weaknesses, opportunities embraced or lost by default, often accounts for mediocrity in a school system.

On the other hand, the extent to which mutual understanding and exchange of ideas can be developed is directly reflected in improved quality and vitality in the educational system.

How such a desirable condition may be brought about cannot be reduced to a formula. It will vary in different communities.

In general, it is much easier for boards to take the initiative in this get-together process than for teachers to do it, although tactful members of either group may lead the way.

The school superintendent, if he is in sympathy with the idea, as he should be, may help greatly in bringing the two groups together.

On the formal side, board members may visit classrooms and teachers may visit board meetings.

On the informal side, some boards arrange, through the superintendent, more leisurely meetings with small groups of teachers, taken in rotation during the year, to discuss aims and procedures at different levels of the school system or with different elements in the curriculum.

Some boards concern themselves with the personal welfare of the teachers, especially those coming into the system for the first time, as regards housing, social acceptance in the community, freedom from discriminating taboos, and the like.

Some teachers groups make it a point to invite board members to their meetings as guests or speakers, to ask board members for written contributions to teacher publications, and to commend boards for praiseworthy action.

Out of all such relationships, the members of the teaching staff gain a new feeling that their best efforts will be expected, understood, and appreciated, and a new sense of belonging to a great enterprise for the common good.

By the same token, members of the board of education gain a new understanding of the endless applications of the educational process to individual needs, and greater confidence in the persons to whom they have delegated responsibility for teaching in their community.

Together, America's teachers and boards of education should operate as a team, a team playing for the highest stakes in human history—the right of each individual to develop to his utmost, the triumph of representative democracy, and the freedom and peace of the world.

What School Boards Can Do

There are many ways in which boards of education may contribute directly to the welfare and efficiency of the teaching staffs in their local school systems, and indirectly to an increase in the supply of qualified teachers for the public schools of America as a whole.

Specifically, it is suggested that school boards should:

1. Remember first, last, and always that the education of children and youth is dependent on the character, ability, and dedication of their teachers more than on any other single factor in the school system.

2. Keep local standards high. Establish the reputation of employing only fully qualified teachers. Never let the bars down.

3. Pay salaries which will attract and hold top quality teachers and reduce turnover to a minimum. No investment will pay bigger dividends.

117

4. Treat teachers as accepted members of the community, entitled to genuine respect and appreciation for their public service.

5. Be generous in the provision of working and living conditions which will remove handicaps to effective teaching and give to teachers a sense of well-being and genuine accomplishment.

6. Establish a policy which will give competent and qualified teachers assurance of support and freedom to teach without fear of unjust criticism and reprisal.

7. Provide maximum opportunities for teachers at all levels of tenure and experience to grow in service so that year by year their effectiveness increases as teachers and as leaders in the community.

8. Encourage administration-staff relationships which will result in welding the professional personnel into a loyal, smooth-working and cooperative team.

9. Inaugurate a system of guidance which will include the early discovery of students in the schools who appear to possess the characteristics of successful teachers, and provide for their consistent encouragement toward such a career, to the end that the local community may contribute as many or more excellent recruits to the teaching profession as it requires fully certified teachers to fill the positions on its instructional staff.

10. Stimulate community provision of scholarships for promising candidates to the teaching profession who might otherwise be unable to pursue their educational preparation for such a career.

What Teachers Can Do

Teachers who realize that they represent the most constant and influential liaison between the schools and the community, discover various ways in which their attitudes and actions may strengthen the hands of the board of education and the superintendent in promoting good public relations.

118

Specifically, it is suggested that teachers should:

1. Believe sincerely that citizen interest in the work of the schools is both desirable and essential, and let their words and actions reflect this belief.

2. Make certain that they understand the policies and program of the local school board and administration so well that they can answer convincingly when people ask them questions. This means that occasionally teachers will drop in at a board meeting just to get the "feel" of things. It means even more that administrators will assist their teaching staffs to become thoroughly versed in these matters.

3. Learn to receive criticism of the schools without showing irritation or resentment. When the motive behind the criticism seems sincere, teachers should be at pains to help bring out the true facts which will then either convince the critic that he is in error or reveal to them where improvement may actually be made.

4. Express appreciation to parents and other citizens, both inside and outside the school, for interest and support of the schools, and encourage wider study and participation in school affairs on the part of the people in the community whenever opportunities offer.

5. Cooperate freely with the various media of communication between the school and the community—press, platform, radio, television—whenever teachers are called upon or have something of special significance to contribute.

6. Be faithful attendants at P.T.A. meetings, even when the meetings are held in the evening (to accommodate the men folk) and they would rather be doing something else. At the same time, teachers should be careful that their role in the P.T.A. is not the dominant one, but seeks rather to stimulate the lay members to assume leadership and active participation.

7. Recognize, finally, that their greatest means of stimulating adult interest in the schools at all times is through their students.

School Board Leadership in America

In classroom teaching from day to day, teachers should take advantage of natural opportunities, or even deliberately create opportunities, to help the boys and girls to understand and appreciate our American system of public education, including:

How the schools are supported by the people as a whole for the benefit of all children, youth, and adults.

How our plan of control by local boards of education, made up of citizens of the community, helps to carry out the wishes of the majority of the people and to adapt the schools to particular needs and conditions.

How wonderful it is that our forefathers created this means of educating all the people, young and old, in order that we may gain the intelligence and judgment needed to govern ourselves.

Board Relations with Teacher Organizations

It is only natural that teachers should associate together in some organized way for their professional, economic, and social welfare and also, hopefully, for the welfare of the schools.

Such associations exist at the local level in individual school districts, and merge or affiliate with more extensive organizations having similar objectives at county, state, regional, and national levels.

In recent years, two general types of teachers organizations have been growing in prominence and in their basic contrast and opposition to each other—a rivalry which portends nothing but trouble for school authorities.

On the one hand are the older, and usually larger, professional Teachers Associations culminating in the National Education Association (NEA) which includes both teachers and school administrators in its membership, and is not affiliated with any other segment of the total population.

On the other hand are the more recent, smaller except in the big cities, workers Teachers Unions, headed up by the American Federation of Teachers which excludes school administrators from its membership, and is affiliated with the labor segment of the population represented by the AFL-CIO.

120

School Boards and School Teachers

School boards find themselves increasingly beset by problems arising from both types of teachers organizations, often both in the same community, and must learn to deal with them openly, wisely, and firmly in carrying out legal board responsibility for decision making in the field of public school operation.

The American Federation of Teachers emphasizes the right of unions of teachers to insist on "collective bargaining" with school boards concerning salaries and working conditions, as do labor unions with employers, and the right of teachers to "strike" if their demands are not met. Major difficulty arises when the unions demand, as they usually do, that they be the "sole" bargaining agency for the entire teaching staff, union members and nonmembers alike.

The National Education Association emphasizes the right of associations of teachers to present their views to school boards with respect to salaries and other matters, but it does not believe that teachers should strike, "any more than parents should." On the other hand, it substitutes for the strike a system of "professional sanctions" against a district, or even a state, which fails to provide what it considers to be adequate support for teachers and the schools. Such sanctions take the form of refusals to sign contracts and blacklisting the district to association members.

The effect of sanctions, no less than that of strikes, is to close the schools and deprive children and youth of the day-to-day education to which they are legally entitled. The general public is inclined to view any such situation with disapproval and impatience no matter which side—the teachers' organization or the school board—appears to be more in the right, and to insist upon prompt settlement of the dispute.

Moreover, there is considerable legal precedent to the effect that public employees (which teachers are) have no right to institute strikes or sanctions against the authority of the state; or even to insist on the process of collective bargaining with an employer who, strictly speaking, is the whole people, and where no profit motive is involved, as it is in industrial disputes.

Both unions and associations of teachers have gone so far in certain instances as to seek collection of their dues *in toto* from

121

the school district by the process of withholding the payments from teachers' salary checks. This is questionable practice from a moral and ethical standpoint even though it may not actually be illegal in certain jurisdictions. It amounts to forcing compulsory membership on teachers, and violates the principle of voluntary personal decision which lies at the heart of our democracy.

The trends indicated above hold many dangers for the future of American public education, and school boards find themselves at the very heart of the situation. In seeking sound solutions, boards should hold the following principles firmly in mind:

1. However constituted locally, the school board's legal authority derives from the state and it is responsible for operating under state laws that govern public education.

2. The board's responsibility is to operate the schools efficiently and economically, but it is equally obligated to operate them at the highest attainable level of support. Money should be spent wisely, not saved at the sacrifice of quality or variety in the educational program.

3. In relation to the professional staff, it should be the board's constant endeavor to set such high standards of qualification, remuneration, equipment, scheduling, and welfare that teachers will eagerly seek the contracts offered by the board.

4. In making policy, including salary schedules and staff working conditions, the board would be well-advised to seek and give consideration to the views of every individual and group involved, and then, on the basis of the combined testimony it receives, to arrive at its independent decision as to the greatest good of all concerned including, primarily, those whom the school is designed to serve—children and youth in the community.

5. The board must represent impartially the *total* school community, and no segment of the community—professional, political, economic, social, religious, or other— should be permitted to dictate policy in any area of school operation.

School Boards and School Teachers

Some Personal Views

It is this writer's conviction that teachers have no business joining any organization which identifies itself with union labor.

The aims of organized labor have little in common with those presumably held by a profession dedicated to the highest development of children and youth and to the general advancement of culture and intelligence among mankind.

Organized labor generally imposes limitations upon the performance of individual union members. For each occupation it seeks to establish a common standard of effort and output for one day's wages—so much, and no more.

Creativity and initiative among union members are seldom encouraged, and sometimes are actually prohibited. Emphasis is on uniformity rather than on differences. But uniformity has to be geared to average ability, and it results in a mediocrity of performance which must be frustrating and repugnant to the self-respect of any individual who knows he can do better.

The above restrictions should never apply to teaching which is, in the best sense, a creative and individualistic performance that involves working with the plastic minds and spirits of growing human beings. A true teacher limits neither time nor effort in helping his pupils to grow.

The drive to unionize the teachers of America grows out of a belief among union leaders that here is a large body of underpaid public employees which can readily be induced to join union ranks by a claim that this will lead swiftly to higher salaries and improved working conditions. They have little else to offer, and even this claim is deceptive.

On the other hand, it is equally this writer's conviction that the professional associations of teachers have responsibilities, far beyond any so far exercised, for policing their own ranks to weed out and keep out any members who do not meet high standards of training, personality, ability, and skill in the teaching profession. Then association membership would stand for something that boards of education could count on both in employment practices and in dismissal necessities.

123

THE VALUE OF OPEN DISCUSSION

"Men are never so likely to settle a question rightly as when they discuss it freely."

— THOMAS B. MACAULAY

Most of us have lived long enough to know that, concerning matters on which there is a sharp division of opinion, the right answer is rarely to be found at either extreme, but is usually somewhere in between. The process by which extreme views are gradually brought to a common focus is through discussion—full, free, and informed discussion. Every aspect of a question must be considered in the light of all the evidence that can be brought to bear upon it. Expressed opinion, unsupported by facts, cannot stand against the facts which must be taken into account in any wise decision. The freest possible exchange of information and ideas among the members of a group or a community is the surest guarantee that questions at issue will be settled "rightly." — E. M. T.

CHAPTER 16

Public Relations
in Public Education

The American plan of local lay boards of education for the control of public schools is unique. There is nothing like it anywhere else in the world (see Chapter 1).

Instead of centralized national control, or even of state or local control of the schools by political parties or the educational profession itself, we have seen fit to adopt a cooperative plan under which representatives of the people at large, in consultation with the professionally trained administrators and teachers, adopt the policies which guide the schools and then leave the carrying out of those policies to a staff which is employed for professional competence (see Chapter 6).

Even though this system may not be perfect, most Americans seem to believe it is sounder than any alternative. In the truest sense our local lay boards of education represent democracy at work for its own perpetuation and advancement. (For a discussion of current challenges to local control, see Chapter 32.)

While there are frequent stumbling blocks to school board effectiveness (see Chapter 5), we are constantly striving toward the ideal which is entirely within reach and which might be expressed as follows:

To secure in every school district a non-partisan, broadly representative, team-spirited board of education, having clearly defined policies based on a thorough understanding of the educational process, conducting its business in open sessions as a committee of the whole, and possessing fiscal independence for the operation of its educational program under the administration of a chief school officer.

The responsibility of the board of education toward its community is not only legal, but has civic, social, economic, and moral aspects which are no less important.

With the greatest good to the greatest number as its goal, the board should seek at all times to carry out the considered wishes of the majority of the people of the community, within the framework of the law, whatever that may be.

The board must stand firmly against the pressures of minority groups and special interests of any kind (see Chapter 8).

It is a wise board, therefore, which uses every channel of communication to establish and maintain effective public relations. These channels include the press, radio, and television, the P.T.A., community organizations, citizens' study and advisory committees of all kinds (see Chapter 17), and the contributions of the school staff, professional and non-professional.

No board should wait until it is forced to take a defensive position in the face of uninformed or unfriendly criticism (see Chapters 9 and 18). *At all times the school board should take the initiative with regard to school affairs.*

An Example of Initiative

Several years ago there was received at the office of the National School Boards Association, copy of a resolution adopted at a regular meeting of the board of education in Battle Creek, Mich.

The resolution, which is reproduced below, speaks for itself, but it is recommended as a working example of the way in which a school board anywhere, while maintaining its full prerogatives and responsibilities, may act to link together more closely the school system and the community, and to interpret each to the other.

"Recognizing the growing importance of public education in American Democracy, and being in complete agreement with the point of view that the schools should remain close to the people and that they should maintain constant contact with all elements in the community;

"and accepting the principle that all concerned with the work of public education—pupils, parents, and teachers—should have a part in developing the educational policy in the schools;

"we, the members of the board of education of Battle Creek, hereby go on record endorsing the instruments of democratic cooperation now functioning in our educational program, including the Parent-Teachers Association, Educational Advisory Council, the Teachers Association, the Engineer-Custodian's Association, the Secretaries' Association, and the City-Wide Student Council.

"As a board, we wish to encourage study, discussion, and active participation by all concerned through their several organizations in the promotion of the best possible program of education for our community.

"We believe that effective education for democratic living takes place only when adequate provision is made for actual practice in democratic action.

"In recognizing the above mentioned cooperating organizations in the educational program of the Battle Creek public schools, and by encouraging their active participation in educational policy-making, we wish to make it clear that in no way does the board wish to escape its responsibility to the citizens of the community as the official governing body responsible to the people for a final decision on all matters of policy and educational programs.

"Under the statutes of the State of Michigan, the board assumes its full responsibility in all matters relating to the program of public education in the City of Battle Creek, and invites fullest cooperation from all groups through suggestion, discussion, and recommendation."

Public Relations Policy

The resolution just cited is an illustration of school board policy regarding one aspect of public relations. The details would, of course, vary from district to district.

127

Another aspect of relationships between a school system and the community it serves revolves around the various media of communication—the press, radio and television, and motion pictures.

Contacts with these media should not be haphazardly left to chance, for that usually results in a lot of unreliable publicity over sensational happenings and controversial issues, with little or no consistent and constructive information to the reading and listening public on fundamental educational programs and progress.

After full consultation with representatives of the various communications media, school boards should establish clear-cut policy with respect to contacts between these media and the school authorities and school staff, seeking, in principle, the greatest possible frankness and cooperation (see pages 44 and 143).

It should never be lost sight of that public schools belong to the taxpaying public which furnishes the money for their operation, supplies the students—young and old—who attend, indicates in the final analysis what shall be taught, and absorbs into its society the graduates of the school system.

The character of our society—its strength, its integrity, its effectiveness, its freedom—is definitely determined by the degree and quality of the education of its individual members.

That character is never static. It is either improving or it is deteriorating.

When the schools are neglected or inadequately maintained, society inevitably deteriorates. If such a condition persists, the very foundations of the nation are threatened. During the depression, World War II, and the early postwar years, America skirted the brink of such disaster. It took gigantic efforts on the part of numerous agencies, organizations, and individuals, both educational and non-educational, to turn the tide.

Even so, the masses of our people have only begun to develop an understanding interest and a generous support of public education as the foremost *constructive* instrument they possess for perpetuating and advancing those things they unconsciously hold dearest—such things as the integrity of the individual; his right

128

to maximum development; his freedom to learn, and earn, and yearn, and to express himself; his obligation to his fellow men, his country, and his God.

Boards of education, especially, have an obligation to do their utmost to keep public interest in public education glowing and growing until its sincerity and persuasiveness permeate every school district and it shall never again lapse into indifference and apathy.

We need to make bigger plans, to aim higher in our aspirations and in our efforts (see page 18). Walter Lippman dramatically expressed this idea in his speech at the Fifth Annual Dinner of the National Citizens Commission for the Public Schools in San Francisco, when he said:

"We must lift ourselves as promptly as we can to a new and much higher level of interest, of attention, of hard work, of care, of concern, of expenditure, and of dedication to the education of the American people."

The solution seems to lie in a continued and stepped up crusade to help the American people to acquaint themselves with the potentialities of their schools and with the significance of a universal system of free, public education in a world where the worth, dignity, and freedom of the individual are being challenged as never before.

> *"I know of no safe depository of the*
> *ultimate powers of society but the*
> *people themselves; and if we think*
> *them not enlightened enough to exercise*
> *their control with a wholesome discretion,*
> *the remedy is not to take it from them,*
> *but to inform their discretion by education."*
> — THOMAS JEFFERSON
> In a letter to W. C. Jarvis, 1820

INCENTIVE

*"Forced-to-go never gits far,
ye know."*

— CAPTAIN LEEZUR
in *Vesty of the Basins*
by Sarah P. McLean Greene

Just as individuals get further when the urge to accomplishment comes from within, so do communities. Compulsion, even by qualified authority, seems inevitably to breed opposition and discontent. As Samuel Butler expressed the matter nearly 300 years ago, "He that complies against his will, is of his own opinion still." No matter how good the reasons given, people grow stubborn when they feel forced into making a decision for which they are ill prepared—such as voting a school bond issue, for example. But when, by participating with local authorities in a study of conditions and needs, the people convince themselves that the best interests of their community will be served by a new bond issue, they pass it readily and take pride in its success. This is the keynote of all sound progress— to develop incentive rather than to apply force. — E. M. T.

CHAPTER 17

School Boards and Citizens
Must Work Together

In a local district the board of education has a leadership function in making certain that all the people of the community are thoroughly acquainted at all times with the facts concerning school conditions.

This acquaintance must extend beyond the current resources in finances, buildings, teachers, equipment, and courses of study, to the anticipated needs two, three, five, or even ten years hence.

It takes years to prepare qualified teachers and to acquire sites and erect buildings.

Many communities are changing rapidly both in total population and in its distribution within the district boundaries.

In increasing numbers, districts are being combined into larger units for greater administrative and financial efficiency.

Much planning ahead is required under all these circumstances, and a school board needs the active support, not only of parents, but of citizens and taxpayers generally.

In behalf of our public schools we must all work together more closely. Too often we dissipate our efforts in many different directions and sometimes for things that are trivial in comparison to major issues and needs.

Public education concerns us all, and it is far wiser and more statesmanlike to seek ways in which we can combine our efforts with those of other individuals and agencies all directed toward the same big problems, so that the total impact shall be concentrated rather than dispersed, and cooperative rather than competitive.

School Board Leadership in America

Enlisting Citizen Participation

Where people are accused of apathy toward the schools, it is usually because they do not know the facts regarding school conditions, needs, and potentialities.

The surest way for citizens to get such facts is to help collect them, organize them, study them, and recommend appropriate action to their boards of education.

People are best informed when they are self-informed!

Boards of education, therefore, are seeking more and more the assistance of citizen groups in an endeavor to reflect true community opinion.

Conversely, citizen groups and organizations concerned about the schools are offering help to their school boards.

Experience has shown that the best schools are to be found in those communities where citizen interest and participation are the greatest.

A wise school board takes the initiative in involving the people of its community in school affairs and does not wait until some crisis forces contact along less desirable lines (see Chapter 18).

When all the people have all the facts all the time concerning their schools, crises are anticipated and resolved before they occur.

Some boards of education are still afraid that to suggest or approve the formation of citizens committees to study the schools is an admission of weakness or "buck-passing" on their part.

Just the reverse is true!

It takes more strength and ability on the part of a board to work consistently with the public than to work apart from it, but the rewards are infinitely greater.

Principles Involved in Working Together

We have learned that the process of cooperation between citizens and boards of education is a two-way street, not just either side "telling" or "selling" the other, but both working together toward a common goal.

132

Boards and Citizens Must Work Together

It must be recognized that this working together is not easy, because all kinds of people are involved, and tact, patience, and self-control are needed to keep from getting off on side interests or selfish interests to the neglect of the primary objective which is, of course, the best educational opportunities that can be provided by the community for its children, youth, and adults.

Out of the experience of many communities where school boards and citizens have worked together, three basic principles have evolved that must always be observed if citizen participation is to be helpful rather than harmful to the educational program.

These three principles cannot be repeated too often or emphasized too much or applied too strictly. They are:

1. That citizens committees or advisory councils, or whatever they may be called, shall always be broadly representative of the entire community. By this we mean that the group as a whole shall not manifest a pre-conceived bias in any direction, but shall be a genuine cross section of the varied interests and attitudes which exist in every community, and shall strive to reconcile these variations and come up with recommendations approved by a substantial majority.

2. That the study, findings, and recommendations of the citizens committees shall be based on facts as they can be obtained by research and investigation, and not on opinions, ideas, guesses, or emotions which too often come to the fore in the early stages and which seldom are substantiated without modification when all the facts are in hand. It is axiomatic that in arriving at the facts on any given problem, the public and the professional school staff must work together and not separately or at cross purposes.

3. That a clear understanding shall exist from the start that, while the citizens committees are free to carry on their work in the manner which seems to them best, there shall be a close working relationship with the established school authorities, and that the recommendations of the committees shall be channeled through the board of education for final approval and action.

133

In no sense is any citizens group intended to replace the legally constituted school board or even to compete with it in the eyes of the community.

If in the end, it should become clear that a majority of the citizens of a community desire changes and improvements in the schools which the board is not willing to grant, then it is time to secure a board which more truly reflects the wishes of those it is supposed to serve.

That is the way in which we operate in the representative democracy which is America.

Questions for Cooperative Study

There are questions in every school district on which the board of education could make policy with a good deal more assurance if it could have the benefit of community-wide study and the recommendations of the citizenry at large.

A list of suggested questions is given below.

Depending upon their urgency in a given community, any of these questions might be assigned to a committee of leading citizens and representatives of community organizations who would work with members of the professional school staff to discover answers and report their conclusions to the school board.

1. Are the schools of this community seeking to provide for the balanced growth of our children and youth as human beings and as citizens?

2. How can our school system insure proper emphasis upon the fundamentals of instruction?

3. Should the schools promote character and spiritual development, and if so, how?

4. Are parents satisfied with the methods of reporting their children's progress in school?

5. How many young people are dropping out of high school, and why?

6. What does the community as a whole think about discipline and how it should be handled in the schools?

7. What changes, if any, should there be in the secondary school curriculum to best meet the needs of the community, state, and nation?

8. What procedures should be followed to recruit better teaching personnel?

9. Is adequate provision made for the orientation of new teachers and for the inservice growth of all teachers?

10. How do salary schedules in the schools of this community compare with those in neighboring communities and with other occupations that compete for personnel?

11. What is the status of the teachers as regards living conditions, personal freedom, social acceptance, and the like?

12. Is there any way in which teachers of superior ability can be recognized and rewarded?

13. What has been done about modernizing school buildings and equipment that depreciated during the depression and war years?

14. Are the school facilities—buildings, land, and equipment—going to be adequate in the next five to ten years for the children already born into the community?

15. Is the school plant being used for maximum service to the community?

16. What is the best method of financing school construction programs in this community?

17. What proportion of our school support is coming from local, county, state, and federal sources, and what shift, if any, seems to be indicated?

18. For this community, what about kindergartens? Vocational education? Junior College? Adult Education? etc.

19. Is the community satisfied with the method of selection, quality of membership, and effectiveness of service of its school board?

20. How can most effective relations between the school and the community be established and maintained?

FOOLISH EXTREMES

"In times of crisis we must avoid both ignorant change and ignorant opposition to change."

— JOHN STUART MILL

Ignorance is dangerous, whether it leads to action or to delay. Equally to be shunned are those who advocate rushing ahead with ill-considered plans and those who insist on maintaining the status quo at any cost. One course leads quickly to catastrophe through error; the other, to defeat by default. The only basis for wise decision on what to do, and when, and how, in any given situation, is full possession and careful weighing of all the facts. School boards will be well advised to remember this during crises that arise in public education, so that in all matters foolish extremes may be avoided and sound courses of action may be taken. — E. M. T.

CHAPTER 18

School Crises—Reasons
and Remedies

W hen we consider the number of people involved in making school policies and in carrying them out in the thousands of separate school districts in this country, it is not suprising that every year a few districts get into serious trouble. And in a good many others, future trouble may be brewing unaware.

If the standards and principles presented and discussed in this book could be followed consistently, there is little likelihood that a school district would get into serious trouble. But to acquaint board members, school personnel, parents, citizens generally, and the leaders of organizations and enterprises in the community with these underlying principles, and to ensure their application in practice, is a gigantic and never-ending task.

It is the purpose of this chapter to set forth some of the disrupting influences that develop in school districts and the sources from which they spring. Recognition of such "seeds of discord" may prevent their growth to devastating proportions in the first place, and may indicate how they can best be dealt with at any stage.

Damage from Dissension

It is a sad and sobering experience for any community to live through a controversy involving its public schools.

Even though conditions may seem to be better after a solution has been reached, the improvement is purchased at a price that the community should never have had to pay.

Every controversy leaves scars that are long in healing. Those most deeply scarred are the children and youth in the community, who are hurt in two ways:

First, the spectacle of their parents and other grownups engaged in dissension that is usually marked by emotion, prejudice, and ignorance instead of by calmness, reason, and understanding, is bewildering and embarrassing to young people.

Second, as a result of any controversy over schools, the quality of the educational program inevitably deteriorates for a period of time, often for months or years, and students in the schools during this period are deprived of the progress they should have made—progress which can seldom be regained.

People are often quick to take sides without troubling to get at the real facts. So what usually starts as a comparatively small difference in viewpoints, is often fanned into the flames of a major controversy involving the whole community.

Seeds of Discord

Seeds of controversy and discord are always present in any school district because so many different people must work together to support and carry on the enterprise—board members, administrative staff, teachers, parents, taxpayers, leaders of organizations, and citizens generally.

Also, because so many different elements are involved—the school program with its greatly varied offerings and methods of approach, the school plant with its sites and buildings that are more or less adequate, the school equipment which is either too meager or too lavish, the school budget and its resulting tax rate, inequities in assessments on real estate, and a hundred and one other things over which there can be differences of view.

Seeds of discord in a school district are like weed seeds in a garden. We all know that if a garden is well managed and thoroughly tilled, the weed seeds may sprout but the seedlings are quickly snuffed out before they can do any damage to the crops. Contrariwise, if a garden is neglected, and the sprouting weeds are not uprooted and killed, they thrive mightily and soon begin to crowd out the legitimate plants and to rob them of the resources of soil, sunshine, and moisture that should be theirs to bring an abundant harvest.

In the same way, if a school district is well and properly controlled and operated, seeds of discord may appear, but they are quickly neutralized by timely and sensible action. Conversely, in a school district that is hampered by overlapping authority, unwritten policy, inefficiency, inadequate support, or lack of vision, seeds of discord may easily grow into crises that rob the students of the resources of harmony, equality of opportunity, discipline, and educational values to which they are entitled and which they must have to grow into an abundant adulthood.

Seedbeds of Controversy

In any controversy involving the public schools, the *school board* will inevitably find itself at the center, sooner or later. Sometimes, unfortunately, the board is the center from the beginning because the seeds of discord are in the board itself and are not properly controlled—seeds of partisanship, of rivalry, of ambition, of self-interest (see Chapter 5).

A serious example of partisanship on school boards is the growing number of members whose loyalty is to parochial rather than to public education. However capable in other respects, such persons violate a primary qualification for school board membership because, no matter how much they protest to the contrary, their attitude can never be non-partisan. In any critical issue between public and private schools in their districts, they must vote in the interest of the parochial system or be subject to discipline by their church authorities. Public education in communities where such persons constitute a majority on the school board is doomed to starvation and mediocrity until the unbalance is remedied by the voters, or else it loses its public nature and becomes essentially parochial in character.

Any board that lacks complete devotion to public education, that is unable or unwilling to get at the real facts in all situations, to reach policy agreements which are based on the facts, and to take the lead in helping the community to understand and accept the facts and the policies, is a seedbed of controversy that may easily spread throughout the district.

Sometimes the seeds of discord lie in the *school administration* if the superintendent turns out to be a dictator rather than a leader, and is uncooperative or incompetent. This rarely happens if the board has followed recommended procedures in selecting its administrator, but occasionally even the most careful screening fails to reveal weaknesses (see Appendix F).

Whenever administrative weaknesses become apparent, the board should frankly consult with its superintendent about them in the hope that he will be willing and able to improve his ways. But if not, then a change must be made and this sometimes precipitates a crisis in the school system unless the reasons for it have been made clear to the community as a whole and public understanding established.

On the other hand, there are superintendents doing an excellent job of serving the community with competence and loyalty, who happen to incur the displeasure or enmity of some individual or group which sets out to "get him." Under such conditions, it is the board which must defend and protect the superintendent against a minority attack and see that it is defeated by the good sense and courage of an informed majority.

Sometimes the seeds of discord lie in the *teaching staff*. So many conditions are involved in keeping a body of teachers happy and effectively functioning that it takes an alert administration and an informed school board to ensure their acceptability. Remuneration, while important, is not the only consideration affecting the welfare of teachers. Other factors are physical plant and classroom equipment, class size and scheduling, freedom from interruptions by too many special assignments or outside demands on their teaching time, reasonable provision for sickness and other necessary absence, clear channels of communication to and from the offices of administration, and a whole host of added considerations.

Problems of tenure and of contract renewal are sometimes sources of difficulty. These involve individual teachers and can usually be settled by frankness and kindness. Occasionally, a teachers' organization protests a real or fancied injustice to some of its members. In such case, the board and administration must act promptly, firmly, and wisely to adjust the differences and to prevent the controversy from involving the entire community (see Chapter 15, section on "Board Relations with Teacher Organizations," page 120).

Political Interference

In far more cases than we commonly realize, the seeds of discord in school affairs lie in the political organization of the community and district.

Most political leaders are concerned primarily with two things: power and money. In the case of schools, they often use their power to nominate and elect partisan board members and to control policies, and they often deny money that is badly needed by the schools through their control of assessments, taxes, and budget appropriations.

School control and party politics should never be mixed, because their aims are not the same. The former must be altruistic, all-embracing, far-sighted, and generous in its provision for our nation's future through education. The latter is too frequently opportunistic, narrow, short-sighted, and greedy in its desire for party aggrandizement and perpetuation.

Nevertheless, politics and schools are both elements of our American scene that are present in all communities and that must live together. Fortunate are those communities where they may live as neighbors and not as bedfellows—where the school board is independent of political domination in its membership, in policy development, and in fiscal control.

Unhappy and handicapped are those communities where politics and schools are wedded to any degree that dictates board membership as party patronage, that limits policy to expediency, and that restricts school budgets to the bare necessities without any desire to invest generously in the education of children, youth, and adults as the surest basis for building a better community, state, nation, and world.

141

In such districts the seeds of discord are like perennial weeds which endure and spread year after year by means of underground roots. Political roots are deeply embedded in the soil of community history, custom, and practice. For the most part, the political bosses take pains to avoid controversy and to suppress rumblings of discontent and starvation in the schools by firm controls and limited doles.

Occasionally things get so bad that the school community rebels and a major crisis is precipitated with charges and countercharges and, in the end, a general housecleaning. The benefits of such an upheaval will outweigh its scars, in the long run, if it results in giving the school board and school administration independence in policy making and fiscal control, with sole responsibility to the total citizenship of the community.

Critics-at-Large

Very often school crises have their birth outside the official school family. In every community, fortunately or unfortunately depending on one's viewpoint, there are individuals and groups who consider themselves self-appointed watchdogs over the schools, and crusaders against whatever they believe to be wrong.

A charitable view is to look upon such persons as serving to keep the school board and administration on their toes. An uncharitable view is that such persons are inborn eccentrics and troublemakers. In any case, they have to be dealt with.

Someone has pointed out that the two most common criticisms of the public schools are (1) that they are not good enough in this, that, or the other respect, and (2) that they cost too much. Often the same critic will use both arguments without realizing how inconsistent he is in demanding that improvements be made at the same time that costs are reduced.

Other targets of critics-at-large include (1) certain courses which can be labeled as "fads and frills" or as "controversial," (2) certain methods of teaching that are regarded either as outdated or as too advanced, (3) certain text or library books which are said to be subversive, un-American, obscene, or otherwise objectionable, (4) a certain person on the board or school staff against whom damaging charges are made. All of these have in them the "seeds" of a major school crisis if permitted to grow.

An early effort should be made to discover the *motives* behind any criticisms of the schools that threaten to become seeds of discord in the community. Motives are never easy to get at, but they must be understood if outside critics are to be dealt with before they precipitate a crisis.

One of the best ways to discover motives is to invite the critic to appear before the school board at the next meeting and present his criticism in written form. If he is honest and sincere in his criticism, he will be glad to do this the best he can.

If, on the other hand, the critic's motive is not honest, but springs from a desire to discredit or weaken the public school system, then he will be unlikely to accept the board's invitation to present his criticism openly, but will prefer to work under cover in secret meetings with others of his ilk, to distribute inflammatory pamphlets or sudden press releases, to distort facts, to attack personalities, and to use all the smear tactics employed by subversives.

Reference is made here to Chapter 9 on "How Should School Boards Meet Criticism?" It is to be hoped that whenever in a district criticism threatens to flare into a conflagration, the board will take prompt steps to broaden the base of understanding by involving the total community in a serious and constructive investigation of the facts.

The Role of the Press

The media of communication—press, radio, and television—bear a responsibility to a school community that transcends their usual role of purveyors of any and all "news."

Because the public schools belong to and serve the total community, and because they are primarily devoted to the training of the young, it is especially important that information put out through the communications media shall be accurate, complete, and unbiased rather than partial and sensational—that its purpose shall be to inform rather than to inflame.

143

Editors, announcers, and emcees should be particularly sensitive to the effect that whatever they print, pronounce, or picture concerning school affairs will have on their audiences. As leaders in the creation of public sentiment and opinion, they have an obligation to make sure that items relating to public education shall be constructive and not destructive.

This is not to say that the items must always be rosy and uncritical. It is to say that, whether a report is good or bad, it shall aim to build up rather than to tear down the school system.

Often the communications media are the first to detect "seeds of discord" in a school community. But the sudden publication of an inflammatory letter, interview, or article is a great disservice to the educational system. A proper sense of responsibility will dictate that the school authorities be consulted before broadcasting the criticism.

Ideally, the school authorities—board and administration—should at all times be in cooperative contact with the communications media. Then, in any developing crisis, the media are in a strong position to present facts, to advocate reasonableness, and to guide public opinion in reaching a sound and constructive solution to the difficulty.

School Surveys

A common outcome of school controversies and crises is the suggestion that a *survey* be made to establish the facts and to make recommendations. This suggestion may or may not have merit depending on a great many factors in the district's history, experience, current status, and areas involved in the controversy.

There are numerous kinds of school surveys covering all possible variations between a brief study by a special local committee and an extensive and expensive investigation by an outside agency employed for the purpose.

Perhaps the most common and one of the best types is the *self-survey* in which a committee representing the board, the school staff, and the community, with the advice of one or more experts from nearby schools of education, studies the problems at issue and makes recommendations for improvement.

If a commercial firm of educational consultants is employed on a fee basis to make the survey, special precautions should be taken to check their reputation and experience, to qualify the survey staff as to objectivity and competence in the areas under study, and to orient them to the district situation.

Whatever the size and scope of the survey, there are certain guiding principles which should be followed. Among the more important of these are

1. The survey shall be officially authorized by the school board, and its purpose, scope, methods of conduct, and terminal date clearly outlined in writing.

2. Individuals or agencies designated to conduct the survey shall enjoy the confidence and good will of all elements in the community.

3. In its efforts to establish true facts, the survey group shall be given the fullest possible cooperation by all concerned, both within and without the school system.

4. The survey report shall be submitted first to the school board and to any individuals who may be personally and directly involved; the board, in turn, shall promptly make the report available to the communications media and interested organizations in the community.

5. As rapidly as possible after receiving the survey report, the school board shall discuss and act upon the various recommendations taking pains to make clear to the community its reasons for adopting or rejecting each recommendation.

Too often school surveys have been made with a great deal of publicity, and voluminous reports have been prepared and submitted, only to have their recommendations languish and die for lack of serious consideration and action by the boards which authorized the surveys.

A small and timely survey, carefully considered and thoroughly implemented, is far more valuable in accomplishing needed improvements in a school system than is an elaborate and costly survey whose report is filed and ultimately forgotten.

SERVICE TO SOCIETY

*"No man has come to true greatness
who has not felt in some degree that
his life belongs to the race."*

— PHILLIPS BROOKS

Voluntary service to his fellow men is a privilege
enjoyed by the citizen of a free society like ours in
America. Thousands accept such responsibility and
discharge it conscientiously. Among these, none
serve to better purpose than do the men and women
on local boards of education throughout the land.
Chosen for integrity, ability, and devotion to the
public welfare, they spend long hours seeking the
best for America's children and youth, without
thought of remuneration in most cases. Their reward
is expressed in the quotation above, and the degree
to which their lives are dedicated to the improvement of a race of free men in a peaceful world
measures that inner sense of "true greatness" to
which Phillips Brooks refers. — E. M. T.

CHAPTER 19

New School Board Members

Over and over again in this book the conviction is expressed that the school boards of America and their associations occupy the key position in maintaining and advancing our system of public education.

Standing as they do between the people of their respective communities and the professional staffs of the schools, seeking to carry out the wishes of the former through employment of the latter, boards of education bear the responsibility for interpreting each group to the other and for developing, with the help of both, the policies which shall combine ideas and activities into the most effective operation of the schools.

In the nature of things, school boards are composed simply of human beings with varying degrees of strength and weakness. Voluntary service of this kind, however, should call for the highest type of integrity and ability that can be found in each community.

On the whole, in spite of occasional shocking examples to the contrary, there is evidence that in recent years standards of school board membership and service have been steadily advancing.

Evolution, not Revolution

Public schools must provide a continuing, non-partisan service to the entire community.

Always a steady stream of young people is flowing through the schools between the entering and the graduating points. Their growth and welfare are greatly dependent upon the stability of the school program which, in turn, is dependent upon harmony and consistency of action by the school board.

Ideally, schools should be going through a continuous process of evolution toward greater effectiveness, but they should not be

147

subjected to a revolution in programming or personnel which sometimes happens when membership on the school board undergoes too radical a shift as a result of dissention or controversy in the district.

As a matter of principle, it is unwise to change a majority of the membership of a school board in any one year.

It should never be forgotten that, when things go wrong in a school system, *it is the children who suffer,* and their entire lives can be adversely affected by such a state of affairs.

Only in the rarest of cases can a community undergo a controversy involving its public schools and emerge without enduring scars (see Chapter 18).

This does not mean that needed changes cannot be brought about by an orderly process of discussion and decision based upon actual facts and majority views. That is the sensible procedure to follow in a democratic society.

Turnover in Membership

There are probably in this country somewhere between 100,000 and 150,000 school board members (also known in certain states as school trustees, or school directors, or school committeemen). The number declines as districts reorganize (see page 41).

Each year, the turnover in membership is very considerable, perhaps from a fourth to a third of the total. This means that every year, at a conservative estimate, 25,000 or more new members are chosen for service on local school boards.

These new members—men and women from among the citizenry of their communities—take office with little or no comprehension of the duties and responsibilities involved in school board membership.

On the other hand, each change in membership, each injection of "new blood" should offer the board an opportunity to re-evaluate its services and to reorganize for greater effectiveness.

Parenthetically, it might be indicated how unwise it is for members of existing boards to concern themselves too actively with the selection of new board members, or even with their own re-selection, thus risking the charge of self-perpetuation.

It is equally unwise for members of school staffs, who are employees of the board, to get involved in school board candidacies, except to exercise their right to vote as individual citizens.

Length of Service

On the average, school board members are reported to serve for about seven years, but a conspicuous few serve a much longer time which means that corresponding numbers serve shorter terms.

Ideally, a qualified board member should serve long enough to reach maximum understanding and competence in the job, but not so long that his usefulness is outgrown because his actions have become perfunctory or routine.

No one can place exact limits on this ideal length of service, because individuals vary so much in their ability

(1) to orient themselves quickly to their new responsibilities, and

(2) to maintain their zest and freshness of approach over a long period,

but we might venture a guess that in most cases service of from 5 to 15 years will yield the best returns to the community, other things being equal.

Should School Board Members Be Paid?

The predominating experience of the past indicates that membership on a school board should represent voluntary service by persons of the highest caliber. Reference is made again to the early chapters in this book.

Wherever school board service is recognized at its true worth by the people of a community, there is little difficulty in attracting top-level citizens to membership without promise of remuneration, arduous though the duties often prove to be.

In those few places where salaries have been attached to

149

school board membership, the results have revealed two basic objections to the practice:

1. Salaries can never be large enough to attract the really big people who are willing to render this public service voluntarily.

2. Since experience nationwide has demonstrated for years that the highest type citizen service is available on a voluntary basis, there can be no justification for including salaries for board members in the school budget—the money is better spent for other things.

On the other hand, it is entirely legitimate to reimburse members for out-of-pocket expenses connected with board business. Further, legitimate financial provision for the board and its members includes budget items for membership in school boards associations (see Chapter 22), and for travel expenses of representatives of the board to attend state and national school board conventions and study conferences (see Chapters 26, 28, and 29).

Qualifications for School Board Membership

Chapters 2 and 3 in this volume reveal many of the essential characteristics of school board members who are qualified to accept leadership responsibilities as educational statesmen.

At this point it is suggested that the reader turn to Appendix B, page 288, and read the statement entitled "Boards of Education —American Plan."

Follow then with a study of the "Thirty Critical Requirements for School Board Membership" by Dr. Richard E. Barnhart (see Appendix C, page 290).

These several statements give a pretty clear picture of what kind of a person the school board member should be to serve his community, state, and nation most effectively.

No single individual can hope to combine in equal degree all these desirable qualifications, but at least they serve as a guide and a goal toward which to strive.

That board member is likely to serve best who combines in fair measure most of these characteristics in contrast to one who is conspicuously distinguished for certain qualities but woefully lacking in others.

Methods of Selection

Comparatively little research has been done in the school board field, and there are few nationwide statistics concerning composition of boards, length of terms, methods of selection, etc.

A study of *Local School Boards: Organization and Practices*, published by the U. S. Office of Education in 1962, supplied a great deal of information from over 4,000 districts having 1,200 or more pupils enrolled. This and various area studies make possible some estimates which are probably not very far wrong.

It is believed, for example, that approximately 85 per cent of school board members in America are elected by the people, and 15 per cent are appointed by some civil authority—by the mayor, city manager, or city council; by county commissioners; by judges, courts, or grand juries; by a special agency created only for that purpose in one state; by the legislature in another state; and by the governor in still another.

Appointed boards are most commonly found in the larger cities—about one-half of the boards in cities of over 500,000 and one-fourth of those in cities of over 100,000 are appointed.

Elections of school board members are variously conducted. About 40 per cent appear to be held at the same time as are regular political elections, and in perhaps half of these cases the names of school board candidates are included on the regular ballots, following nomination by the party machines.

About 60 per cent of school board elections are held at a different time than political elections with the intent of focusing attention on them from a non-partisan standpoint.

Advantages and disadvantages can be cited for any method of appointment or election. Far more important than the method are the ways in which candidates are nominated and the motives behind their selection.

A recurrent threat to school board unity and effectiveness is the new board member who, without undergoing a period of

151

assimilation, sets out single-handedly to accomplish some declared reform or to lead a crusade toward some personal objective.

Any motive except an unselfish desire or willingness to serve the best interests of the total community in the most effective operation of its schools is open to suspicion.

Motives are more readily suspect when a candidate seeks the office than when the community seeks a candidate. For, aside from inner satisfaction, little return is normally to be expected from school board service than a lot of hard work, considerable criticism, and the unexpressed appreciation of fellow citizens.

The narrower the base of candidate selection, whether by individual petitions, official bodies, groups, or organizations, the greater the danger that partisan motives will govern the choices.

Conversely, when the base of selection is broadened to involve the whole community to the widest possible extent, the best qualified candidates are likely to be nominated.

This brings us to the caucus plan which is coming to be used in an increasing number of communities as citizens seek better ways of selecting school board members.

Nomination by Caucus

A caucus is a body of representatives of a school district voluntarily associated together for the purpose of convassing, screening, and nominating the best available candidates for school board membership, whether the final selection is to be by popular election or by appointment.

Caucus members are usually selected from the civil subdivisions of the district or from community organizations, but may be chosen on some other or combination basis, bearing in mind the underlying principles involved, which are as follows:

1. The caucus body shall be so broadly representative of the school district as to deserve the confidence and support of the entire community.

2. The caucus body shall be completely independent of any other civil, political, or community organization.

3. Members of the caucus body, whatever the basis of their selection, shall serve in their individual capacities, dedicated to the best interests of the district as a whole.

4. Membership in the caucus body shall be on a rotating basis with a one-third to one-half carryover of old members into each succeeding period of operation.

5. The period of service of a particular caucus body shall extend from one school board election (or appointment) through the next, with a sufficient number of meetings to accomplish the following things:

   a) organize the caucus body with a chairman, secretary, committees, etc., as per constitution and bylaws.

   b) carry on a campaign to secure from citizens generally suggestions of qualified candidates for board service;

   c) secure complete data on each potential candidate and go through a process of screening;

   d) interview and secure consent from candidates finally chosen by the caucus;

   e) present the names of candidates to the proper appointment or election authorities;

   f) publicize the caucus selections to the district with supporting data, and urge widespread and active community backing for the candidates;

   g) and finally, arrange for the proper selection of new members of the caucus body for the next period, and for their adequate orientation.

Breaking In on the New Job

Whatever previous experience or exercise of judgment the new member brings with him to his school board duties, in the vast majority of cases he finds himself confronted with a whole set of facts and conditions with which he is more or less unfamiliar.

Until he can build up a background of understanding, not only of the local school situation, but of the place and potentiality of public education in the state and nation, his decisions with regard to board policy cannot be of sound and enduring value.

153

It is not always easy for a mature and experienced adult to accept the fact that he will need to invest some solid time and effort in preparing himself for effective service in the new assignment. But such is the case, and a candidate for school board office should be aware of this necessity when he accepts the nomination.

After he succeeds to board membership, how is a new incumbent to secure the needed background knowledge most readily and rapidly? Various ways are open to him, both on his own initiative and with the help of the older board members and of the school administrator and staff.

If there is an interval of time between his selection and the date for taking office, during which the current board holds one or more meetings, the incoming member should be invited to sit in as an observer. The matter of extending such an invitation rests with the president of the board.

At every first meeting following the addition of a new member to the board, the board president should extend an official welcome and make a point of explaining how the board operates and the duties and responsibilities of board members.

In advance of taking his place on the board, or as soon as possible thereafter if the new member is seated immediately following his selection, he should make an effort to do the following:

1. Have a personal conference with the school administrator.

2. Spend some time in the schools to gain a first-hand impression of the school plant and personnel.

3. Talk informally with the other board members in the community, present and past, to obtain a variety of viewpoints for the purpose of planning his own course of action for greatest effectiveness.

4. Make for himself a little private code of the most important guides to his conduct as a school board member. Expressed in his own words, these guides would involve such principles and attitudes as

   a) The board member has no legal authority outside the sessions of the board.

b) It is the board member's responsibility to represent the best interests of the *total* community, not of any particular segment of it.

c) Under no conditions should school board status be used for the personal privilege or advancement of a member of the board.

d) At all times the utmost in board harmony and "teamwork" should be promoted.

e) As long as he is on the board, a member should give time enough to school board service to do it well.

f) A board member should insist on having all available facts before being called upon to render a decision.

g) During discussions on the board, a member should listen more than he talks, should state his views briefly and clearly, and when he must disagree do so without being disagreeable or cherishing grudges.

h) Once board policy is adopted a member will firmly uphold it whether or not he favored its adoption.

i) A board member will refer complaints or suggestions that come to him personally through proper channels in accordance with board policy.

And many other points that the member will work out to fit the local situation.

5. Get hold of, for reading and study, all pertinent printed materials, both local and general, including

a) A copy of the *state law* governing schools and school board duties and responsibilities.

b) *Minutes* of preceding board meetings as far back as the new member is interested to go. These will give him not only an understanding of procedures and policies but knowledge of the attitudes and reactions of both his predecessor and colleagues on the board which may be very significant and useful as he seeks to fit into the board "team" smoothly and efficiently.

c) The written or printed *policies* of the board which are currently in force.

d) The *rules and regulations* promulgated by the administrator for carrying out policy in the day to day operation of the schools.

e) The *annual reports* of the school district for the past several years, including copies of the budgets and statistical records.

f) *Books and pamphlets* which may be recommended to him as of particular value. It is to be hoped that the board, with the help of the superintendent, has built up a small working library on school board functions and activities including many of the items listed in the Bibliography on pages 283-87.

Nor is it a bad idea for a board member to obtain personal copies of those items which he finds of most help to him so that he may keep them at home for easy and frequent reference.

g) At least one of the standard *periodicals* in the school administration field, especially one which carries material of particular interest to board members.

6. Finally, the new board member will want to assure himself that his board

a) is a member of the State School Boards Association and of the National School Boards Association;

b) takes advantage of the services offered by associations in the way of publications, consultation, research, etc.;

c) encourages all board members to attend regional school board conferences and workshops, at least half of the members to attend state association meetings, and one representative member each year (on a rotating basis) to attend the National Convention with the superintendent.

PART II

AMONG SCHOOL BOARDS ASSOCIATIONS

"TEAMWORK"

"For there's no lone hand in the game we play,
We must work to a bigger scheme;
And the thing that counts in the world today
Is how do you pull with the team?"

— EDGAR A. GUEST

The whole purpose of associations of school boards is to develop greater teamwork. The individual board member belongs to the "team" represented by his local board. The local board belongs to the "team" represented by its State School Boards Association. The state association belongs to the "team" represented by the National School Boards Association. And at every level—local, state, national—school board groups are members of bigger "teams" comprising councils or committees representing every lay and professional organization having any concern with public education. As we develop and strengthen this teamwork in every part of the nation it will become a mighty expression of faith in and support of the public schools. — E. M. T.

CHAPTER 20

In Association
There Is Strength

Why should a local school board be a member of its state association of school boards?

Why should a state association affiliate with the National School Boards Association?

These are frank questions. They call for equally frank answers.

The responsibility for maintaining a system of public education in this country, as has been pointed out in Part I of this book, is vested legally in the state governments.

Traditionally the states have left to local boards of education a large measure of the actual direction of school affairs within the framework of the state regulations.

We cherish this heritage of local control of public education, and rightly so.

But while our public schools are designed to be locally controlled and directed, this does not mean that each district should stand alone and unrelated to adjoining or surrounding districts.

No school board can do its most effective work in isolation!

It is true, of course, that conditions in no two school districts are exactly alike. Communities differ just as people do; each has distinctive characteristics.

There are principles of human conduct and experience in living, however, which guide us as individuals no matter how unique our own personalities may be.

We grow most soundly as persons when we profit wisely from the experiences of others with whom we come in contact.

The wiser we are, the more we seek an understanding of how other men and women have faced life's realities and solved its problems.

In just the same way there is a common ground of experience in school affairs that reveals underlying principles on which local adaptations may be based.

That school board is wisest and most successful in its work which seeks to know and to understand how other boards have operated in meeting problems similar to those it faces.

Here, then, is the basic reason for a state school boards association—to provide a clearing house and exchange center for many experiences of local boards which, widely cited and discussed, will encourage every board to give its own schools and community more effective service.

So, too, the National School Boards Association provides a medium for an exchange of ideas and information among the states.

There is much variation in the pattern of school administration from state to state. None is perfect, but each has outstanding features which have significance for others.

The more rapidly each state is able to learn about, adapt, and adopt features which have proved their merit elsewhere, the faster will be our progress in education as a nation.

Another important function of both state associations and the national association is to give school boards their proper voice among the numerous statewide and nationwide organizations that take an interest in the public schools.

Some of these agencies are professional by nature; some are groups of laymen representing business, labor, farming, women, veterans, and others.

Two organizations in particular involve both educational professionals and laymen—the Parent Teacher Association and the School Board (see Chapter 8).

In Association There Is Strength

More and more conferences are being held, and councils or committees are being formed, which bring together representatives of many groups in the interest of public education on local, state, and national levels (see Chapters 16 and 24).

On the local level, the individual school board can meet the situation.

But on the state and national levels, there is no way that school boards can be represented and make their voices heard unless they have effective state and national associations.

For in association there is strength!

Now, "association" does not mean union, and "strength" does not mean power.

There are vast distinctions between these terms which are important in their relation to public education.

School boards voluntarily *associate* with one another to *strengthen* their services to education; they do not unite to display their power.

Power implies the external application of force or pressure. This is not what school boards are after.

Strength implies internal effectiveness; that is the school board's goal!

School boards associations belong to the school boards of this country. They are more than nice societies in which it is pleasant to hold membership and to attend an occasional meeting. They are serious working organizations whose influence for the constructive improvement of public education at all levels is beyond calculation.

Every local board should be an active member of its state school boards association, and every state association should be a fully affiliated member of the National School Boards Association.

On a broader basis, State Boards of Education and the boards of state supported colleges and universities are more and more finding it advantageous to identify themselves with the state and national associations of school boards.

WHICH WAY—UP OR DOWN?

*"I find the great thing in this world
is not so much where we stand as in
what direction we are moving."*

— OLIVER WENDELL HOLMES

Members of school boards, guardians as they are
of America's future, may well ponder these words
of one of the famous poets and philosophers of the
past century. Which holds more promise for the
years ahead, a good school system that is growing
poorer or a poor school system that is growing
better? No system should, nor indeed can, stand
still. It is always moving in some direction for better
or for worse. Nor is any system ever perfect no
matter what its attainment. There is constant room
for a higher degree of perfection in the investment
by the community in its schools, in the quality and
quantity of personnel, in the utility and beauty of
the physical plant, in the effectiveness of the equipment, and in the adaptability of the curriculum to
life as it must be lived in community, state, nation,
and the world. — E. M. T.

CHAPTER 21

Growth of the
Association Movement

There is a thrill in watching school boards associations rise in strength and vigor to tackle the problems of American public education in their own right.

A period of careful foundation building has gone on in recent years.

Now the associations are beginning to blossom into a maturity which will bring forth much good fruit in due season.

This is not to say that school boards or their associations can solve the problems of education by their own unaided efforts.

On the other hand, neither can any other organization—professional, semi-professional, or lay—solve these problems alone.

Solution will require the united efforts of all Americans working together toward the common goal of a more effective system of universal public education.

But the growth of associations of school boards in the states, and their federation into the National School Boards Association, brings to bear an important factor which heretofore has not been present in any such degree.

Until the National School Boards Association established a headquarters office (see Chapter 27) and began to keep in regular contact with the state associations, little collective information was available regarding them.

School Board Leadership in America

The Situation in 1949

The first directory of state school boards associations compiled by the N.S.B.A. identified 37 such associations. Eleven states had no associations, but several expressed interest in forming one.

The oldest association was in Pennsylvania which had had a continuous existence since 1896. Six others were organized by 1920, 19 more by 1940, 11 others by 1949 (see page 169).

Every degree of variation was found among the associations with respect to membership, financial support, paid personnel, services, publications, etc.

Memberships varied from 100 per cent of the local boards in a few states having a small number of districts down to a tiny fraction of the eligible boards in states having thousands of small rural districts.

Association dues varied from none at all or a $1 nominal fee to a maximum of $250.00 in two states for boards with the largest jurisdictions.

Six states reported full-time paid executive secretaries and eight others part-time paid secretaries, men or women. The secretaries of the remaining associations served on a voluntary basis to hold the organizations together. Over the years, the services of such loyal volunteers have been incalculable, and the highest tribute is due them.

Sixteen states reported some type of regular *News-Letter*, *Bulletin*, or *Journal* to their memberships, and a dozen had developed or sponsored *Handbooks* for school board members.

Association after association reported that its officers and executive committees were making plans to revise the schedule of dues upward and work toward 100 per cent membership so as to provide a state headquarters, a full time executive secretary, some regular printed or mimeographed publication for members, more frequent and effective regional and statewide meetings, wider cooperation with other lay and professional state organizations particularly with regard to needed school legislation, and active support of the National School Boards Association.

164

A Challenge to Growth

In closing his report to the National Convention in February 1952, the executive secretary of the N.S.B.A. attempted to look ahead at American public education and the relation of the school boards association movement to it, in the following words:

"All of us are aware to a greater or lesser extent, depending on our contacts and background, that there is a rising tide of public interest in the public schools of this country.

"It goes without saying that, for better or for worse, school boards stand at the very heart of all this discussion.

"The question is, Are we ready to meet the added responsibilities and opportunities which this renaissance in public education is inevitably bringing?

"My answer, based on the widespread observation which it has been my privilege to enjoy as your executive secretary, is that by and large we are just beginning to get ready, but that we have at hand the machinery with which to work.

"This machinery is our school boards association movement, state and national.

"The time has come for us to recognize in this movement something more than a helpful device for our own self-improvement.

"School boards hold legal responsibility for the quality of public education in this country.

"That quality is manifest at every local level, rural and urban. It is reflected at the state level by the adequacy of the statewide educational program. It is focused nationally by the sum total of the progress that is being made in school finance, building construction and equipment, teacher supply, curriculum adjustment, and a whole host of other problems with all of which the American people are vitally concerned because they supply the children to be educated, they pay the bills, and they absorb the product of the schools into the social, economic, and civic life of the body politic.

"No longer are school boards going to be permitted to

165

operate in exclusive isolation, and if we are smart we will take the lead in extending cooperation rather than wait until we are pushed into it.

"We are going to have to stand up and be counted whenever and wherever questions arise regarding our public schools.

"We are going to need countless facts about school conditions, local, state, and national, which we do not now as a whole possess.

"We are going to have to understand better than we do the process of universal public education and why it is so vital to the future welfare of our representative democracy.

"We are going to have to meet more courageously those selfish pressures for preferential favors which are contrary to our commitment to operate the schools without fear or favor in the interest of all the children of all the people.

"We are going to have to learn to recognize and deal with certain vicious and insidious attacks upon our public schools from forces which do not want our future citizens intelligently equipped to maintain a free economy and self-government in these United States.

"We are going to have to examine with open minds honest criticisms of our schools from whatever source they come.

"We are going to have to learn to accept, nay, even to initiate and encourage, offers of assistance from citizens and professionals to the end that the entire community shall participate in the formation of educational policies.

"Through all of this, we are going to have to carry the responsibility which is legally ours to make the final decisions in the light of all the facts solely in the best interests of those whom the public schools are designed to serve.

"I submit again, that school boards as a whole are just beginning to realize the implications of these things in relation to their own local operation.

"This realization is coming through the contacts established by membership in school boards associations.

"Let us redouble our efforts to develop in every state at the earliest possible moment a school boards association which will embody in greatest measure standards of independence, an adequate working budget, 100 per cent membership, a full-time executive secretary, effective media of communication, stimulating statewide and regional meetings, cooperation with other state organizations concerned with or interested in the public schools, and affiliation with the National School Boards Association.

"And let us build the National Association through the state associations to the point where it will render maximum service to its federated membership and will truly become the voice of the school boards of America in the cooperative councils and conferences which take place at the national level."

The Situation Today

In the years since the preceding challenge was offered to the school boards associations of America, phenomenal growth has taken place in the number, membership, strength, and influence of these associations.

Nevertheless, much remains to be accomplished, and the challenge is as true in essence today as when it was made. Perhaps even more so, because it seems that changes in the demands on our schools occur at an increasingly rapid pace from year to year, which means that school boards and their associations must act to meet these changing demands with ever greater promptness, courage, and wisdom.

Organizationwise, every state now has its association of school boards, and all continue to grow more or less steadily. A number still operate with volunteer and part-time paid employees and too limited budgets.

Association leaders would do well to study the chapters which follow dealing with association finance, staffing, services,

167

legislative relationships, and work-type meetings, and to step up their efforts to increase the strength and effectiveness of the school board association movement all along the line.

Criticisms of our American system of state and local control of public education are being heard with increasing frequency and emphasis (see Chapter 32). If these are to be met, the highest type of dedicated and enlightened service on the part of the controlling agencies—local and state boards of education—will be demanded. The surest way to acquire the needed information and inspiration for such service is through the contacts and exchanges made possible by school boards associations.

A Word to the Shortsighted

Some state associations report difficulty in convincing certain local boards that they should be members of the association.

It seems almost incredible that this should be so in view of the public obligation which each board has assumed to render the most effective service possible to its community.

The way things are today, no board can be effective without knowledge and understanding of how widespread and interrelated are the problems facing schools everywhere, and without a frank exchange of views and experiences with other boards in its region, state, and the nation as a whole.

One fundamental difficulty may be a misconception of what a school boards association really is and what it is for.

Non-member boards too often think of the state association as something outside and apart from themselves which wants them to join for its own benefit.

The truth is the exact opposite—the association is not apart from the local boards, it *is* the local boards. Membership does not primarily benefit the association, *it benefits each member board.*

So a school board that does not belong to its state association becomes its own worst enemy and defrauds its community of assistance to which the community has a right.

This is plain speaking, but it needs to be said!

Growth of the Association Movement

Since public schools belong to the public, those delegated by the public to operate the schools—the boards of education—are derelict in their duty if they refuse to take advantage of the greatest resource at hand to increase their own efficiency—their school boards associations.

In one state, the act of the legislature legalizing the association of school boards went a step further and made it mandatory that every board in that state must be a member. This may not be the wisest plan, and most other states argue that a local board should be left free to join the association voluntarily.

But the fact remains that because of its 100 per cent membership, the association in the state mentioned above is able to take concerted action in behalf of public education that associations with memberships of a third or a half or even two-thirds of the local districts cannot accomplish.

Only the united voice of *all* the school boards in a state can speak with authority and command a respectful hearing when it calls attention to the needs of the schools.

When a local board exercises its freedom of choice by refusing to associate with other boards in attaining the best possible education for the children, youth, and adults of its own community, it offers a poor example of judgment, foresight, and devotion to the task for which it was created.

Chronological List of Association Origins

1858 Hawaii (Ter. Bd.)	1932 & 1946 Iowa	1948 Arizona
1896 Pennsylvania	1936 Kentucky	1949 Alabama
1896 & 1919 New York	1936 & 1942 Missouri	1949 Indiana
1903 & 1914 New Jersey	1936 Vermont	1949 Michigan
1906 Virginia	1937 North Carolina	1950 & 1955 N. Mexico
1913 Illinois	1938 Louisiana	1951 Georgia
1918 & 1946 Kansas	1939 Connecticut	1951 & 1956 Mississippi
1918 Nebraska	1939 & 1949 S. Dakota	1951 South Carolina
1921 Wisconsin	1939 Tennessee	1952 & 1955 Arkansas
1922 Minnesota	1940 Colorado	1952 West Virginia
1922 Washington	1941 & 1949 Texas	1953 Rhode Island
1923 Utah	1943 Idaho	1955 Alaska
1926 Montana	1944 Oklahoma	1955 Ohio
1926 North Dakota	1945 New Hampshire	1957 Nevada
1930 California	1946 Delaware	1957 Maine
1930 Florida	1947 Massachusetts	1957 Maryland
1930 Wyoming	1947 & 1953 Oregon	1958 Dist. of Columbia

VISION

*"My interest is in the future, because
I am going to spend the rest of my life
there."*
— CHARLES F. KETTERING

We all know persons who, grown old, live largely
in the past. Still greater numbers, caught in the heat
and hurry of middle life, live wholly in the present,
with scant thought as to what may lie ahead. But
youth are always looking in the future, wondering
what life will hold as they grow into manhood and
womanhood. Fortunate individuals, like the noted
engineer and inventor quoted above, never lose
their interest in building for the future. Well aware
that "tomorrow is only a vision," they are also
convinced that "today, well lived . . . makes every
tomorrow a vision of hope." Through such people
the world moves on to better things. It is the reason
why maximum educational opportunities for Americans, young and old, is so magnificent an investment. — E. M. T.

170

CHAPTER 22

Financing School
Boards Associations

The school boards association movement has reached the stage where it seems desirable to set forth certain fundamental considerations concerning the adequate support of these associations, state and national.

The plain truth is that, except in a few states where legal authorization is still pending, the local school boards of this country have the means at hand to support their state and national associations to whatever extent they deem necessary. Why then, don't they?

The situation is confused by a lack of informed leadership, by the variety of different patterns used, by unfounded timidity about increasing dues for fear of losing memberships, and by too much wishful thinking about outside support instead of self-support.

If we cut straight to the heart of the matter, the whole process is a good deal simpler than it appears to be.

Recalling Some Basic Principles

1. School boards are legally constituted bodies, organized locally under state authorization for the conduct of the public schools.

2. School boards traditionally are composed of lay citizens representing impartially all the people of their districts, and serving in most cases without salary and, in the beginning, without experience.

3. The increasingly complex and mobile society of today makes it virtually impossible for school boards any longer to operate effectively in isolation. They need the benefit of pooled experience, and a broader outlook toward public education in the state and in the nation as the surest means of continuing the strength and freedom of our American way of life.

4. Associations of school boards at various levels offer the means through which local boards may increase their effectiveness by acting cooperatively, and through which they may make their collective voice heard concerning educational advancement.

5. The expense of this voluntary process of joint self-improvement and of concerted action is a legitimate charge against the district funds administered by each board, as evidenced by the legal authorizations existing in a majority of the states.

In no case will this expense ever amount to more than a tiny fraction of one per cent of the district expenditures, even were the school boards associations to be supported to render services far beyond the present conception of any of us.

Basically, the associations of school boards in this country should be maintained and supported by the school boards themselves with the use of public money and for purposes which are clearly evident to the public at large.

These associations must never be subsidized by private monies or foundation grants which could be the means, or even be imagined to be the means, of influencing their activities in some particular direction.

However, there are opportunities for special contributions for particular pieces of research or study or promotion which the governing body of an association feels would be desirable above and beyond its basic continuing program, and which some private source might be interested in assisting the association to undertake, without any strings attached.

The Principles Applied

Universal application of the principles outlined above would mean that the school boards of America have the means to create, support, and profit from the services of their own associations to whatever extent they feel it to be in the public interest.

In so doing, they are acting as boards, not as individuals. Membership in a state association should be *by boards*, and voting membership in the national association *by state associations*.

The individual board member, of course, receives benefit from his board's membership in the state organization, and from his state's membership in the national organization, but solely to the end that he may be a more effective member of his board since he has no authority outside official board meetings.

It is clear, then, that there is an ample legal reservoir of support for school boards associations, to be appropriated and used according to the judgment and decision of local school boards.

Two Kinds of Returns

With most undertakings in this world, we are likely to get out of an enterprise about what we put into it—in money, in interest, in participation, and in loyalty. This is true of school boards associations.

If a local board puts none of these things into its state association, it naturally gets little in return except some gratuitous service supported by other boards and given for the good of the cause, though undeserved in such an instance.

If a board puts only a nominal fee into an association whose schedule of dues is so low that its budget is inadequate to provide continuous helpful service, then the board can expect only a nominal and intermittent return.

But if a board contributes its proper share of a carefully considered state association budget, designed to provide adequate organization, staff, and service activities, then it can expect to receive more nearly a real return on its investment, even though that investment is relatively much greater.

However, when a local board tries to measure returns against contributions solely on a dollar for dollar basis, it reveals a narrowness of viewpoint and a lack of understanding of the varied nature and purpose of the association of which it is a part.

Direct service to each school district and to each board member is, of course, a major function of a state school boards association and, as has just been pointed out, will be most effective when adequately financed.

But there is an *indirect return* that is probably of equal importance though not so easy to measure in dollars and cents.

This indirect return is the impact on the educational program, state and local, that comes from a united school board voice.

No group carries more weight in educational circles and with legislative bodies than do school boards, because their only concern is the welfare of children and youth and they cannot be accused of self-interest.

But a state association, to be effective in educational councils at the state level, must represent as nearly as possible 100 per cent of the boards in its state.

The question association officers and committees are most often asked is "Do you represent all the school boards, or a majority of them, or only a few of them?"

On the answer to this question depends the influence which the association can bring to bear for the sound solution of school problems and the improvement of public education.

A local board should never fail to recognize the indirect as well as the direct returns it receives from the dues it pays to its state association.

Just one case in which the association helps to secure increased state aid for schools, or assistance with schoolhouse construction, or the liberalization of debt limitations, or some other item affecting local districts financially, may mean to a given district a hundred or a thousand times the amount of its association fee.

All that has been said concerning the two kinds of returns which each local district receives from its state association, applies with equal truth to the returns that the boards in each state receive from the National School Boards Association.

Direct returns in the way of useful materials and reports, of

174

consultative services, of participation in conventions and workshops, can be measured in some degree.

The indirect return that comes from supporting a united school board voice at the national level can rarely be measured, although it is a tremendous asset to every school board in America as is becoming increasingly evident with each succeeding year.

What Is Needed to Do the Job

What it takes to operate a state school boards association effectively is not guesswork. Over a dozen associations are operating on budgets of from $50,000 to $250,000 a year.

Those associations which are trying to operate on less than a $25,000 minimum find that they cannot render continuous service to their membership. The sooner such associations take courage and raise their sights, the sooner the whole association movement will be contributing more nearly its essential part to American public education.

There has never been a case where an association has lost ground because it increased its dues. Exactly the reverse happens because, even though a few boards may drop out for a year or two, the total income is always greater and in consequence the services are so much better that boards seek affiliation and membership grows.

Basic items in an association budget must include:

1. The salaries of a qualified full-time executive secretary with at least one office assistant (see Chapter 23).

2. Maintenance of a headquarters office with adequate facilities for answering mail, keeping records, distributing materials, and providing consultative services (see Chapter 24).

3. The publication and distribution of some kind of a regular newsletter, bulletin, or journal that will reach local boards at least once a month.

4. Expenses for travel by the executive secretary, by association officers, by the board of directors and other committees within the state, and the sending of two official voting delegates

to annual conventions of the National School Boards Association.

5. The holding of an annual convention which will be largely attended and widely effective in promoting the collective influence of the association.

6. Provision for regional meetings of local boards two or three times a year in all sections of the state, and for an annual workshop for new school board members (see Chapter 26).

7. Expenses connected with the work of a legislative committee in promoting constructive school legislation in cooperation with other educational agencies in the state (see Chapter 25).

8. Development and distribution of a *Handbook* for school board members, and interpretations of new school legislation.

9. Provision for payment of the full-goal affiliation of the state association with the National School Boards Association.

Nor are the above nine items the only services which can be rendered by school boards associations, although they are the first and most essential ones.

As an association's budget increases many other opportunities present themselves for consideration by the board of directors:

a) opportunities for definite pieces of investigation and research leading to special reports and publications, especially in the field of school board policies;

b) opportunities for promoting the selection by communities of highly qualified board members and for their in-service education;

c) opportunities for providing consultative services to local boards on special problems;

d) opportunities to build up an effective loan library of books, reports, bulletins, records, films, and other audio-visual aids which the state office can supply on request to local boards for use in meeting critical situations;

e) opportunities in almost endless variety for working cooperatively with other lay and professional groups for the advancement of public education;

and so on and on.

Financing School Boards Associations

Figuring Out the Dues Schedule

To produce any given state association budget, the contribution of each local board should depend on the size of its jurisdiction and the number of boards in the state. States with fewer boards must assess higher dues per board.

Schedules of dues customarily include a number of classes graduated according to the size of school districts as indicated by one or more of the following factors (figures for which can be obtained with statistical accuracy from State Department of Education reports):

a) The number of teacher units in the district.

b) The number of pupils in the district: A.D.A., census, enrollment, etc.

c) The assessed valuation of the district.

d) The amount of district income for current operation.

e) The size or type of district as indicated by some state designation.

In many cases, more careful study needs to be given by school board leaders to the development of schedules of dues which will provide their associations with adequate budgets and an equitable distribution of the load among local boards.

The advancement of public education to the position it must occupy in the future welfare of our nation depends in large measure on the degree to which boards of education strengthen their own effectiveness by collective action and self-help through their school boards associations.

> "I read, I study, I examine, I listen,
> I reflect; and out of all this
> I try to form an idea into which I put
> as much common sense as I can."
>
> — MARQUIS de LAFAYETTE

CAREER

"There are two just reasons for the choice of any way of life: The first is inbred taste in the chooser; the second, some high utility in the industry selected."
— ROBERT LOUIS STEVENSON

Fortunate indeed is the man or woman whose work from day to day meets the ideal set forth above. To earn our way in the world doing something worth while that we *like* to do is a veritable blessing. Too many, through circumstance or lack of guidance, fall into tasks which are distasteful and from which there seems no escape. Sometimes, under such conditions, a person of strong character may cultivate the taste which was lacking at the start and come in the end to enjoy his daily breadwinning. The test of "high utility" will have many degrees of interpretation, but at least we hope the work we do will qualify as an honest and necessary contribution to the welfare or comfort of our fellow men. — E. M. T.

CHAPTER 23

The Association Staff

Practically every state school boards association got its start through the volunteer services of devoted secretaries and other officers whose pioneering efforts should never be forgotten.

But, as we learned in Chapter 21, the number of full-time and part-time paid employees has been rapidly increasing and we may expect this development to continue.

It might be well, therefore, to devote a short chapter to the association staff, its scope, qualifications, and duties.

The key person in every state, of course, is the executive secretary, or executive director as he is sometimes called, particularly after others are added to his staff.

The Ideal Executive

To be a full-time executive director of a state school boards association is to occupy one of the strategic positions in the field of public education today.

What are some of the qualifications which will best fit an executive to serve the varied interests of his association and its local member boards? Among others, we suggest the following:

1. A degree of maturity and practical experience with school affairs which will command the respect and confidence of those with whom he has to deal—school board members from every walk of life, professional educators from the state superintendent to the classroom teacher, members of the legislature, leaders of all types of statewide organizations, his fellow executives in other states and in the National School Boards Association.

2. A robust constitution and good health to insure pursuit of the arduous responsibilities which cover an entire state.

3. A personal integrity which reflects a sincere liking for people, enabling him to meet strangers easily, to evaluate their worth instinctively, to enlist their cooperation, and to establish and maintain enduring personal and professional friendships.

4. A combination of vision with organizing ability and a mastery of detail which will insure the accurate and effective conduct of activities once they are projected.

5. Ability to write simply and interestingly and to speak clearly and convincingly to varied groups and audiences.

6. The will to drive himself because he must be his own boss so large a proportion of the time in carrying out the program of his widely scattered board of directors.

7. Ability to contribute constructively to the policy making of his association leaders and to put policy, once adopted, into effect with dispatch.

8. Ability to plan for, direct, and work with his staff in a spirit of friendly cooperation.

9. Courage to persevere in the face of setbacks, opposition, or defeat, and to acknowledge and rectify as far as possible the inevitable mistakes that every active leader sometimes makes.

10. Patience to allow programs, ideas, and suggestions time to mature in the minds of those who must approve and support them, before urging acceptance.

11. A generous spirit that does not fret over who receives credit so long as essential work gets done.

12. An abiding faith in the American system of free public education, under school board control, as the chief instrument for insuring and promoting our democratic way of life.

The qualities listed above cannot be said to be in any particular order since for practical purposes they are nearly coordinate in importance. To them might be added other factors which we have come to associate with leadership and which each reader will phrase for himself (see Chapter 2).

Truly, all this represents an ideal that never finds complete expression in one individual. But these qualities are worth striving toward by any person facing the opportunities for constructive service offered the executive of a school boards association.

Who Executives Are

Actually, executives for state school boards associations have been drawn from many varied backgrounds.

Some have been board members—farmer, business man, lawyer, legislator, postman, housewife, etc.

Some have been school administrators in city or county systems.

Some have been members of college staffs.

Some have been experienced in other fields—finance, economics, advertising, newspaper work, public relations, etc.

There is no best source of supply. The right person may turn up anywhere.

In brief, the *man* is more important than his background, though both should be considered in selecting an association executive.

Pattern of Staff Expansion

The key to expansion is, of course, the size of the association budget. As more money becomes available and more services are demanded, more staff assistance is made possible.

In the beginning, the executive secretary is likely to do all the work himself, with some hourly help from a typist.

Then comes the day when a full-time office assistant can be employed who ideally is a combination receptionist, stenographer, typist, bookkeeper, mimeographist, mailing clerk, and general "right hand man" to the executive. Many an association owes its successful operation to such a person.

Services most in demand tend to govern the order of further additions to the staff. Assistants to an executive director may be one or more of the following:

a *field secretary* to plan and attend regional meetings and travel around the state in response to requests for consultation;

an *editor* responsible for getting out the monthly *Bulletin, Journal* or *News Letter,* and other incidental publications;

a *research person* who can conduct surveys and compile statistics;

a *legislative assistant* especially knowledgeable and skilled in working with the state legislature (see Chapter 25).

Assistants to an office manager (first girl, promoted), may be one or more of the following, singly or in combinations of duties:

a bookkeeper

an expert mimeographist and mailing clerk

a typist for routine letters and manuscripts

a membership list and file clerk

What the Executive Does

Following is a list of activities reported on one occasion by the executive director of one of the largest state school boards associations as his actual responsibility:

Managerial functions and staff problems

Consultant service

General services—correspondence, etc.

Clearing house services, *Journal,* etc.

Field services

Research services

Directors' meetings and committees

Membership

Dues and other sources of income

House organ and special publications

Convention programs and exhibits

Sectional meetings

Public relations

Correlation with other educational, governmental, and lay
  organizations and agencies
State Department relationships
Legislative work and bulletins
Trade association kinships
Etc. etc. etc.

Staff Executive Get-Togethers

In recent years, the annual conventions and occasional study
conferences of the National School Boards Association have
provided needed opportunities for the executives of the federated
state associations to sit down together in meetings of their own
for half a day or a day at a time.

At such meetings several things happen, but most important,
executives from all parts of the country come to know one another
personally and to establish contacts which can be continued
throughout the year by correspondence with assurances of
sympathetic response.

Of almost equal value is the direct exchange of experiences,
practices, and ideas with respect to association services, which
are possible only by word of mouth.

No state association has done everything, but every state
association has done something that may have significance for
those who have not tried that particular thing.

The pooling of experience leads to the multiplication of
worth-while practices and speeds up the effectiveness of the whole
association movement.

At times, part of the executives' meeting is devoted to expert
instruction in some particular phase of association service as, for
example, publications, public and press relations, legislative
relations, or research procedures.

In addition to these nationwide get-togethers, state association executives have met with one another and with other state
leaders in a number of regional conferences (see Chapter 29).

All such face to face exchanges are desirable and profitable
in building association staff morale and effectiveness.

WORK IN FAITH

*"All work that is worth anything is
done in faith."*
— ALBERT SCHWEITZER

Someone has said that hope is confidence in the future but that faith is confidence in the present. And it is the present with which we have to deal. The Bible warns us that faith without works is barren. Conversely, a great humanitarian and Nobel prize winner implies in the quotation above that works without faith are of little worth. It takes a combination of the two—faith and works, works in faith—to guarantee results of lasting value. In the field of education, we may be certain that generous service performed in a spirit of confidence, like good seed sown upon fertile ground, in due season will yield a rich and rewarding harvest. — E. M. T.

CHAPTER 24

State Association Services

A state association must plan to serve all the school boards of its state, from those in the largest cities to those in the smallest rural districts.

Problems may differ in kind and degree, but the common purpose of public education in our American democracy is the controlling and cementing influence.

Problems can be solved when all concerned will bring together the pertinent facts and seek solutions which are in the general interest without favor to some at the expense of others.

Rural-Urban Relationships

The American system of public schools is dedicated to the education of all the children of all the people.

It makes no difference whether the individual unit is a one-teacher school out in the open country, a huge, fully graded building in the heart of a congested city, or anything in between. The goal in every case is the same—the best in education that can be provided.

Nowadays our population is very fluid. Many people born and educated in rural areas eventually settle down to live and work in urban centers. In some cases the reverse takes place.

There is a constant shifting going on between communities and between states. Few boys and girls know with any certainty where they will go or what they will do when school days are over.

Therefore, the schooling of our young people must be broad and basic. It must develop and equip them to meet whatever circumstances they encounter, to embrace whatever opportunities are offered, to lead happy and successful lives wherever they may be, and to develop a spirit of service to their fellowmen.

All this means that there should be no conflicts in aims and interests as between school boards of varying jurisdictions.

There are a few states where this has not been understood and accepted, where rural boards and urban boards set themselves in opposition to each other in matters of legislation and other concerns of education.

Such a situation is unfortunate and short-sighted, and the children are the ones who suffer as a result.

A little effort on the part of each school board to understand the problems of other jurisdictions, a little willingness to extend cooperation and to receive it in return, will work wonders.

State associations of school boards offer the best medium for bringing about this spirit of cooperation among all the boards of a state, whatever the size or peculiarities of their jurisdictions.

Special effort should be made to enroll all types of district boards in the membership and to develop a program of service to all.

When this is done, a new strength is imparted to the educational program statewide, and rapid progress is a foregone conclusion.

Such a policy of service calls for farsighted leadership and generous effort. Its rewards are great and enduring.

Service Involves Participation

As a general principle, the vitality and success of a state school boards association is determined by the degree to which its members feel an active, personal interest in the work of the organization.

This feeling is not something which can be built up hurriedly or sporadically. It comes through continuous contact between the officers, the staff, and the membership all during the year and over a series of years.

It comes best when a good many members are assigned definite pieces of work in connection with state committees, regional meetings, local surveys, and other association activities. Through such assignments members realize that they have a part in a worthwhile undertaking and they want to see it succeed.

School boards on the whole have not had much practice as yet, in many states, in sharing experiences and working together. That is exactly what a school boards association is designed to promote.

It is natural, of course, that younger and weaker associations have to devote more time to working out sound methods of organization, membership, and finance, preparatory to reaching their most effective service basis (see Chapters 21 and 22).

The older and stronger associations, with their lines of service well established, are nevertheless constantly finding new ways to serve their local boards and to cooperate with other lay and professional organizations in the interest of public education.

Services to Member Boards and Board Members

It seems desirable to summarize at this point the more important kinds of direct service rendered by a state school boards association to its membership.

Inevitably there will be some duplication with discussions in other chapters and cross references are given where they are particularly significant or will take the place of more elaboration here.

Headquarters Office. Establishment and maintenance of an association headquarters in some central location in the state (often in the state capital) is a first important evidence of service.

Members like to know that there is a place to which they can address their questions and requests with assurance of receiving prompt attention.

In the headquarters office, membership and financial records are kept, correspondence answered and filed, telephone calls received, callers welcomed, publications prepared and mailed, etc; in short, this is the "heart" of the association.

Publications. Practically every association sends out some kind of monthly communication to its membership. In the beginning this may be only a mimeographed *News Letter* which soon changes to a printed form of four pages or more.

In states not having 100 per cent membership, a commendable practice, where resources permit, is to mail an occasional *News Letter* of particular significance to non-member boards in the hope that through it they will come to see the value of affiliation.

More elaborate *Bulletins* and *Journals* are now published by many associations either on a monthly or a quarterly basis. In some cases, part of the cost of publication is met by selling advertising to school supply and equipment agencies.

The preponderance of material in association publications should naturally relate to school board operation, but there should always be items relating to state educational problems and association activities, and a few dealing with the national scene. A good balance between local, state, and national content is ideal.

State associations are more and more sponsoring the publication of special pamphlets or bulletins. The most widespread of these is a state *Handbook* for school board members, often prepared with professional assistance from the State Department or State University.

Other special publications deal with a calendar of legal requirements for school boards, with the policy-making function of boards, with insurance problems, with school buildings, with convention and workshop reports, etc. etc.

As association budgets grow, there is really no limit to the useful material which can be prepared and furnished to local boards.

Legislative Service. Chapter 25 deals specifically with school board association relationships with the state legislature.

In this connection two items should be mentioned here, though they might also come under the head of publications.

Many state associations now make a practice in legislative years of mailing frequent (as often as weekly) special mimeographed reports to member boards on the introduction and progress of school legislation.

Following the adjournment of the legislature, at least one association has for years devoted an entire issue of its *Journal* to an annotated listing of new school laws for the guidance of local boards and administrators.

Regional Meetings and Workshops. This phase of association service is discussed separately in Chapter 26.

The Annual Convention. All state associations hold an annual convention at some time during the year.

The majority of such meetings come in the fall and winter months, but a number are held in the spring; in fact, they occur in every month except July and August.

There are states in which the convention of the school boards association is looked upon in educational circles as the most important meeting of the year, and as time goes on it may logically become so in all states.

There are states which hold two and three day conventions. Attendance at some exceeds 3,000 board members, though numbers are not so significant as percentages. A convention attended by 400 out of 500 board members in one state carries more weight than a convention attended by 3,000 out of 10,000 in another.

There is a definite trend in convention programming away from a lot of speechmaking in favor of more panel and audience discussions.

More and more associations are staging *commercial exhibits* in connection with their annual conventions. The results are mutually gratifying—the exhibitors are able to display their wares to the people who actually pay the school bills—board members —and the association gains some added income from the rental of exhibit booths.

One feature of every convention that is vital to the continued welfare and growth of the association is the *business session.*

Unfortunately there have been too many occasions when only a handful of members has transacted association business.

Experience indicates that the business session should be scheduled at the very height of the convention with attractive program features preceding and following. This will ensure a maximum attendance of voting members when it comes to a consideration of important plans and policies for association activities in the year ahead.

A popular feature of the annual convention in a growing number of states is an award to the outstanding board or board member of the year. This may be handled in a variety of ways to conform with local ideas and conditions.

Research. As times goes on it seems evident that state school boards associations are going to be in a position to promote some of the research that is so much needed in the school board field.

In two or three cases already, staff members have been added to devote part-time attention to research. Usually these are graduate students at a nearby university.

In other cases, the association contributes toward maintaining a research person at a university provided he will give some or all of his time to school board problems.

Another much needed service in relation to research is the interpretation of studies already made in language that can be understood by the average board member, and the widespread distribution of such information.

No area of association activity offers greater promise for the future than does this one of cooperative research. In many matters we must *find* the facts, *filter* the facts, and *face* the facts, before we can intelligently *follow* the facts. Only the barest beginnings have yet been made.

Lending Library. A growing number of associations are establishing lending libraries at their headquarters consisting of books, pamphlets, slides, film strips, recordings, and even motion pictures that can be loaned on request to local boards for limited periods.

One association, after accumulating several hundred such items over a period of several years, finally had them organized and catalogued by a professional librarian. Then it published these references under major headings of interest to board members and school administrators in a *Lending Library Bulletin* and sent it to the association's mailing list with an invitation to borrow any item by mail without charge.

Obviously, immense opportunities for direct service are indicated by an extension of this idea.

Consulting Service. Of course the executive director and other members of an association staff are available to consult with local boards whenever they are able to meet such requests.

The amount of this service is naturally limited by the staff personnel and the funds available for travel.

One association has gone further and created what it calls a *Council of Consultants.* It has compiled an approved list of competent persons in the state who are qualified to assist local boards with various problems such as those relating to school buildings, budgeting, taxation and assessment, community relations and surveys, staff relationships, population studies, and other areas.

Consultants are made available through arrangement with the association's executive officer and expenses are met in whole or in part, depending on circumstances, from the association budget.

Here is an idea capable of indefinite expansion with untold possibilities for the more rapid solution of educational problems on the local level.

Service Areas of Broader Concern

A few areas of almost universal concern at the state level are suggested as indications of the unlimited opportunities for association initiative and service.

1. The setting up or strengthening of some kind of a state-wide Advisory Committee, or Council, on Education, composed of representatives of lay and professional organizations and of leading citizens; this committee to act as a clearing house and exchange medium among all those concerned with the advancement of public education.

States where such committees, or councils, have been tried have found them the most effective means of securing wider understanding of educational needs and greater unity of support for a common program of action.

2. The creation of joint committees, either on a continuing or temporary basis, between the State School Boards Association and any important group at the state level, as, for example, the Association of School Administrators, the Congress of Parents and Teachers, the Education Association, the Taxpayers League, the State Chamber of Commerce, or any other organization where opportunities may be uncovered for cooperative endeavor in the interest of better schools.

3. Plans for reorganizing and improving the State Department of Education including the State Board of Education and an appointed state superintendent where such condition does not now exist.

4. Increased financial support for the construction and maintenance of schools to provide a basic educational program. This usually involves consideration of the whole tax structure and state budget procedure.

5. Provision for securing an adequate supply of qualified teachers. This involves proper laws relating to accreditation and certification, reciprocity, minimum salary schedules, tenure, retirement, etc., as well as adequate support of teacher-education institutions, scholarships, etc.

6. Plans for the most effective organization of school administrative units. In a few states this has been accomplished; in most states much more needs to be done.

7. Codification of the school law. Only a few states have any recently combined and simplified School Code.

8. The status of nursery schools and kindergartens at one end of the scale of public education and of junior or community colleges at the other end. Many states have not yet accepted and made possible these expansions of the range of public education in local communities.

192

In Summary

The constitutions of state school boards associations include many statements of purpose, but they all revolve around the following areas of general and/or specific service:

1. The general advancement of public education.

2. Efficient and effective support and administration of the public schools.

3. Service to and among local boards which will be to their mutual advantage in handling school problems.

4. Support of beneficial, and opposition to injurious, school legislation.

5. Cooperation with all individuals and organizations concerned with public school education.

The Salutation of the Dawn

Listen to the Exhortation of the Dawn!
Look to this Day! For it is Life,
The very Life of Life.
In its brief course lie all the Verities
And Realities of your Existence:
The Bliss of Growth,
The Glory of Action,
The Splendor of Beauty.
For Yesterday is but a Dream,
And Tomorrow is only a Vision;
But Today well lived
Makes every Yesterday a Dream of Happiness,
And every Tomorrow a Vision of Hope.
Look well, therefore, to this Day!
Such is the Salutation of the Dawn.

From the SANSKRIT

FIRST ORDER OF BUSINESS

"I view education as the most important subject we as a people can be engaged in."

— ABRAHAM LINCOLN

Most Americans agree with Lincoln's view—in principle. In practice, the agreement is not so evident. Too often it would appear that other things seem much more important than education, as evidenced by our expenditures of time, effort, and money. Where does education stand today on a list which includes automobiles, radio and television, highways, organized sports, liquor, tobacco, public entertainment, jetplanes, atom bombs, and space exploration? Not too high, unfortunately. Yet America cannot be kept great by means of gadgets or through self-indulgence. Only by persistent cultivation of intelligence, morality, character, and industry in young and old can we continue increasingly to be the respected, responsible, resourceful people needed to lead the world to freedom and to peace. It is time to put education first in fact as well as in theory. — E. M. T.

CHAPTER 25

Association-Legislative

Relationships

There are some persons who say that a state school boards association is simply another organization designed to put pressure on the state legislature. They accuse it of being a lobby group, using the word "lobby" in its sinister meaning.

The accusation is false and unjustified!

In the first place, as we have seen in Chapter 20, the *primary* objective of a school boards association is not to influence legislation, but to assist local board members to increase their own understanding and effectiveness in the job they have to do in their respective communities.

At the same time, however, an association does have a state-wide interest and responsibility in helping to make certain that laws passed in relation to schools are good and helpful laws.

Assisting the state legislature is one important function of a state school boards association.

Legislators cannot know all about everything they are called upon to enact into law.

Legislatures rely on agencies which have the facts on the basis of which they must decide what had best be done. Such agencies present their evidence and their views, pro and con, at hearings before committees of the legislature.

This is lobbying, or pressure, if you please, in the best sense, and it is the way we handle all matters of legislation in our representative democracy.

The most important factor to discover in all cases is the *motive* behind the requests and demands that are presented to legislators and legislatures by various individuals and groups.

Is the motive a selfish one seeking special privilege? Or is the motive one of public spirited interest in the general welfare?

Ask yourself what motive school boards have for expressing their collective voice for or against legislation.

Certainly school boards, voluntary servants of the public as they are, have no selfish interest. The only interest school boards can have is to secure the best possible education for the children, youth, and adults of their communities.

School boards represent the will of the people with respect to schools, just as legislators represent the will of the people in all aspects of public welfare.

It makes good sense to suppose that a well-organized, well-conducted school boards association, with a membership composed of all or a majority of the local boards in the state, should be the most important and most reliable asset that a legislature can have in determining what is best for the schools.

That is the way things are working out in many states today, and that is the goal toward which every association should strive —a friendly, cooperative, mutually respected relationship between the state school boards association and the state legislature.

Rough Going for School Legislation

In state after state in recent years bills for increased support and the advancement of public education have been killed or drastically curtailed in committees or voted down in legislative sessions.

There have been some notable exceptions which only serve to point to the gains that could be made in every state.

Competition by other groups for the tax dollar; unrelenting and richly financed lobbying by selfish interests that will deny children the right to an education to save themselves a few dollars; lack of laymen (including board members) to join the educational profession in asserting that the public schools must be more adequately supported—these are important factors that have spelled the defeat of needed school legislation.

Some Concrete Examples

Example 1. "If there had been even one lay citizen—a businessman—to testify in support of the need for school buildings it might have changed the vote."

So spoke the legislative chairman of a state education association to the leaders of the state schools boards association and the state P.T.A.

A bill to extend the limit on bonded indebtedness from five to ten per cent had been up for hearing in a senate committee.

The representatives of the school administrators and teachers who had testified were accused of promoting needless expenditures and their own self-interest.

The vote in committee was a tie. The chairman broke the tie by voting "No" and the bill died.

At least two more years would go by before many districts in this state could hope to raise enough money for needed schools.

"We've gone as far as we can alone," concluded the education association representative. "The public will have to help."

Perhaps if the state school boards association had been strongly represented in the hearing just described, the story might have been different, and the lives of many children made brighter.

Example 2. Writing in his monthly *Bulletin,* the president of another state school boards association had this to say:

"The action, or inaction, of the legislative session just concluded seems to me to be inexplicable.

"I do not wish to be vindictive or unfair. I am puzzled, hurt, and disappointed.

"Perhaps I am too naive and should not have expected our representatives, senators, and the governor to keep simple faith with 300,000 school children and the school boards of our state."

197

After a complete review of the facts of the situation, this state president concluded the statement to his fellow board members as follows:

"We and the people of our great state must face realities and make a choice.

"We must decide what we want for our children and our children's children educationally. And then we must make a strenuous effort to see that our decision becomes a reality.

"In this endeavor, school boards must show leadership but the job is much too large for school boards alone.

"Every organization interested in education, including the very effective State Education Association and the P.T.A. and others, would have to work untiringly.

"Frankly, I again admit that I do not know the answers. But I do know that our responsibility as school board members of the State of _____ is to make proper provision financially and otherwise for the education of our children.

"Therefore, I am convinced that we must find the answers and prepare for whatever action is necessary to guarantee the fulfillment of our obligation."

Here is a rallying cry from a dedicated state school boards association leader which should bear fruit in years to come.

Example 3. Speaking before the annual meeting of a state school boards association, the chairman of the State School Aid Commission, and a board member himself, had the following advice to give:

"While it is true that there is a general acceptance of the Commission's plan by the people of the State of _____, I must be frank with you and report that such acceptance is a long way from the legislation needed to make it effective.

"If this program to broaden the base of tax support for schools is to become a part of the state tax structure, then you board members, you school heads, and others who understand the problem firsthand must now take the initiative and put the case before the people of your communities, the representatives in the legislature, and the governor.

"As you know, in spite of its professed interest in public education, the State Taxpayers Association has opposed our program of State Aid from the beginning.

"I would suggest that you look over the list of the board of directors who, I think, we can assume, support the Taxpayers Association and control its policies.

"If any of them live or work in your community, I would suggest that you invite them to sit down with you to discuss your local cost of education, your program, and your problems....

"I'd like to see you people do that. You can do it at the local level; nobody on the state level can do it....

"The people of the state have charged you with the responsibility of protecting their schools and educating their children.

"The youth of this state will hold you responsible if you give them a second class education.

"But if you as board members fight for our schools, the battle can be won."

Here is a challenge that could be repeated in many states. Through the school boards associations, local boards and board members can be kept alerted and informed as to how such battles for the public schools may best be fought and won.

Association Leadership

A study of the messages of governors to their respective legislatures in recent years, reveals that, with some exceptions, the states are in sound financial condition.

But it is politically expedient and popular to avoid any increases in state taxes.

So the game to play is to take the income that is anticipated under existing tax laws and divide it up among all the state services, each of which, including the schools, is clamoring for more because of three basic conditions:

(1) curtailments during the depression and war decades;

(2) increases in the constituency to be served; and

(3) the rising level of costs due to inflation.

In this game of snap-the-whip, the schools are usually at the tail end where the going is roughest and the chances of success are least.

But much of the general advancement of public education, statewide, depends on legislative enactments, and the school boards associations can and should take the lead in rallying the support of all interested agencies.

Chief among these agencies, to begin with, will be the State Congress of Parents and Teachers and the State Education Association. These two, with the State School Boards Association, constitute the "big three" in every state.

Working together, this "big three" can easily become the nucleus around which other groups of educators and lay citizens may concentrate their cooperative efforts in behalf of the schools. This pattern is being followed in an increasing number of states with beneficial results.

School boards associations should build up their membership and organizational strength until they become the key link in this chain of school support.

No group can speak with less prejudice and with a greater "voice of authority" in behalf of public education than can the school boards. It is time they learned their associated strength and used it to good purpose.

A concrete example is provided by the Iowa Association through the holding of what is called a "Representative Assembly" on the state level preceding each legislative session.

Proposed school legislation is first discussed by board members in small meetings throughout the state, and instructed delegates are selected from every county and large city to attend the meeting of the Assembly.

The great benefit from a program of this kind is to focus the attention and concensus of local boards on the enactment of new laws which will strengthen their efforts to maintain good schools.

Association—Legislative Relationships

Some Personal Views

It is this writer's belief that the greatest single threat to the perpetuation and advancement of our American system of public education is the inroads being made by parochial school systems in seeking tax dollars for sectarian education.

These inroads occur at every opportunity and at every level —national, state, and local. Gains, once achieved, are never relinquished, but become stepping stones to further infringements.

It is common knowledge that the desires of a majority of the American people for greater participation by the federal government in support of public schools could have been realized years ago except for the insistence of the powerful Catholic lobby in the Congress that private as well as public schools must share any federal appropriations for education.

In state legislatures, numerous efforts are made every year to secure passage of bills which will authorize the use of public money for tuition grants to students in church schools, for transportation of parochial pupils, for textbooks, health programs, and other special services where claims can be made that private schools should receive a share of state and local tax dollars. Threats have been made that failure to secure this public money will lead to the transfer of pupils from parochial to public schools, and this has actually been done in some cases.

School boards, through their associations, should be alert to defeat all such special legislation, designed to break down the constitutional separation of church and state. Locally, the way to deal with transfers of pupils is to accept them promptly into the public school system under public school policies and regulations, and to keep the district taxpayers fully informed. It is safer, sounder, and cheaper to meet these costs directly than to have tax money used to subsidize parochial systems.

Board associations need to be equally alert for other types of special privilege legislation, including efforts by teacher organizations to legalize collective bargaining, withholding dues from paychecks, and other practices leading to board coercion and the suppression of individual rights.

THE COURAGE OF CONVICTION

*"Nothing will ever be accomplished
if all possible objections must first be
overcome."*
                    — SAMUEL JOHNSON

School boards are more than debating societies.
In the final analysis, they are agencies for decision
and for action. True, they should decide and act on
the basis of all available evidence, pro and con, in
any given situation. Their endeavor at all times
should be to serve the expressed desires of the
greatest number of an informed and understanding
citizenry. But no matter how right and desirable a
goal or policy may be, there are always some who
fear a new course, who advise against following
an untried path because of difficulties and dangers
that may lie ahead. Were such objections to prevail,
no progress would ever be made. In public education, as in everything else, some risks must be taken,
some pioneering must be done, some courage of
conviction must be displayed. — E. M. T.

CHAPTER 26

State Association

Work-Type Meetings

The primary motive for any meeting of school board members— local, regional, statewide, or national—should be the promotion of more effective service to public education.

Unless it helps members to perform their duties with greater wisdom and skill, there is little excuse for holding a meeting.

On the other hand, a well-conducted exchange of ideas and practices can tremendously stimulate those who participate.

Time was, not so many years ago, that meetings of school board members, scheduled by their associations, followed the usual pattern of a full program of speeches with little opportunity for audience participation.

Those on the receiving end of such meetings felt more or less repaid for attending, depending on the quality and appropriateness of the speeches they heard.

But the audience always left with a lot of unanswered questions and a feeling that members could have contributed something of value from their own experience if they had been given a chance.

Program planners are now scheduling fewer speeches and are providing time for discussion periods of various kinds.

Sometimes panels of "experts" discuss selected topics among themselves in front of the audience and then invite questions and comments from the audience in whatever time remains.

Too often, just when real interest and general participation begin in such a meeting, the time runs out and again there is a lot of audience frustration.

Much depends on the skill of the chairman, or moderator, in holding both the panel and the audience to brief, pointed comments, clearly related to the subject under discussion.

Long-winded, rambling remarks and the airing of personal experiences or grievances having no general interest can ruin any discussion period.

Still more effective is the true workshop or study-type conference where most of the time is spent in small discussion groups with *everyone* participating.

Usually, it is essential to provide a certain amount of factual information as a basis for profitable discussion. This can be given in an opening presentation by a recognized authority, or it can be furnished in printed form in advance of the conference.

In any case, each group of ten to twenty persons needs a capable *chairman* and a good *recorder* who can summarize and report the outcomes of the discussion.

Another helpful arrangement is to include in each group a *consultant* or two having experience in the subject under discussion, provided the consultants are wise enough not to dominate the discussion.

Sometimes an *observer* is added to the group to watch for outstanding developments and to advise with the chairman on the conduct and progress of the discussion in order that the meeting may be of greatest benefit to all.

Various Plans for Holding Meetings

The discussion-type conference seems to be particularly effective for meetings within a state where a high percentage of board members from a comparatively small area can be brought together for a few hours or a day.

If careful advance planning is done to select topics for discussion which the members themselves have indicated they are most interested in, and if leaders are chosen for their ability to put a small group quickly at ease and to encourage participation by everyone, a profitable experience will result.

State Association Work-Type Meetings

Most state associations have regional and/or county sub-divisions in which more frequent meetings are held than is possible on a statewide basis.

More and more association leaders are finding that a regular series of regional meetings does more than any other activity to build interest and to assist local district boards.

The plans for scheduling such meetings vary, depending on local conditions and board member preferences.

In many states, a series of one-day regional meetings is held in rapid succession over the state in the fall or spring months. In at least one state, the regional meetings are all held on the same night which focuses statewide public attention on effective school board service.

Programs for such meetings usually include current problems of statewide interest in relation to educational legislation.

By the time the meetings have all been held, two major purposes have been accomplished: (1) A large number of board members over the entire state has had a chance to discuss the issues first hand; and (2) association leaders have gained a pretty clear idea of the concensus of school board views, pro or con, concerning each issue.

In one state having long experience (and in a growing number of others which have adopted a similar pattern) very successful meetings are scheduled in each of eleven regions in the fall and again in the spring.

These are late afternoon to early evening meetings designed so as not to cut into the board member's business day too severely and to get him home at a reasonable hour.

The meetings convene at 4:00 to 4:30 p.m. in a series of four or five group discussions on selected topics of timely interest. Board members make their own choice of the group they will attend.

A chairman and several discussion leaders are selected in advance for each group, but every effort is made to promote general participation by *all* who are present.

These discussions last for an hour to an hour and a half. After a brief interval, all the members who have been attending the several group sessions gather for dinner and a general session. (Effort is made to rotate the meetings to different centers in each region, with the local school board acting as host.)

At the conclusion of the meal, various items of business and reports of progress may be presented, and then there is a talk by some prominent lay or professional leader on a topic of interest to the whole group, followed by questions from the floor as long as time permits up to adjournment at 9:00 p.m.

A few states are conducting real workshops for board members on a statewide basis in addition to their annual conventions. In some cases these cover a period of two or three days of intensive study and discussion, and are often held in rotation at state institutions of higher education.

These workshops are designed primarily for newly selected board members, a large majority of whom are persuaded to attend, but there is also a considerable number of older board members present who find the experience profitable year after year. Always they learn something new.

Suggestions for a systematic program of self-study, either by a single board, a regional group, or a statewide workshop, will be found in the "Outline for a Ten-Session Workshop Study of School Board Functions and Relationships" in Appendix E.

Suggested Topics for Discussion

As an aid to those who are planning group discussions and program talks at various regional and statewide meetings of school board members, the following list of topics has been compiled.

These topics and questions have been gathered from many sources and, while by no means exhaustive, they do include most of the subjects of greatest current interest to school boards in all parts of the country.

For any given meeting, selection should be made of a limited number of the topics that are most pertinent and timely to the local situation.

State Association Work-Type Meetings

I. School Board Policies and Procedures

How Should the School Board Be Organized?

What Are the Special Responsibilities of the President of the Board?

Policies, Procedures, and Records of School Boards

What Are the Discretionary Powers of School Boards?

What Are the Advantages of Written Board Policy?

How the New School Board Member Can Best Learn His Job

What Makes a Good Annual Report?

How To Select the Superintendent of Schools

The School Office and Its Functions

Population Trends in the School District

What Should School Boards Know About Textbooks?

What Are the Legal and Administrative Aspects of School Discipline?

The Need for Long-Range Planning by School Boards

What Is Needed *Most* to Improve Our Schools?

II. The School Program

What Are We Aiming At in Public Education Today?

Let's Take a Look at the School Curriculum

What Interest Should the School Board Take in the Curriculum?

What Goes On in the Classroom?

What Is Meant by the School's Responsibility for the "Whole Child"?

Are We Preparing Youth for Life in a Changing World?

What Is a Good Counseling Program?

Can Something Be Done to Reduce the "Dropouts" in the High School?

What Are We Doing for the Gifted Child?

What Are We Doing for the Retarded Child?

How Closely Are We Meeting the Individual Needs of All Children?

How Is the Education Program Related to Physical and Mental Health?

What is the Place of Athletics and Other Extra-Curricular Activities in a School Program?

The School Safety Program, Including Civil Defense

Do We Have a Balanced Program of Vocational Education?

Are We Making Full Use of Audio-Visual Aids?

How Should the Schools Teach Moral and Spiritual Values?

Should Religion Be Included in the School Curriculum?

III. *School Organization*

The Reorganization of School Districts into Larger Tax and
Administrative Units

The Case For and Against a High School of Fewer than 400
Students

Problems of School Transportation

How Important Relatively Is Elementary Education?

How To Secure Better Articulation Between Elementary and
Secondary Education

What Are the Special Problems of Small Rural Schools?

What About an Intermediate Unit District for Special Services?

Can Class Size Safely Be Increased?

What Is the Place of Nursery Schools and Kindergartens?

Do We Need a Community (Junior) College for the 13th and
14th Grades?

Should the High School Try to Hold All Youth to Age 18?

How Fully Should Public Schools Provide for Adult Education?

What About Camping Education and the Extended School
Year?

Are There Educational Uses for Farm and Forest Land for
Schools?

How Effective Are the State Board, the State Superintendent,
and the State Department of Education in This State?

IV. *Professional and Staff Relations*

Desirable Human Relationships in Successful School Operation

School Board—Administrator Relationships

Qualifications of a School Administrator

Are School Boards and Administrators Wasting Each Other's
Time?

What Guides Should Be Used in Building Salary Schedules?

What Responsibility Does the Board Have for Teacher Employment and Evaluation?

Evaluation of Teachers—Pro and Con

Would Merit Pay Insure Better Teaching?

School Board—Staff Relationships

Should Teachers Tell the School Board Their Problems, Needs,
and Aims?

The Pre-School Workshop and Its Importance to the Teachers'
Progress

What Can Be Done To Improve Teaching Standards?

Valid Requirements for In-Service Training

What Are Desirable Tenure and Retirement Policies?

How Can We Recruit an Adequate Supply of Competent
Teachers?

How Do Accrediting Agencies Operate—and Why?

V. *Finance*

Good School Accounting Procedures
Making the School Budget
Are Assessment and Taxing Procedures Equitable?
Tax Objections and the Problems They Present
What Can be Done About Delinquent Property Taxes?
How to Float a Bond Issue
What Kind of Insurance Program is Needed for Adequate Protection Under Present Conditions?
Things School Boards Should Know About Fire Insurance
When Are School Boards Liable?
How Much Should Education Cost?
State Support—How Much and How Administered?
Federal-State-Local Relationships in School Finance

VI. *Building Policies*

How to Go About Making a Local Survey and a Master Plan of School Facilities
How Much Land Is Desirable for Schools?
What About Building Problems in the Next Few Years?
Trends in Schoolhouse Design and Building Materials
What Is Meant by Functional Design?
Modernizing the School Plant
How Well Are Schools Equipped with the Tools of Learning?
Planning Plant and Playground Facilities for the Physical Education Program
What Wider Use Can Be Made of the School Plant?
How to Win Community Support for a School Building Program

VII. *Public Relations*

What Are the Duties of the School Board in Public Relations?
Citizens Committees and Community Councils—Their Organization and Function
How to Get Community Support for Schools
How to Deal Effectively with Pressure Groups
What to Do about Criticisms of the Schools
Press, Radio, and TV Relationships
Responsibility of the School Board Toward Needed Legislation
How Schools Aid in Developing Community Resources
How Do Communities Go About Finding Board Members of Outstanding Ability?
Current Trends in Home and School Cooperation

NOW AS THEN—WHY?

"Fellow citizens, why do ye turn and scrape every stone to gather wealth, and take so little care of your children, to whom one day you must relinquish it all?"

— SOCRATES (468-398 B.C.)

If you reject the idea that here in prosperous, powerful, twentieth-century America we also take too little care of our children, why not face the facts? Consider the decline in wholesome family living and the mounting record of juvenile crime and delinquency. Consider the number of children who spend their school days in obsolete and unfit buildings, without needed grounds, facilities, and equipment. And the number assigned to double shifts, or to classes too large and too crowded to permit attention to the individual needs of each child. And the number who, because of the shortage of qualified teachers, are receiving a substandard education. In brief, consider how small a percentage of our fabulous national income we spend to insure in the nation's children those qualities of body, mind, and spirit which they must have to lead worthy and useful lives and to keep America strong and free. These things being true, what is *your* answer to the question, Why? — E. M. T.

CHAPTER 27

The National

School Boards Association

The organization now known as the National School Boards Association, Inc. had its origin in 1940, but not until 1949 were more than a handful of school board leaders and school administrators aware of its existence.

In the latter year three things happened which started the Association on the period of rapid development and wider recognition which still continues. These three events were:

1. Appointment by the Association's executive committee of a full-time executive secretary.

2. Establishment of a national headquarter's office for the Association in Chicago.

3. Incorporation of the National School Boards Association under the laws of the State of Illinois.

These developments led to recognition of the revitalization of the N.S.B.A. as one of the "Ten Major Educational Events of 1949" as determined by ballots submitted to members of the Education Press Association of America.

Brief Early History

In 1940, the already well established school boards associations in California, Illinois, and New York took the lead in organizing the National Council of State School Boards Associations.

The executive secretary of the California School Trustees Association, Mrs. Florence C. Porter, is generally recognized as the founder of the movement, and she was elected first president of the National Council at a meeting in St. Louis, Mo., February 28, 1940, held concurrently with the annual convention of the American Association of School Administrators (A.A.S.A.).

In February 1941, the First Annual Meeting Luncheon Conference of the N.C.S.S.B.A. was held in Atlantic City with some 65 persons in attendance. A Second Annual Meeting Luncheon Conference was held in San Francisco in February 1942, but by August 1942, World War II intervened to such an extent that the National Council lay dormant for several years.

In the fall of 1945, a small group of state leaders met in Springfield, Ill., decided to revive the National Council of State School Boards Associations, elected Arthur J. Crowley of New York as the second national president, and called a meeting to be held in Chicago in March 1946.

At this 1946 meeting, which was attended by 12 persons from 9 states, the most important decision reached was "that it should be the policy of the National Council to become a strong, independent organization cooperating with all other agencies in education."

Meetings were held in Atlantic City in 1947 and 1948 in conjunction with the February conventions of the A.A.S.A. Attendance at one of these reached approximately 100 persons from some 23 states. Dr. David J. Rose of North Carolina became the third president, and Robert M. Cole, executive director of the Illinois Association of School Boards, continued to serve as secretary-treasurer of the National Association.

At the 1948 meeting the name of the National Council of State School Boards Associations was shortened to the National School Boards Association which it has remained ever since.

In February 1949, the meeting was held in St. Louis with 45 board members from 19 states and 8 guests in attendance.

As at all previous meetings, major discussion centered around the problem of financing the N.S.B.A. and of finding someone to carry on its work the year round. The treasurer's report indicated that, after all bills were paid, there would be approximately $3,500.00 in the treasury.

At the close of this meeting, Edward M. Tuttle, editor-in-chief of Row, Peterson and Company, textbook publishers, who had been one of the guests during the program, stated that he planned to retire on April 30, 1949 and offered his services as a full-time executive secretary to the N.S.B.A. without stipulation as to remuneration.

After considerable discussion by the executive committee as to the possible success of such a venture, using the $3,500.00 reserve and what little more might come in, the committee authorized the incoming fourth president, J. Paul Elliott of California, and Mrs. Porter, founder and first president, to make such arrangements with Mr. Tuttle as seemed mutually acceptable.

On Monday, May 2, 1949, Mr. Tuttle established the headquarters of the National School Boards Association at 450 East Ohio Street, Chicago 11, Ill. in a building owned by Northwestern University which for the next four years charged the association only a nominal rental.

By fall, the executive secretary had incorporated the N.S.B.A. under the "Not for Profit" laws of the State of Illinois, and had gotten out a first Directory of the presidents and secretaries of the 37 state associations found to be in existence in various stages of development.

Which Type of Association

From the beginning, the founders of the National School Boards Association were faced with two alternative types of organization:

1. Should the National Association seek direct contact with local boards in matters of membership, finance, and service? or

2. Should the National Association work primarily with and through the state school boards associations?

There had been a short-lived attempt by another group in the late 1930's to organize a national association of local board members, and this was one factor which hastened the organization in 1940 of the National Council of State School Boards Associations (later to become the N.S.B.A.) designed to be just what its original name implied.

However, the alternatives of direct local memberships versus the federation of state associations kept bobbing up in all the early meetings, because the original constitution assessed all state associations a flat membership fee of $25.00 per year, and provided that local boards might voluntarily become sustaining members without vote by contributing $1.00 per board per year.

Not until the 1950 Convention in Atlantic City was the issue apparently settled by a unanimous vote of delegates from 28 states in support of a motion that

> "the National School Boards Association be a federation of state school boards associations, and that the National Association serve the state associations, and indirectly local boards through the state associations."

A constitution was adopted embodying this principle and eliminating the sustaining memberships.

Because of the subsequent restoration of memberships for local boards and for individual board members, and because the nature of the structure of the National School Boards Association is so fundamental to its enduring strength and success, it seems desirable to set forth the distinctions between the two types of organization, as brought out in the discussions of 1950.

1. *Direct memberships by local boards* would produce a type of national association which could

    a) compete with each state association for the interest and allegiance of the boards in that state. Some boards would join both, some would join the state and not the national, while some might join the national and not the state.

    b) A large amount of clerical machinery in the National Office would be needed just to keep itself going and its membership and mailing lists current.

    c) Service to the local boards would have to be of a rather general nature since state laws and regulations are all different and are best interpreted by the respective state associations.

    d) A national association publication to which local board

memberships would provide subscriptions would be an almost immediate necessity.

e) In the annual conventions all members would expect to be voting members and the association would become an action group with a lobbying role in national legislation based on the will of the majority.

f) Participation by the association in cooperative councils with other national agencies would be limited by the extent of its local memberships, and would always be a partial rather than a potentially universal representation.

2. *State-association memberships* would produce a different type of national organization.

a) The National Association would look for its primary support to a maximum membership of 55 state and territorial associations, and it would grow *with* them rather than in competition to them.

b) Maintenance machinery in the National office would be held to a minimum and efforts could be concentrated on acting as an interstate exchange to promote the strength of the state associations to more nearly their maximum effectiveness.

c) A National School Boards Association publication would not be so immediately necessary because contributions from the National office would find outlet to local boards through the state school board journals and news-letters, and through the voluntary cooperation of *The American School Board Journal* and other existing commercial publications with a national circulation.

d) The business of the Association would be done at the annual conventions by a body of voting delegates from the state associations.

e) The N.S.B.A. would become an action, or lobbying, organization only in cases of complete policy agreement among its state memberships. On national issues where differences in views were manifest, action would be left to the several states, pro or con.

f) In counsel and cooperation with other national agencies, the N.S.B.A. would potentially represent all the school boards of the nation, since every local board on becoming a member of its state association would automatically become a member of the national association by reason of its state's affiliation.

N.S.B.A. Finance

The problem of finding a sound basis of financial support troubled the National School Boards Association from the date of its origin.

Delegates to the 1950 convention squarely faced the fact that a pro-rata dues formula for the several states, making possible an adequate national budget, was the desirable solution, but that many state associations were themselves too weak financially to support such a formula 100 per cent and would have to drop out.

After prolonged discussion of every possible alternative, the delegates adopted a compromise plan which established a dues *goal* for each state, but granted membership in good standing to all state associations which paid a certain minimum amount. Over the years, this minimum has gradually been raised until today practically all states have reached their full goal memberships in the National Association.

In addition to its basic income from affiliated state associations, other sources of revenue for the N.S.B.A. are (1) convention fees and the sale of space to commercial exhibitors, and (2) dues from the other classifications of memberships provided by amendment of the By-Laws in 1958, as follows:

School Board Memberships: Any State School Boards Association that is an Active Member of the National School Boards Association, Incorporated, may authorize the National Association to issue an Active Membership Certificate to any board of education which has paid $10.00 membership dues to the National Association during the fiscal year.

Individual Members of School Boards: Any State School Boards Association that is an Active Member of the National School Boards Association, Incorporated, may authorize the National Association to issue an Active Membership Card to any individual school board member who has paid $5.00 membership dues to the National Association, during the fiscal year.

State Boards of Education: Any State School Boards Association that is an Active Member of the National School Boards

Association, Incorporated, may authorize the National Association to issue an Active Membership Certificate to their State Board of Education which has paid $100.00 membership dues to the National Association during the fiscal year.

Associate Membership, as defined in the Constitution, may be attained upon payment of $5.00 membership dues to the National School Boards Association, Incorporated, during each fiscal year.

Sustaining Membership, as defined in the Constitution, may be attained upon recommendation by the Executive Committee and upon payment to the National School Boards Association, Incorporated, of such annual dues as the Executive Committee may establish; provided that such dues shall not be less than $100.00 annually.

The earlier fear that the N.S.B.A. might be competing with its affiliated state associations if it encouraged national memberships by local boards and board members is relieved by the provision that all such memberships *must be authorized* by the respective State School Boards Associations.

The provision for sustaining memberships by "commercial or professional service organization personnel," in the judgment of this writer, is open to serious objections. Cooperation by such persons and/or organizations should be extended through the channels of exhibits and advertising and not through identification with school board membership.

Foundation Grants

During the years since 1949, while the National School Boards Association has been steadily building its organizational structure, it has been the recipient of a number of grants for special projects.

On the whole, the results of these subsidized activities were beneficial to the association movement and to public education in general and they came at a time when they were most needed.

There are legitimate ways in which further grants might be used to establish patterns or to experiment with ideas which may point the way to permanent association activities in the future.

However, such subsidies present a danger which always accompanies too sudden and too abundant riches—the temptation to rely on such extraneous support to the neglect of basic development, and the establishment of levels of spending during the short periods of the grants which cannot be maintained afterward.

Those who cherish the thought of a sound and enduring National School Boards Association in these United States for all time to come hope that its officers and directors through the years will be given the wisdom to guide its progress surely and safely through prosperity as well as through adversity. As its resources increase so do its responsibilities and its opportunities for service to American public education.

N.S.B.A. Functions

The Constitution of the National School Boards Association defines its purposes as follows:

1. To promote the general advancement of education for the youth of the United States and its Territories.

2. To study the educational programs of the different states and territories and to disseminate the information as a service function to the State School Boards Associations and the membership.

3. To encourage the most efficient and effective organization and administration of the public schools.

4. To work for the adequate financial support of the public schools.

5. To study educational legislation proposed in Congress to the end that the various State School Boards Associations and the membership may be informed of such legislation.

6. To implement and accomplish such programs, or proposals consistent with the purposes of the Association, as may be approved by vote of the Delegate Assembly or by the Board of Directors.

Seeking to carry out the purposes set forth above, the National School Boards Association has identified the following objectives and functions as among the most important to which it is committed:

1. To *aid* state school boards associations to improve and strengthen their state organizations in effective service to local school boards.

2. To *maintain* channels for exchange of ideas and to prepare and distribute to state associations, and through them, to local school boards, educational information and literature, as well as to encourage workshops and study groups where school board members may prepare and qualify for more effective service to the public schools.

3. To *inform* state school boards associations, and through them, local school boards, on successful techniques of school board operation, school administration, educational trends, and solutions to current school district problems arrived at in the various states.

4. To *give* the school boards of America, through their state and national associations, a voice in educational policy making at all levels.

5. To *foster* such objectives and policies of education as will preserve our American concept of democracy and develop each individual child for successful living and good citizenship.

6. To *improve* the quality of school programs toward the highest type of education offered in the various states, seeking a balance of curriculum content and instructional methods which will utilize the best ideas of modern education while retaining established and proven techniques.

7. To *encourage* the most desirable and efficient working relationships on the local level between boards of education, school administrators, the school staff, and the public.

8. To *provide* a constructive program of information and good public relations on the national, state, and local levels in order to inform parents, communities, states, and the Congress in Washington of the aims, potentialities, and needs of our public schools.

9. To *work* in cooperation with every national agency, educational and lay, which is sincerely desirous of advancing universal public education to higher levels of effective service to the children, youth, and adults of America.

Just as local school boards are urged to adopt written policies and to keep them up to date (see Chapter 6), so the National School Boards Association has adopted a *Statement of Beliefs and Policies* in the field of public education and of school board procedures on which its affiliated membership is in agreement. First adopted in 1955, and added to for several years thereafter, the Statement was completely revamped in 1962 under the following main heads: Introductory Statement; (I) Control and Support of Public Schools; (II) Responsibilities of Local School Boards; (III) The Educational Program; (IV) Relationships with State School Boards Associations; (V) Relationships with Other Groups; and (VI) National Legislation.

The activities of the National School Boards Association, in carrying out its stated objectives, fall into two general categories:

1) services to its affiliated state associations which are chiefly discussed in this chapter, and

2) services to public education on the national level which are discussed primarily in Chapter 30 on "N.S.B.A. Cooperative Affiliations."

Services to the States

Up until the establishment of a national headquarters in 1949, the activities of the N.S.B.A. were practically limited to the holding of an annual convention (see Chapter 28), where some of the leaders from the states could meet together for a program and exchange of views.

As soon as the national office opened, it began to build up a comprehensive *file* on the state associations, and twice a year to issue and distribute an up-to-date *Directory* of state presidents and executive secretaries. Currently it is issued periodically.

Monthly *releases* (since January 1959 printed and titled *School Boards*) are mailed to state leaders. These cover reports on state and national activities in the school board field, and a wide variety of timely items sorted out and condensed from the great mass of educational literature received at the N.S.B.A. office. State asssociations find increasing use for some of this material in their *Bulletins, News Letters,* and *Journals* to local boards.

In 1962, the N.S.B.A. Delegate Assembly authorized the institution of an *Information Service Program* available to individual board members anywhere in the nation on a subscription basis. In brief, this service includes (1) *School Boards,* the monthly publication of the Association; (2) a regular series of Information Service *Bulletins*—short, one and two page items of interest to board members on current topics; and (3) selected booklets and pamphlets on pertinent subjects. The Program is designed as an effort to step up the flow of vital information to school board members from the headquarters of the National School Boards Association. Subscriptions are promoted through the state associations.

Special N.S.B.A. Studies are conducted by committees of the Association in areas of current concern to the school boards of the nation, and reports are made to delegates and others at the annual conventions. Areas in which such studies have been instituted include (1) the drafting of A Code of Ethics for School Board Members (see Appendix D); (2) a poll of board members throughout the nation on their attitude toward federal assistance to education; (3) an exploration of teacher-superintendent-board relations; and (4) a study of state and local school finances, designed to encourage increased support of public education. Similar studies will undoubtedly be continued in the years ahead as needs arise and as resources permit.

Correspondence at national headquarters has steadily increased in volume and significance. It comes from the member states, from a wide variety of cooperating organizations on the national level (see Chapter 30), and from individuals.

Some states write much oftener than others and in general this is a good index of the activity within a state. Many of the letters ask for specific help or raise questions that require time and consideration to answer. Practically none of the correspondence is of a routine or perfunctory nature, and it never should be. Letter exchanges are direct evidence of those cordial, personal working relationships which constitute the very life blood of the N.S.B.A., and correspondence must always have top priority as a direct service to the state associations.

Visits to States. In his first year of service (1949-50) the N.S.B.A. executive secretary was able to visit twenty-six states. In seventeen of these, he attended and addressed the annual state association meetings. In the others, conferences were held with the state officers and executive committees. Evidence of increased vitality in the whole association movement was the fact that a dozen states associations at their 1949-50 meetings adopted new schedules of dues, revised upward.

The trends just indicated have accelerated through the years. More and more, the N.S.B.A. presidents and other officers, as well as the executive director, find it possible to accept invitations to visit states for consultation and to participate in state programs. Their voluntary service and devotion to the association movement have acted as a tremendous stimulus.

Meetings and Conferences. Beyond a doubt, the most effective service the N.S.B.A. renders to its affiliated states is to make it possible for state leaders to meet together and enjoy those personal friendships and exchanges which nothing can replace.

At first, such meetings were limited to the annual conventions of the National Association (see Chapter 28), but gradually other opportunities presented themselves in the form of regional and nationwide study conferences (see Chapter 29).

Since school board leadership within the states is constantly shifting, there will always be tremendous value in bringing the leaders together as often as such conferences can be well planned and financed. Here is a phase of N.S.B.A. service which has unlimited possibilities for considered development in coming years.

Looking to the Future

Comparatively speaking, the National School Boards Association is a young organization. Of necessity, it has had to go through a period of much more rapid expansion in the demands upon it than in the resources with which to meet those demands.

In short, the N.S.B.A. has growing pains, plenty of them. But this is a healthy condition, for it is much safer in the long run to have real work to do with limited means than it is to have to hunt for ways to justify the expenditure of an overabundance.

In addition to a steady and normal growth of the services which have been described in this chapter, there are other ways, as yet barely touched, in which the N.S.B.A. will grow in stature and service in the years to come. Without attempting to go into particulars, these services are likely to fall into three broad areas:

1. A wide variety of publications for board members.

2. The stimulation of research in the school board field and popular interpretation of the results of research.

3. Continuous relations with the general public through the use of all modern media of communication.

As has been pointed out in Chapter 22, the school boards of America have in their hands the means to promote their own effectiveness to whatever extent they consider necessary.

In 1958, *headquarters* of the National School Boards Association was moved from the original Chicago address (see page 213) to 1940 Sheridan Road, Evanston, Ill., opposite the Northwestern University campus. The building is a former residence, owned by the University, and provides ample room for the expanding activities of the Association.

> *"The crisis of our times is moral as well as material, and the spirit of man is stronger and hungrier than the body."*
> —ADLAI STEVENSON

ORDEAL

*"Say not that this or that thing came
to thwart you; it came only to test
you."*

—MURIEL STRODE

Sometimes problems and difficulties appear to be
insurmountable—in our personal lives, in our business affairs, in our efforts at public service. Yet over
and over again it has been proved that a resolute
facing of a problem, with the will and determination
to solve it, leads directly to its solution. There is
great encouragement in the quotation above, which
says, in effect, that no problem we are called upon
to face is beyond our power to meet, if we will but
rise to the test. For individuals and for organizations, including school boards, each test, met with
courage and skill, gives added strength for the next.
Thus we grow in ability to accomplish the seemingly
impossible. — E. M. T.

CHAPTER 28

The National
School Board Convention

Although the National School Boards Association is primarily a federation of state school boards associations, with two voting delegates from each legally affiliated state association, the National Convention is open to all local board members.

The number of school boards and school board members in this country provides a tremendous potential, and if the National Convention continues to grow as it has since 1949, within a few years it will be among the largest and most influential educational meetings in America.

Who Should Attend?

Local boards should consider carefully their relationship to the annual convention of the National School Boards Association. Following are some suggestions in this connection:

1. Each local board should be represented each year. It is of increasing importance that school boards should broaden their understanding of the relationships in educational policy on local, state, and *national* levels in order to serve their own communities most effectively.

2. One or two members from a board should attend—rarely the whole board, except in some unusual circumstance such as having a high-ranking national officer from the local district. In no sense should the national meeting be regarded as the occasion for a "junket" at public expense.

3. Representation should be rotated from year to year, so that during his term of office each member of the local

board will have at least one opportunity to participate in a national convention and to gain the insight and inspiration it can give.

4. New board members should be a little seasoned before they attend a national convention. This seasoning should come from attendance at area and statewide meetings of their state school boards association, which are designed primarily to help them with their local problems. After they begin to understand educational relationships *within* the state, they are in a much better position to understand educational relationships *among* the states and in the nation as a whole.

5. Travel and subsistence expenses of local school board representatives to the N.S.B.A. Convention should be paid from school board funds. This is a legitimate investment designed to develop increasingly effective service to the community. Most board members serve without remuneration and at considerable personal sacrifice. If they contribute time away from their businesses to attend a national meeting, they should not be expected to be out of pocket for the legitimate expenses of the trip. In states where such reimbursement is not legally permissible at present, the school boards associations should take steps to secure an authorization by legislative enactment.

6. Local boards should insist that their representatives to the national meetings bring back as complete reports as possible and share all that they have been able to learn with their fellow board members.

Conventions of the Past

The first annual convention of the National Council of State School Boards Associations (forerunner of the N.S.B.A.) was held in Atlantic City in February 1941 in conjunction with the meeting of the American Association of School Administrators. About 65 persons were present.

Thereafter, conventions were held each year except 1943 and 1944 when they were prevented by travel restrictions due to World

War II. Attendance never exceeded 100 until 1950, the first Convention after the N.S.B.A. established a headquarters with a full-time executive secretary (see Chapter 27). In 1954, attendance passed the 1,000 mark for the first time, and five years later totaled over 3,500.

Until 1950, the N.S.B.A. Conventions were held at the same times and places as those of the A.A.S.A., but from 1950 to 1957 inclusive they were scheduled at the end of the week preceding the A.A.S.A. meetings so that, while the two conventions were separate in time, one led directly into the other.

Board members were often accompanied by their administrators for part or all of the School Board Convention, and a good many board members stayed over for part or all of the Administrators Convention.

In 1957, by a cooperative arrangement, the great commercial and architectural exhibit of the A.A.S.A. opened on the Friday of the N.S.B.A. Convention in order better to serve both meetings. This plan met with approval from board members, administrators, and exhibitors alike.

First Independent Convention in 1958

Notwithstanding the recognized benefits that had been experienced from holding the meetings of the two associations together in sequence, the N.S.B.A. Board of Directors voted to hold the 1958 Convention at a different time and place from the meeting of the A.A.S.A. Several reasons led to this decision:

1. Most important was the desire to move the school board convention from February to a later date in order not to conflict so seriously with sessions of state legislatures which school board leaders were reluctant to leave at such a critical time for school legislation.

2. Attendance was growing so rapidly that difficulties were being encountered in room reservations for the two big groups, especially where members wanted to attend both meetings. Seemingly, it was inevitable that the separation must come sooner or later. Then why not make the begin-

ning in a year (1958) when the A.A.S.A. was holding three regional meetings instead of a single national meeting?

3. It was felt by many state and national school board leaders that board members would feel a greater sense of autonomy in holding their own convention at a time and place not related to any other educational meeting. This feeling could only be confirmed or disproved by trying the plan.

4. It was hoped that an independent convention could stage its own commercial exhibit for more direct study of school construction, equipment, and maintenance materials by board members and with some resulting income to the N.S.B.A.

The Convention was held in Miami Beach, April 17-19, 1958, and exceeded all expectations. Over 2,100 board members registered from the 49 states and Hawaii, with 31 school trustees from Canada, a 50 per cent increase over the convention in Atlantic City the year before. Including guests, the total registration was 2,909.

The theme of the convention, "School Boards and the Curriculum," was extremely timely. A wave of criticism of the American educational system had followed in the wake of the scientific successes scored by Russia. The President of the United States had urged school boards throughout the nation to "scrutinize the school's curriculum and standards to see whether they meet the stern demands of the era we are entering" (see Chapter 10).

Every general session and discussion group during the three-day convention was packed with listeners and participants. Comment in the lobbies described this as the most profitable meeting the board members present had ever attended.

The First Convention Exhibit was an auspicious beginning to this phase of future N.S.B.A. activities. Seventy-one (71) leading firms filled 109 booths with displays of their latest offerings in construction materials, school equipment, and maintenance supplies. They expressed gratification at the eager interest shown by the school board members who sought firsthand information that would be of real assistance to them in supporting purchases recommended by their administrators.

In subsequent years, Conventions of the National School Boards Association increased steadily in attendance, in variety and extent of programs, in exhibit displays, and in action by the official Delegate Assembly representing the federated state associations. By 1963, attendance exceeded 5,000, and the prediction made in the second paragraph of this chapter seemed on the way to fulfillment.

A Broad View Is Needed

At each convention of the N.S.B.A., two-thirds or more of the board members present are attending the national meeting for the first time. Some of them are inclined to feel that more help should be given them in solving their local community problems.

It is not the primary function of the National Convention to attempt to solve local school problems, though it may often help to do so indirectly.

Since, in this country, responsibility for public education is vested in the several states, and there are wide variations in legal authorizations and restrictions among the 50 states, it is obviously impossible to discuss details of local policy and procedure at a national meeting without a lot of waste motion and disregard of broader principles and relationships.

State association meetings and workshops, annual and regional, should be the places to tackle problems of local concern, where there can be an exchange of ideas and experience within a given legal framework (see Chapter 26).

The National Convention, in contrast to state meetings, provides the best opportunity board members have to inform themselves on nationwide relationships in the field of public education, relationships that are becoming increasingly important.

As a federation of state associations, the N.S.B.A. cannot take a nationwide position on any question where there are differences of views among its affiliates without destroying its own usefulness as the united voice of the school boards of America.

But the N.S.B.A. can provide, in its annual conventions, a place where local board members and state association leaders may gain information and perspective on many issues, controversial and otherwise, so that they will be in a position to express their own views intelligently on any level—local, state or national—when occasion demands.

There is a growing host of concerns that have nationwide significance which need to be understood and taken into account by local boards if they are to do the most effective job of developing local policy and of planning ahead for their own communities. Some of these concerns are:

1. The extreme mobility of our population in these days of rapid transportation and communication. This means, literally, that a poor school anywhere hurts the nation everywhere.

2. Keen competition for trained manpower at top levels. This includes not only scientists and engineers but those who must make up the supply of teachers and administrators, as well as the leaders in all walks of life.

3. Shifting impacts on communities by reason of military or industrial expansion. The more board members can learn about why, when, and where such impacts may come, the more intelligently they can reach decisions with respect to their own communities.

4. The manner in which local, state, and national agencies are inextricably interwoven in our whole tax structure.

5. Rising costs of all public services, including that of public education, and the increasing competition for the tax dollar.

6. The nation's stake in the basic goals of education for all its citizens, present and future, which should undergird local and individual adaptations. The furore of criticism of public education that followed the launching of the first man-made satellites by Russia in the fall of 1957 is a striking example of this national concern (see Chapter 10).

7. The position of the United States Office of Education in the structure of the Federal Government in the years ahead. Shall it be (1) a division within an Executive Department of the Government, as at present, or (2) an Executive Department itself headed by a Secretary in the President's Cabinet, or (3) an Independent Agency of the Government under the jurisdiction of a Board of outstanding lay citizens which shall appoint the Commissioner of Education and adopt policies governing the conduct of the Agency in accordance with the law?

8. The criticisms of our established system of local control of public education that threaten to replace it with a national controlling authority, and what needs to be done to offset such a threat (see Chapter 32).

There are other national concerns that could be cited, but those listed above should be convincing evidence of how important it is that somewhere, somehow, board members who are responsible for the operation of America's public schools should have an opportunity to discuss and seek to understand such nationwide problems and relationships.

If those who attend N.S.B.A. Conventions will come with this broader view of what to expect at a national meeting of school board leaders, then we may anticipate that year by year the National Convention will become more meaningful and valuable.

"No matter whose the lips that would speak,
they must be free and ungagged.
Let us believe that the whole of truth
can never do harm to the whole of virtue;
and remember that in order to get
the whole of truth you must allow every man,
right or wrong, freely to utter his conscience,
and protect him in so doing."

— WENDELL PHILLIPS

"IT IS MORE BLESSED"

"The strength of a democracy is judged by the quality of the services rendered by its citizens."

— PLATO

The most significant word in Plato's shrewd observation, made centuries before Christ gave the world its "Golden Rule," is in the phrase *"by its citizens."* Why did he not say that the quality of services rendered *to* its citizens indicates the strength of a democracy? Who constitute a democracy? Is it not the people themselves—all the people? If each citizen seeks to receive greater services than he gives, how long will there be any reserve of services to render to anyone? But if each citizen assumes a measure of responsibility for helping to promote the general welfare, then the total reserve of services grows in strength and quality, and the level of democracy rises and carries its constituents to higher purposes, achievements, and standards of human living. — E. M. T.

CHAPTER 29

Regional and Nationwide
Study Conferences

Just as it is important for the members of local school boards to have opportunities to get together in area and statewide work-type meetings (see Chapter 26), so it is equally essential that the leaders of state school boards associations should have opportunities to meet for periods of more concentrated study than can be provided in the midst of the National Conventions.

Moreover, it became evident between the years 1949 and 1952, as the National School Boards Association began to grow, that one of its greatest handicaps was financial inability to bring its officers and directors together for consultation and planning except once a year at brief meetings of the Board in connection with the National Convention.

What the association movement, state and national, needed to give it surer guidance and increased momentum was to find some way to get its leaders together between conventions in one or more real working conferences.

But early efforts to secure assistance in financing such nation-wide study conferences failed of realization.

The Midwest Regional Conferences

A first break in the seeming impasse described above came when Dr. Francis S. Chase, director of the Cooperative Program in Educational Administration (better known as the Kellogg Project) at the Midwest Administration Center of the University of Chicago, offered to subsidize a study conference for school board association leaders in the Midwestern states during the summer of 1952.

233

School Board Leadership in America

A three-day conference was held at Chicago University in August, attended by the association presidents and secretaries of ten midwestern states, together with the officers and executive secretary of the National School Boards Association.

The areas of discussion set up by the planning committee for this first regional study conference served, with some natural variations, as a basic pattern for later conferences, both regional and national. They centered around the following questions:

1. What are the proper functions of school board members?

2. What help is needed by board members in order that they may understand their functions and know how to perform them effectively?

3. In what ways can a state school boards association most effectively provide the assistance needed by school board members?

4. What can be done to develop or to strengthen a state school boards association so that it may provide the assistance needed by board members?

5. In what ways can the National School Boards Association assist state school boards associations in providing the services required by board members?

After the First Midwest Regional Conference was over, some of the comments from participants were:

"The best meeting I ever attended."
"I wouldn't have missed it for anything."
"I have gained a realization of the need for state and national school boards associations that I never had before."
"I'm going back to try and do a better job for my state association."

In reporting this meeting to the National Convention six months later, the N.S.B.A. executive secretary made the following observations:

"In my judgment, the most important event of the past year in relation to a sound future growth of the school boards

234

association movement was the Study Conference for the leaders of ten midwestern states held at the University of Chicago . . .

"More concrete progress in mutual understanding and in exchange of ideas was made during these three days than at any meeting of school board leaders I have ever attended, and I am confident that the results will be increasingly evident.

"The major question for us all is how to secure a similar opportunity in other sections of the country, so that ultimately the leaders of every state association will be able to attend such a conference every year.

"A few years of this kind of intensive study would, I believe, advance our state associations to a degree of strength and effective service to their local member boards beyond anything that we can now imagine."

A second Midwest Study Conference was held with equal success at the University of Chicago in July, 1953, with one-half of the expenses borne by the Midwest Administration Center and the other half by the associations.

In 1954 the Conference was held in Des Moines, Iowa, with the Iowa Association acting as host. One-fourth of the expenses were subsidized that year, after which the Midwest Administration Center dropped out of the picture financially upon assurance that the state school boards associations could carry on alone.

In subsequent years, other state associations in the Midwest have acted as hosts to the annual summer study conference. This rotation plan affords the various association leaders an intensive glimpse of the setup in each state visited, in addition to the stimulation that always results from getting together.

First Nationwide Study Conference

Based upon the experience of the Midwest Regional Study Conference, the National School Boards Association, in 1953, submitted a proposal to The Fund for the Advancement of Education, which resulted in a grant of $50,000.00 (extended through the

School Board Leadership in America

National Citizens Commission for the Public Schools) to be used for the holding of two Nationwide Study Conferences for School Board Leaders, one in 1953 and one in 1954.

The first of these conferences was held in Evansville, Ind., on November 13-15, 1953, marking what may well be looked upon in years to come as an historic date in school board service in this country.

Participants in the Evansville Conference came from 45 states and included 16 national officers and directors, 34 state association presidents, 25 other state leaders—vice presidents, past presidents, directors, and board members—38 state association secretaries or their direct representatives, and a half dozen guest authorities on association work who helped as moderators and consultants.

Nothing like this had ever happened before, and these 119 leaders, after an opening session on Friday evening, divided voluntarily and quite evenly into five working groups and spent Saturday examining the purposes and accomplishments of state school boards associations with respect to

A. The Selection, Orientation, and In-Service Education of Individual Board Members

B. Improving the Operation of Local Boards of Education

C. Defining and Solving Educational Problems Which Cannot Be Solved on the Local Level

D. Perfecting the Organization and Financing the Activities of State School Boards Associations

E. Developing the Prestige of a State Association

In the afternoon, the same groups met again for three hours and, on the basis of the background discussion of the morning, sought to discover

1. Areas of weakness in state programs

2. Ways in which help could be given the states by the National School Boards Association

3. What additional activities should be performed by the N.S.B.A.

Regional and Nationwide Study Conferences

Because the conclusions and recommendations of the First Nationwide Study Conference have served ever since as a challenge to association development and as goals toward which to strive, and because later conferences were designed largely to follow through on the Evansville Findings, they are reported here in considerable detail.

Great progress has been made in the intervening years in realizing many of these recommendations; others have barely been approached; and still others lie in the future, perhaps to be achieved in time to come by some of the readers of this book.

GROUP A reported its unanimous conclusion that state and national school boards associations have a definite responsibility to improve the process of selecting school board members, to give added status to school board membership, and to use every means to arouse and inform the public on this important subject.

It urged that much could be done for local boards through wider use of handbooks, consultative services, and workshops, and that far greater use of press, radio, and television outlets should be made in reaching the general public.

It urged surveys and studies as to methods of cooperating with higher institutions to develop research needs, and suggested that the N.S.B.A. should function as a major clearinghouse for research interpretation and the coordination of proposed research.

GROUP B concluded that there is great room for improvement in the operation of local boards of education, and suggested that if a few tape recordings of actual board meetings could be made and played back to board members, ways of improving procedures would quickly reveal themselves.

It urged that all state associations work toward having a full-time secretary, more area meetings within the state, a good publications program, sound legislative activities, and endeavor to secure 100 per cent participation of local boards.

It urged the N.S.B.A. to develop more frequent and regular channels of information to the several states, to cooperate as fully as possible with other organizations on the national level working in the interest of public schools, and to utilize all media of mass

237

communication to make better known the purposes and activities of school boards and their associations throughout the nation.

GROUP C found that educational problems which cannot be solved at the local level, and which require cooperative effort through the state association, fall chiefly in the realm of legislation affecting such matters as the organization of the State Board of Education and the Office of Public Instruction, the amount and distribution of state aid to schools both for maintenance and construction, the development of foundation programs, and problems concerning the general welfare of pupils and school staffs.

It urged that state associations hold more area conferences on legislative matters, and develop methods of speedy communication with all local boards.

It suggested that associations take the lead in co-ordinating the efforts of all state agencies and organizations concerned over public education in developing a desirable and essential working program of legislation at each session of the legislature.

And it hoped that the N.S.B.A. would expand its consultative and publications services to state associations, and develop a legislative committee on the national level to advise with the states and report at the annual conventions.

GROUP D, dealing with organizing and financing the activities of state school boards associations, found that many of its conclusions were reflected in the other reports, but emphasized

(1) that annual dues should be collected from *boards*, not from individual board members,

(2) that dues should be on some kind of a sliding scale dependent on the size of each board's jurisdiction,

(3) that well-planned state and area meetings are important,

(4) that cooperation with institutions and organizations in the state to develop research, workshops, handbooks, etc. should be promoted,

(5) that board members should act as leaders in local and state school affairs,

(6) that associations should take a stand on important state school legislation, and

(7) that a good public relations program is a *must*.

This group urged that the N.S.B.A. gather and distribute to the states more information on how state associations are organized and financed, on the conduct of area meetings and workshops, on the formulation of written policies by local boards, and on national legislation.

Conversely, it urged the state associations to cooperate more fully with the N.S.B.A. by sending in information promptly when called for and by publishing and distributing information whenever it applies to the state situation.

GROUP E felt that the prestige of state and national school boards associations could be advanced

(1) by holding a nationwide study conference like this each year,

(2) by holding regional meetings in different parts of the country, involving every state,

(3) by securing fully qualified association executives at state and national levels and by paying them adequate salaries,

(4) by having national representatives in attendance at all state and regional meetings, and state representatives in attendance at all district and area meetings within the states,

(5) by moving the annual meeting around the country on a circuit over a period of years,

(6) by more frequent meetings of officers and directors of the N.S.B.A.,

(7) by increasing consultative and information services from the national to the states, from one state to another, and from the states to local boards,

(8) by developing an effective public relations bureau within the N.S.B.A.,

(9) by establishing an office in Washington, D.C., and developing a two-way legislative service,

(10) by stimulating more research in the school board field in cooperation with higher institutions of learning and with the U. S. Office of Education,

(11) by continued cooperation with *The American School Board Journal,* seeking to publish more news of the school boards association movement, state and national,

(12) by inviting members of state legislatures and of the Congress, members of the State Boards of Education and of the U. S. Office, and leaders of educational and lay groups to state and national association meetings,

(13) by taking initiative when necessary and by extending generous cooperation at all times in working with other agencies for the advancement of public education at every level.

"We are rolling now!" was the way one state association secretary summed up the Evansville Conference and he spoke truly, as has been reported in Chapter 21, section on "The Situation Today," page 167.

Second Nationwide Study Conference

In late October, 1954, the second Nationwide Study Conference for School Board Leaders, provided for by the 1953 grant, was held in St. Paul, Minn.

In attendance were 141 persons of whom 117 were official delegates from 46 states, N.S.B.A. officers and directors, and speakers and consultants. The other 24 were additional delegates, visitors, and local school board leaders, present on invitation but at their own expense. Among the delegates were 35 state association presidents, 7 past presidents, 10 vice presidents, 10 directors, and 33 secretaries.

In the belief that it would be wise to focus the discussions at this second nationwide conference on the two most pressing problems in education rather than to go over again the broad field so well covered at Evansville the year before, the planning committee adopted as the theme of the St. Paul Conference, "How School Boards Associations Can Help Secure the Necessary Teachers and Facilities for America's Children."

Two noted speakers laid the background of facts as a basis for the discussion of teacher supply and school construction. Conference participants then divided into eight groups, four in each area.

Each of the groups on teacher shortage concentrated discussion on one of the following questions:

1. What should school boards associations do to stimulate the recruitment of teachers to meet the increasing shortage of personnel?

2. What should school boards associations do to improve teacher morale and teacher prestige?

3. What should school boards associations do to effect school district reorganization in order to relieve the teacher shortage?

4. What should school boards associations do to improve salaries, pensions, certification standards, etc., of teachers in order to secure a larger number of teachers in the profession?

The groups on building shortage discussed the following questions respectively:

1. What should school boards associations do to stimulate more functional, serviceable, and economical school building construction?

2. What should school boards associations do to encourage rehabilitation of buildings that are structurally sound?

3. What should school boards associations do to secure greater flexibility in school building codes?

4. What should school boards associations do to improve financing procedures and to secure sufficient funds for constructing school buildings?

School Board Leadership in America

The findings of the eight discussion groups were reported at a final session of the Conference, and were later published in report form by the N.S.B.A., as had been the conclusions and recommendations of the Evansville Conference a year earlier.

Kansas City Symposium

In September, 1955, for the third year in succession, the National School Boards Association sponsored a nationwide conference of school board leaders.

But this meeting in Kansas City, Mo., was different, although a natural "next step" after the two preceding conferences. It was announced as a "Symposium to Explore New Approaches to the Problems of Public Education."

Supported by a direct grant to the N.S.B.A. from The Fund for the Advancement of Education for this special purpose, an invited group of 124 school board leaders from all 48 states, together with 43 professional educators from various levels, met for three days of study and discussion.

To stimulate the discussions, which were carried on in eight groups for a period of eight hours in three sessions, nine prominent speakers from various walks of American life were invited to bring to the conference participants a variety of experiences and ideas that might have some application to the problems of education.

The speakers included the executive secretary of the National Manpower Council, a member of the staff of The Menninger Foundation, a forward-looking school architect, a representative of the Methods Engineering Council, the vice president of the New York Stock Exchange, the director of the New York Hospital-Cornell Medical Center, the director of Station WHAS-TV Louisville, a prominent superintendent of schools, and the Chief of Staff of the Department of the Army.

This notable array of speakers did a wonderful job of throwing out challenging ideas, many of which struck their listeners at first hearing as entirely inapplicable to school conditions. Later, in the group discussions, the participants were not so sure, and began to try to discover whether some new and different approaches might not be possible after all.

242

The chairman of a committee of nine observers, charged with evaluating the Symposium, closed his summary with these challenging and prophetic words:

"We have now arrived at the moment in history when a thoroughgoing reconstruction of the content, the method, and the administrative organization of education is needed for all age groups.

"The outlines of this needed reconstruction are not clear, and no one person or small group of persons can project them. Instead, the answers must be sought through a process which enlists the best thinking of our generation as a guide to public policy for education.

"That is why this Symposium is so important. It has kindled the imaginations of many of us here, and has facilitated some break-throughs into the better education that we can create if we can only imagine it first.

"The real test of this conference is not the conclusions reached in the discussion groups, and is not the import of what speakers have brought to you from this rostrum, but it is the fires which will be lighted in communities from Maine to California, and in the school boards associations and other groups which you represent."

An objective report of the Kansas City Symposium, entitled *New Approaches,* was prepared for the N.S.B.A. by a noted writer in the educational field. In condensed and readable form for popular consumption, more than 90,000 copies were distributed in 1955-56, largely through the offices of state school boards associations, but also through some other organizations. Later, The Fund for the Advancement of Education provided money to reprint *New Approaches* and thus made possible the continued availability of this challenging pamphlet (see page 284).

N.S.B.A. Board Meetings

An important by-product of the three nationwide conferences described in this chapter was the fact that they made possible meetings of the Board of Directors of the National School Boards

Association *between* National Conventions, because of the presence at the study conferences of all the national leaders.

At Evansville in November 1953, at St. Paul in October 1954, and at Kansas City in September 1955 the Board was called together officially to transact N.S.B.A. business, and to participate in the planning of the annual conventions, a process which theretofore had always had to be carried on by correspondence.

The results of these added opportunities for the members of the Board from all parts of the country to meet face to face, to get to know one another better, and to take a more active part in the affairs of the National Association were of far-reaching importance in the critical growing years.

The Southeast and Other Regional Conferences

In June 1954, school board leaders of the associations in the Southeastern States held their first regional conference at Daytona Beach, Fla., in conjunction with the regular annual meeting of the Southern States Work Conference.

Such a regional conference had been talked about by the southeastern leaders during the nationwide conference in Evansville the previous November, and again at the national convention in February, but it only became a reality when Dr. Truman M. Pierce, then director of the Southern States Cooperative Program in Educational Administration (Kellogg Project), centered at George Peabody College for Teachers in Nashville, Tenn., followed the lead of the University of Chicago two years earlier and offered to subsidize the expenses of two school board leaders from each southeastern state at a week-long conference workshop.

This first meeting in the Southeast Region was fully as successful as the first Midwest Regional Conference described earlier in this Chapter. It followed much the same pattern but with particular adaptation to the needs of a region where many of the state school boards associations were struggling with organizational problems and inadequate budgets.

Two comments near the close of the conference will serve to indicate how eyes were opened and opinions changed by the face to face exchange of ideas and experiences. The president of one association which at the time had no real budget said, "I'm coming around to the view that state associations should be supported by local boards with public money." And another, whose association was then identified with a professional organization remarked, "I've changed my mind. I can see now that our school boards association should be independent and have a full-time executive secretary of its own."

Before the conference closed, plans were laid to repeat it again the following year, with promise of partial support from the Peabody Administration Center and a cordial invitation from the Southern States Work Conference to continue the affiliation.

Each year since, a Southeast Regional Conference for School Board Leaders has been held at Daytona Beach in June with delegates sent by the state associations. It differs from the Midwest Regionals in continuing to be held in the same place instead of rotating among the several states, but that can always be done if the associations wish.

Up to 1957, other regions in the nation had not held study conferences for school board association leaders similar to those in the Midwest and Southeast, though some meetings of shorter duration had been held in the Northeast, and at least one in the Southwest; none in the Far West.

Then, at the 1957 Convention of the National School Boards Association an amendment to the Constitution was adopted dividing the United States into five regions for purposes of equalizing the number of national directors at three from each region.

It is this writer's belief that there should never be a formal organization of regions within the N.S.B.A. which would tend to lessen the direct relationships between the national association and its affiliated, dues-paying state association members.

But there is great benefit to be derived from the type of informal regional cooperation demonstrated so well by the Midwest and Southeast states in the holding of one or more workshops or study conferences for their leaders each year. May their number and effectiveness continue to increase!

245

EQUALITY

*"As if it harmed me, giving others the
same chances and rights as myself.
As if it were not indispensable to my
own rights that others possess the
same."*

— WALT WHITMAN

The world is much concerned nowadays with the
question of human rights. If we could all see clearly
and act according to the simple truths set forth by
Walt Whitman in the quotation above, the matter
would quickly be resolved. First, that giving equal
opportunities and equal rights to all men works no
injury to any man. Second, that no man is secure
in his own rights until all men possess those same
rights. Slowly and painfully mankind labors toward
this goal, set back time and again by the jealous
greed and selfish fears of those who covet special
privilege which others may not enjoy. Such self-
seeking ultimately defeats itself, whether in the case
of individuals, groups, organizations, or entire nations. Progress lies the other way, in true equality —
E. M. T.

CHAPTER 30

N. S. B. A.

Cooperative Affiliations

Second only to its function of coordinating and encouraging the development of state school boards associations, is the responsibility of the National School Boards Association to command the respect of and establish cordial working relationships with the leading national organizations and agencies having a concern for public education.

The principle involved here is that since the public schools belong to all the people, *all must work together* in behalf of school improvement, without concern as to who initiates particular undertakings or who receives most credit for achievements.

With its announcement of a national headquarters and full-time executive secretary, the N.S.B.A. began to receive offers of cooperation from many of the established educational organizations and, conversely, their requests for N.S.B.A. cooperation in various projects on the national level (see Chapter 27).

Prior to that time, only a few of these organizations even knew of the existence of the National School Boards Association, but they were quick to recognize the possibilities inherent in its representation of the school boards of America in national conferences and councils concerning the advancement of public education. They welcomed the fact that the school boards now had an association which could be consulted and a voice that could be heard.

As fast as its resources in personnel, time, and money permitted, the National School Boards Association embraced these opportunities for cooperation, trying to establish some priorities which would make its efforts count for most.

With the passage of the years, N.S.B.A. cooperative activities have multiplied and grown in significance and this chapter is an attempt to indicate something of their scope.

A few of these endeavors have come and gone with changing conditions and passing emergencies. One of the most significant and exciting of these at the time was N.S.B.A. cooperation with 85 other organizations in 1950-52 in the National Conference for Mobilization of Education (better known as MOE), working to secure additional allotments of critical materials (steel, copper, aluminum, etc.) for school construction, equipment, and supply. The N.S.B.A. executive secretary was a member of the executive committee of MOE, and appeared before a Congressional subcommittee to emphasize the desperate needs of the schools.

Among the affiliations which the National School Boards Association currently enjoys, a few of the most significant will be described briefly, and others will simply be listed.

Cooperation with the A.A.S.A.

Obviously, the organization most closely related to the National School Boards Association in its basic concerns is the American Association of School Administrators, one of the departments of the National Education Association.

From its earliest days, the N.S.B.A. and its forerunner, the National Council of State School Boards Associations, worked cooperatively with the A.A.S.A., especially in connection with their annual conventions. (See Chapters 27 and 28.)

The N.S.B.A. executive officers, and often its president as well, participate by invitation in the annual spring meetings of the presidents of state school administrators associations, and representatives of the A.A.S.A. have been included in N.S.B.A. study conference discussion groups.

Another area of cooperation has been collaboration on a number of pamphlets sponsored jointly by the two associations (see Bibliography, pages 283-84).

In two instances of late years, officials of the N.S.B.A. have been members of A.A.S.A. Yearbook Commissions, in each case working with the commission for a period of two years.

A representative of the N.S.B.A. was asked to serve as the only lay member of a special A.A.S.A. Committee for the Advancement of School Administration, set up to evaluate and disseminate the results of the Cooperative Program in Educational Administration (C.P.E.A.) supported by the Kellogg Foundation.

Most recently, joint meetings of the N.S.B.A. and A.A.S.A. executive committees have been held to think through the problem of professional negotiations and other common concerns.

Many Contacts with the N.E.A.

It is natural that the National School Boards Association should find many points of contact with the great overall organization of the teaching profession—the National Education Association which celebrated its first 100 years of service in 1957.

From the first, N.E.A. officers and its general staff were generous with advice and suggestions as to the relationships between the young school boards association and various educational groups. Then, in the fall of 1956, after considering the matter for several years, a joint N.S.B.A.-N.E.A. Committee was created with five representatives and the executive officer from each association.

The purpose of this joint committee, which is intended to be a continuing one with rotating memberships, is to provide a ready means for exchanging views between the school boards and the educational profession, to develop better understanding between the two groups, and to plan areas of possible active cooperation in behalf of the advancement of public education.

The National Education Association is composed of numerous commissions, departments, and divisions, with a good many of which the N.S.B.A. is cooperating directly. Chief among these, of course, is the American Association of School Administrators, discussed above. Some of the others are:

American Association of Colleges for Teacher Education (A.A.C.T.E.) one of the groups with which the N.S.B.A. joined in creating the National Council for Accreditation of Teacher Education (see page 253).

Classroom Teachers Association, which is working with both the N.S.B.A. and the A.A.S.A. on a study of teacher competency.

Commission on Professional Rights and Responsibilities, at whose request the N.S.B.A. on several occasions has recommended school board members for investigation committees.

Educational Policies Commission which has more than once consulted N.S.B.A. leaders regarding the school board viewpoint.

Legislation and Federal Relations Division, which has been most generous in keeping the N.S.B.A. and state association offices informed as to the progress of Congressional legislation on schools.

National Commission on Safety Education with which the N.S.B.A. cooperated in sponsoring a motion picture on school community planning and action for safety education.

National Commission on Teacher Education and Professional Standards (T.E.P.S.) also one of the Accreditation Council groups, an organization whose annual week-long study conferences have been closely followed by leaders of the N.S.B.A.

National School Public Relations Association (N.S.P.R.A.), with which the N.S.B.A. has enjoyed most profitable relationships in the development of printed materials and in acting as one of the sponsors of Celebrities Night and Golden Key Awards which is fast becoming one of the notable events of the educational year.

National Organizations Round Table on Public Schools

The idea behind the National Organizations Round Table on Public Schools is that the most effective way to unite the American people in support of public education is through their existing organizations.

But first, the leaders of these national organizations of all kinds—business and industrial groups, farm and labor organizations, service clubs, womens groups, veterans groups, educational and professional associations, and others—must themselves meet regularly face to face around the same table for informal discussion of any and all matters affecting the public schools and colleges of this country.

250

N.S.B.A. *Cooperative Affiliations*

The Round Table grew out of a suggestion advanced by this writer in an article in the January 1951 issue of *The School Executive* magazine calling for a National Coordinating Council on Education. This suggestion was picked up and promoted by the National Citizens Commission for the Public Schools under the leadership of Roy E. Larsen and Henry Toy, Jr., and resulted in the selection of a steering committee of nine, representative of organizations in various fields of American life.

Nearly two years of careful planning by this steering committee preceded the first meeting of the Round Table which was held in Arden House, Harriman, New York on March 23-24, 1953 with one or two top-level representatives of some thirty national organizations participating at their own expense.

It was apparent that a majority of these leaders were meeting each other for the first time, and that there were diverse and conflicting views in the group, but such was the friendly endeavor to work harmoniously that the utmost good feeling prevailed.

It was emphasized from the beginning that the Round Table is not and can never be an action group. It does not commit its component organizations to anything, but by promoting mutual confidence and understanding of conditions in public school affairs, it cannot help but improve the character and effectiveness of approaches made to school problems by national organizations and their state and local affiliates.

Agreement was unanimous that a second National Organizations Round Table on Public Schools be held in October, 1953, in the expectation that this might set the pattern for semi-annual meetings, as indeed it did, for regular two-day meetings of the Round Table have been held in the Spring and Fall ever since.

Continued frank exchanges of views under such conditions should gradually result in greater mutual understandings and in better coordinated cooperation if, in the course of their discussions, these national leaders

1. Consider the facts with respect to all phases of public school objectives, functions, needs, and potentialities, and analyze their relative importance and urgency.

251

2. Learn what the various nationwide organizations are already doing or are prepared to do in connection with the advancement of public education.

3. Reach the greatest possible unanimity of voluntary agreement regarding both short-range and long-range educational policies.

4. Are stimulated to transmit to the state and local constituencies of their respective organizations the understandings they have gained and the cooperative endeavors that have their approval.

In short, by such a process it is possible to embark on a crusade at all levels of organizational activity that has for its goal the ready support of public education by the American people.

An Unmet Need

At one of the early Round Table meetings (see above) this writer exhibited a post card received at the office of the National School Boards Association reading as follows:

"Dear Sir: I am interested in up-to-date and unbiased information concerning public education in America. Will you please send me some information?"

The card was signed by a married woman in the suburbs of one of our great metropolitan areas.

This inquiry points up the fact that while a great volume of literature on public school matters is constantly being issued and distributed by numerous lay and professional agencies, there is no single document anywhere that meets such an inquiry.

What seems to be needed is a fairly brief, simply written, basic statement of the foundations, structure, functions and operation of the American system of public education, so presented that the average interested citizen (like the writer of the post card) could use it as a starting point for further study.

Moreover, were such a statement to be discovered or prepared, its effectiveness would be tremendously increased if it could be published and distributed under the *joint sponsorship of many organizations* rather than by any one group.

Is it too much to hope that such a coordinated effort to give the American people the basic story of American public education may some day be realized?

Participation in Accreditation of Teacher Education

The National Council for Accreditation of Teacher Education was organized in the fall of 1952 after many months of planning and preparation in which the N.S.B.A. participated. The Council is composed of nineteen members selected by the following groups:

> American Association of Colleges for Teacher Education (seven members)
>
> Council of Chief State School Officers (one member)
>
> National Association of State Directors of Teacher Education and Certification (one member)
>
> National Commission on Accrediting—Special Committee (three members)
>
> National Commission on Teacher Education and Professional Standards of the National Education Association (six members)
>
> National School Boards Association (one member)

This is the first time that a representative of the lay public has been included in such an activity in the field of education, and the N.S.B.A. is honored to serve in that capacity.

The N.C.A.T.E. is fully recognized as the national accrediting agency for institutions preparing teachers, and its work is of such far-reaching importance in building up an adequate supply of competent teachers in the years to come that school board leaders should lend every possible support and encouragement to the objectives and activities of the National Council for Accreditation of Teacher Education.

Council of Chief State School Officers

The National School Boards Association and the Council of Chief State School Officers have a lot in common. They are both

253

federations of their state and territorial components. They both represent the legal aspect of public school operation.

One common concern of both the N.S.B.A. and the C.C.S.S.O. was how to render assistance to State Boards of Education (now existing in all but a couple of states) which seemed to occupy a somewhat isolated position between the two federations.

For several years, the N.S.B.A. provided a section meeting at its National Convention for members of State Boards of Education, and the C.C.S.S.O. cooperated by urging its chief state school officers to encourage their State Boards to be represented. Then, in 1958, the Delegate Assembly of the N.S.B.A. amended its Constitution and By-Laws to provide an active membership classification for State Boards of Education (see Chapter 27, page 216).

National Congress of Parents and Teachers

As was pointed out in Chapter 8, the two organizations in this country which stand between the educational profession and the general public and look both ways are the school boards and the P.T.As. This means that at every level—local, state, and national—these two groups need to understand each other's policies and programs and to work together in harmony.

Though different in type of organization—the National Congress having an individual membership of over 12,000,000 and the N.S.B.A. a federated membership of state and territorial affiliates—there are many ways in which each can support the efforts of the other, and these ways their leaders are constantly striving to discover and to emphasize to their constituents.

National Citizens Council for Better Schools

It is interesting that the National Citizens Commission for the Public Schools (forerunner of the National Citizens Council for Better Schools) came into being in New York City in May 1949, the same month that the N.S.B.A. opened its national headquarters in Chicago.

From the beginning, the chairman of the Commission, Mr. Roy E. Larsen, president of Time, Inc., and the Commission's director, Mr. Henry Toy, Jr., (later president of the Council) kept in touch with N.S.B.A. leaders.

N.S.B.A. *Cooperative Affiliations*

The National Citizens Council for Better Schools terminated all its activities at the close of the year 1959, and designated the National School Boards Association, Inc. as the depository of materials produced by the Council for which there would be continued demand by the public (see page 284).

Other Mutually Profitable Relationships

Numerous as are the cooperative affiliations already discussed in this chapter, there are others which deserve mention, however briefly. All possess potential for the advancement of public education along various lines, and as resources permit and opportunities arise, the N.S.B.A. extends increased cooperation.

Adult Education Association—After all, the whole school boards association movement is one phase of adult education for a particular group; moreover, it is the school boards which must authorize provision for increasing the extent of offerings to adults by the schools.

American Council on Education—School boards find themselves having growing concern with many aspects of education beyond the high school.

American Library Association—Most schools of any size have school libraries, and the A.L.A. has a division promoting their advancement and efficiency.

American Textbook Publishers Institute—This is the trade association of textbook publishers to which the N.S.B.A. can turn with assurance for answers to problems in that area.

Association of School Business Officials of the United States and Canada—Second only to the school administrators in their importance to the successful operation of the schools are the business officials which are found in an increasing number of school systems. Ideally, these persons are responsible to the general superintendent (see Chapter 5, point 7), and are of invaluable service to the school board and its administrator. Their national organization was established long before the N.S.B.A. and has been generous and helpful in extending its cooperation.

*Boy Scouts of America—School Service—*A large percentage of Boy Scout troops have their meeting places in school buildings and school boards are usually glad to extend their facilities to promote this worth while youth movement. The same comment would apply to the *Girl Scouts* and other similar groups.

*Federal Civil Defense Administration—*A handbook, entitled "School Boards Plan for Disaster Problems," was developed jointly with the N.S.B.A. in 1958 (see Bibliography, page 284).

Joint Committee on Educational Television and its coordinate *National Citizens Commission on Educational Television—*Both keep the N.S.B.A. office supplied with reports of progress in this field of growing importance.

*Magazine Publishers Association—*The N.S.B.A. has been privileged to participate in several of the fruitful conferences held between educational leaders and magazine editors.

*National Conference of Professors of Educational Administration—*These are the people responsible for the adequate preparation of those who become our superintendents of schools.

*National Safety Council: School and College Conference—*Since 1951, the N.S.B.A. has held membership in this Conference and has usually been represented at the annual meetings in Chicago in October.

National School Supply and Equipment Association (formerly the *National School Service Institute)—*This is the trade association of manufacturers and distributors of school supplies. In 1953 the N.S.B.A. was one of three organizations that worked closely with the N.S.S.I. to produce "A Buying-Selling Code for Schools."

*President's Conference on Fitness of American Youth—*In June 1956, by special invitation from the President of the United States, the president of the N.S.B.A. attended a meeting at Annapolis, Md., to consider ways of improving the fitness of American youth. A representative of the N.S.B.A. is included in the President's Council on Youth Fitness which meets at intervals.

PART III

CHALLENGE

WE FACE OUR ARMAGEDDON

"Marching down to Armageddon—
Brothers, stout and strong!
Ask not why the way we tread on
Is so rough and long!
God will tell us when our spirits
Grow to grasp His plan!
Let us do our part today—
And help Him, helping Man!"

— SIR EDWIN ARNOLD

"Armageddon" is the last great struggle in the world between right and wrong, between good and evil. Whether or not the struggle now going on between our democratic concept of government of, by, and for free men and the communist doctrine of life and death control of the many by a self-chosen few is to be the world's Armageddon, we cannot know. But at least we do know that it is the Armageddon of our lifetime. Accordingly, we must meet it by helping our fellow men from day to day, without complaint when difficulties arise or we grow tired, with faith that a Divine Providence will ultimately reveal the purpose behind it all. None among us possess greater opportunity so to help their fellow men than do the school boards which control democracy's creative instrument for teaching its people, young and old, to live as responsible citizens in a free society. — E. M. T.

CHAPTER 31

Education "by Will" versus
Education "by Order"

"The Russians now clearly are showing their long-term confident conviction that education 'by order' will defeat education 'by will.' This is one of the greatest challenges now facing the American people. It is but little understood by us, in part because it has received but little discussion."

The Benton Report

The statement above occurs near the close of a comprehensive article published in the *1956 Book of the Year* of the *Encyclopaedia Britannica*. The article is entitled "The Voice of the Kremlin" and was written by William Benton, Publisher and Chairman of *Encyclopaedia Britannica*.

In this article Mr. Benton gives his first hand observations on propaganda techniques within the U.S.S.R. and its satellite countries, with particular attention to the educational system and to the control of press, movies, radio, television, and the arts—literature, painting, sculpture, music, dancing, and the drama—in short, every medium which affects the thinking and cultural development of the people.

Mr. Benton, who will be identified as U. S. Assistant Secretary of State for Public Affairs in 1945, and as United States Senator from Connecticut from 1949 to 1953, spent some weeks in the Soviet Union in the fall of 1955 with his family.

After considerable effort he was able to arrange interviews with most of the responsible leaders of the Communist Party and to listen to such statements as the following:

"Ideas can't be stopped by rifles."

"Propaganda is of crucial importance to the final triumph of the Party."

"We teach history as we Communists see it ... The U.S.S.R. is the country of socialism. Our Fatherland is the greatest country in the whole world."

"Revolutionary ideas know no frontiers; they travel throughout the world without visas and fingerprints."

"Religion is still the opiate of the people, but we are strong now and not afraid of it."

"Just because we don't teach Marx in the first ten grades, please do not conclude that our lower schools are non-political. Our aim is Communist education."

At the time, this writer sent reprints of the 32 page Benton Report to the leaders of school boards associations throughout the country stating that it was one of the most significant documents ever distributed to them from N.S.B.A. headquarters because it dealt with the future of this nation and of the world as it will be determined by the extent and quality of our system of education "by will" in contrast to the Communist plan of education "by order."

There are statements and observations in this document which every thinking American citizen needs to be aware of in connection with his understanding and support of public education in this country.

Some Significant Observations

One needs to read the whole report carefully in order to realize what we and the rest of the world are up against in the struggle for the minds of men. Here are just a few of the most striking things that Mr. Benton found out about the Soviet educational system and related phases of cultural development.

The Russians have a ten grade system which by 1960 became compulsory for all young people everywhere. These ten grades are at least equal to our elementary and high school education. Russian children and youth go to school six days a week, ten months a year, and study harder than our American students.

Education "by Will" vs. Education "by Order"

The Soviet system is not designed to meet the needs of the individual, but only the needs of the State. It has two main goals: to find and train the specialists that are needed in every phase of the expanding Russian economy, and at the same time to make certain that every graduate of the schools and higher institutions is completely indoctrinated and loyal to the Communist regime.

Mr. Benton brings out the very interesting dilemma which the Soviets are facing: Can they produce a generation of highly trained and creative people in every field except those of politics and economics where obedience to the Party line must be loyal and unquestioning? His observations led him to think there is a possibility that the Communists may succeed in this unnatural combination. If they do it will constitute a greater threat to the free world than does the hydrogen bomb. It will mean, in brief, that the Communist Party leaders think they can conquer the world with ideas instead of with bombs.

Mr. Benton concludes that "if an uneasy truce in the use of force between nations is now in the offing, for the next decade or the next century, the competitive struggle in the field of ideas will remain."

We should use such a truce to strengthen our own position educationally and culturally so that we "can be of help to human beings everywhere in the development of their own freedoms and well-being."

This is a tremendous challenge. It has been brought home to us most forcefully by the spectacular successes achieved by the Soviets in science, engineering, and space exploration.

People everywhere in the United States need to understand the true facts in the situation, to weigh them carefully, to face them squarely, and to carry out promptly whatever measures are indicated for strengthening our American system of education.

Our Weapon of Offense

The introductory statement of the "Beliefs and Policies" of the National School Boards Association, Inc. asserts "that 'education is the bulwark of freedom,' and that our universal system of

261

free public education is literally the nation's first line of defense and the greatest constructive force in the possession of the American people for the preservation of their freedoms and the advancement of the democratic way of life."

In the light of the Benton report, this writer now ventures to suggest that our educational system "by will" is and must be far more than a "line of defense;" it must be a "weapon of offense" with which we equip our people to compete both at home and abroad with a Soviet system that "milks the best out of all available brains" and then "channels them into the usages of the State."

In America we are dedicated to the policy that our military might shall be used solely for defense and never for offense, and this is right and just.

But in the battle for men's minds, which though bloodless may be no less deadly, must we not prepare ourselves to attack as well as to defend, to be equipped to promote our belief in personal integrity, freedom, justice, and self-government among all the peoples of the earth who long for a peaceful world based on those principles?

What Must We Do?

With this new emphasis on the unparalleled importance of education in the years ahead, what are the lessons we must take to heart and apply with ever increasing strength and effectiveness?

1. We need a clearer definition of the fundamental relationships between our system of universal public education and the future of our democratic republic and a free society.

Many efforts have been made and are constantly being made both by educators and by laymen to arrive at some simple and effective way of stating these relationships so that the masses of our people will grasp their importance and rise to their support. These efforts have not made very conspicuous progress (see Chapter 30, section on "An Unmet Need," page 252).

While it is probably true that there is now greater public interest in the schools than at any time in our memory, we still have hardly begun to reach a majority of the population convincingly.

Education "by Will" vs. Education "by Order"

We must keep working toward this goal of public understanding with renewed vigor and determination, and it would help if some better ways could be found to pool our efforts.

2. This pooling of effort, this pulling together toward common goals is perhaps the greatest problem we face in public education.

In this country, as we all know, the control of education is vested in the states which in turn delegate much of the responsibility to boards of education in local districts.

The total picture of American education, therefore, is like a great mosaic made up of thousands upon thousands of separate pieces (see Chapter 1).

How to help each piece in the "mosaic"—each school board, each school staff, each school community—to see the total picture and to make the greatest possible contribution to the total need is one of our most important and most puzzling challenges.

For we cannot accomplish this goal "by order" from some central authority, and would not do it that way if we could. We have to accomplish it by developing a "combined will" among our people, so well informed, so clearly convinced, so firmly determined that it results in a united, concentrated, effective program.

3. Our system of education, decentralized though it be, is still too much of a mass production process with too little emphasis on individual capacities and needs.

This neglect occurs because we try to do more with the means we provide than those means will permit doing well.

We must provide larger staffs and more facilities so that it will be possible to give each student the preparation which will best fit him to make his maximum contribution as a self-supporting, self-respecting, self-governing citizen.

We have been increasingly concerned with helping the handicapped, and rightly so, but we should be even more concerned to develop our superior people who must become leaders in science and technology, in business and industry, in education and culture, in government and international relations. In this area the Communists are rapidly outdistancing us.

Mr. Benton reported that in Russia there is already a larger "post-high school enrollment" than we have in the United States and that "about 90 per cent of all students in these higher institutions are on state scholarships."

We know that in the United States only about half of our high school graduates capable of profiting by advanced preparation ever get to an institution of higher education.

Failure to develop our most able young people to the fullest measure of their potentialities may turn out to be a costly waste of talent and manpower if we do not speedily correct the situation (see Chapter 10).

4. It should be obvious that we must be prepared to invest a much higher percentage of our national income in public education and all related agencies of cultural development.

The report of the White House Conference on Education stated that we should be spending twice as much as we now are. But how strongly do the American people as a whole believe their investment in the public schools should be doubled, and what must be done to help them to understand the necessity, and to be willing to pay the bill?

Among other things, the first Benton report and other comparisons of Soviet versus American respect for and support of education, if they could be widely read, interpreted and discussed, might make important contributions toward this goal of increased investment in schools.

5. Corollary to the question of the financing of education, especially of tax supported education, is the relationship it bears to other services of government with which under present conditions it too often has to compete to its serious disadvantage.

Education is a creative, constructive process. It differs in this respect from civil services which are largely regulatory, disciplinary, and corrective (police, fire, welfare, sanitation, etc.)

How long will it take us as a people to see that if we were to double our investment in education and do the things we could do to help each individual to normal, healthy, happy, effective living, our bills for delinquency, penal institutions, mental hospitals, illness, accidents, and a whole host of preventable conditions would be reduced far more than the added cost of adequate education?

The chances are that we could actually save two "welfare" dollars for every added dollar spent on education if we had the vision and faith to deal in futures to this extent.

6. We need to make greater use than we have yet planned or imagined of technical aids to education and the cultural development of our people—film strips, motion pictures, radio, television, the press, magazines, books, programed instruction, teaching machines, and all other media for reaching people individually and en masse.

Conclusion

The suggestions above are some of the ways in which we can strengthen our "will" to educate our children and ourselves most effectively on the side of freedom and self government as opposed to those who believe they can "order" the education of people for purposes of the State without regard for the rights and integrity of individuals.

A tremendous struggle for control of the minds of men lies in the years ahead.

If we believe that a well-trained *free* mind is superior to a well-trained indoctrinated one, let us not fail to make certain that free minds in our America have abundant opportunities for maximum development. Then, in time to come, their influence will be felt around the world!

> "To be long lived, republics must invest in education."
>
> — BENJAMIN RUSH

CHALLENGE

"God give us men! A time like this demands
Strong minds, great hearts, true faith, and ready hands."

— JOSIAH GILBERT HOLLAND

These ringing words, written when our country was torn by civil strife, offer no less a challenge in the present crisis. When what Americans do now will affect themselves not only, but the destinies of mankind the world around, how even greater the need for clear thinking, for stout courage, for firm belief in justice and the right, for unremitting toil in the common cause of freedom, security, and peace. Is it too much to ask, or to expect, that the men and women who guide and control our great system of public education shall set an example to young and old in their communities by exhibiting these qualities in fullest measure?—E. M. T.

CHAPTER 32

The Challenge to Local Control
of Public Education

Throughout this book, our American system of public education, based on what we call "local control," has been taken for granted. It has been assumed that this is the accepted way of keeping our schools close to the people and our people close to their schools.

The expression "local" control is used primarily in contradistinction to "national," or "federal," control, and it includes state control. It deals with the legal controls of public education exercised by lay boards of education at state and district levels.

In recent years, voices have been raised in our land suggesting that local boards of education either be done away with completely or be reduced to rubber-stamp functions without any real authority. In their place would be established some form of centralized control for all the public schools of the nation. It therefore seems desirable to add a chapter to this Revised Edition indicating some of the reasons behind this suggestion and how it should be answered.

The Soviet Bugbear

Serious proposals for the nationalization of American public education began to attract attention immediately following the launching of the first man-made earth satellite by the Russians in the fall of 1957. A wave of hysteria amounting almost to panic seemed to sweep the country and to sweep away the reason and good sense of many of our citizens.

267

Looking around for an excuse as to why it appeared that Russia was ahead of the United States in scientific achievement, the easiest scapegoat to point to was our system of decentralized control of public education in contrast to the rigid centralized control prevailing in the U.S.S.R. (see Chapter 31).

Some critics were ready to throw overboard the values inherent to the individual in our system in favor of the demands of the "state" (nation) without regard for the individual. They either did not accept, or were willing to sacrifice, the belief that *if each individual could be educated to his highest potential the nation would find itself in posssession of all the varied and specialized talents needed for leadership and greatness.*

Within a year, Congress passed the Defense Education Act of 1958 subsidizing increased emphasis on the teaching of science and mathematics, and some other items such as foreign languages. It represented a categorical type of federal "aid" to education that inevitably carried certain federal controls and, in many school districts, resulted in throwing the curriculum greatly out of balance (see *The Nation's Stake in Education,* page 86).

Other Influences

Many times in earlier chapters of this book it has been pointed out that the modern age in which we live has largely done away with the provincialism which once marked many of our school districts, and even whole states, and has emphasized, as never before in history, the fact that all Americans have certain needs in common and must seek common solutions.

These solutions are intimately connected with the education of those who must live in the world of today and tomorrow and are complicated by influences to which we are all subject.

The most obvious broadening and unifying influence is the speed of modern transportation and communication. As a consequence, the American people today are much more enlightened and homogeneous in their knowledge and experience than they have ever been in the past.

Another influence is the mobility of our population, a large percentage of which shifts every year from community to community and from state to state. Moreover, hundreds of thousands of Americans are scattered all over the world as military personnel, representatives of governmental agencies and the United Nations, Peace Corps volunteers, agents of private business and investment in foreign countries, and tourists.

Still another influence is the tremendous increase in our knowledge about all subjects, both scientific and humanitarian, to the point where no individual can even begin to grasp it all.

We have also discovered a great deal that is new about the teaching and learning process by which knowledge and skills are passed from one generation to the next, and we are devising all kinds of "tools" to aid in the process.

The pitfalls we face in our educational goals are made clear oy humorous definitions of the specialist and the generalist, as follows:

The *specialist* is a person who learns more and more about less and less until he finally ends up knowing all there is to know about nothing.

On the other hand, the *generalist* is a person who learns less and less about more and more until he finally ends up knowing nothing about everything.

The lesson is clear for each individual. If he aspires to expertness in some special field, he is under obligation to secure enough general education to relate his specialty to life as a whole. Or, if he aspires to a broad humanitarianism in his total outlook, it is highly desirable that he explore at least one field in depth in order to understand the magnitude of all fields, and the degree of attainment necessary to render essential service in any special field.

The Trend Toward Bigness

Education, no less than all aspects of modern life, is caught up by the tendency in business, industry, labor, government, and other areas to organize into larger and larger units under more and more centralized control.

This trend is neither altogether good nor altogether evil. There are obviously greater dangers and hence greater responsibilities in large units of organization in any area of national life than in smaller units wielding less power. When the power of big units grows too great for the common good, the people, through legislation and the courts, ultimately insist on its regulation in the public interest.

There are those who would carry this trend toward bigness to its ultimate limit in the field of public education by centralizing the control of all schools at the national level.

They point to the thousands of school districts with every degree of size, strength, and effectiveness as a wholly unjustifiable system in the light of national necessities and goals.

They insist that coordination and cooperation by these local districts in reaching common goals is too much to expect.

They claim that the determination of educational programs and policies in this modern day is beyond the capacities of lay citizens and should be in the hands of the teaching profession.

They argue vehemently for the development of a national curriculum and a national testing program which will apply to all public schools throughout the length and breadth of America.

They compare our schools unfavorably with those of European nations having a single Ministry of Education.

The School Board Answer

The criticisms listed above are aimed directly at the school boards of this nation, and it is school board leadership that must answer them if our long-cherished system of local control of public schools is to survive.

This leadership must be manifested by individual school boards everywhere and by the state and national associations of school boards. Unless and until school boards as a whole demonstrate by their actions that they can be successful in providing educational programs of highest quality for every individual in every segment of the American people, the challenge to their control will persist.

It will not suffice simply to oppose changes in the *status quo* and to keep operating schools in traditional patterns. Boards must show initiative and readiness to adapt local policies and programs to changing conditions and broader needs—in short, they must stand for dynamic progress year after year in educational standards, offerings, and achievements.

Earlier chapters in this book are concerned with many aspects of school board leadership, but it will be helpful to restate the more important of them here in specific relation to the challenge to local control which is currently pressing.

School Board Orientation and Self-Study. Higher standards and quality in school board service will help to quiet and offset the challenge to local control of public schools.

Boards and board members must strive to improve their qualifications for effectively discharging their responsibilities.

They can do this by advocating a district-wide caucus to screen and nominate board candidates, and by urging greater voter participation in school board elections (see page 152).

They can do it by providing adequately for the rapid and thorough orientation of new board members to the duties and responsibilities of board membership (see pages 153-56).

They can do it by attending board workshops in their district, region, or state (see Chapter 26 and Appendix E).

They can do it by more active support of their state and national school boards associations (see Chapter 21).

School District Organization. There are still far more small, weak school districts in this country than there should be, notwithstanding the considerable progress that continues to be made in reorganizing them into larger and more efficient units of administration and instruction (see page 41).

School boards must support needed redistricting even though, in some cases, it means their own elimination, and must take leadership in helping their constituencies to understand and agree to the wiser planning.

On the other hand, the major cities of the country represent the opposite extreme in school district organization. Their districts are too large for most effective control by a single board, except in matters of broadest policy. Efforts must continue to organize sub-districts under the central authority, each carrying some degree of local autonomy in relation to its immediate community within the metropolitan area.

Financial Support for Education. Every nationwide survey and study of educational needs since the White House Conference in 1955 has concluded that we are spending far too small a percentage of our national income for the adequate education of our people, young and old, and has recommended that up to twice as much should be spent.

Instead of trying to limit school budgets and hold down tax rates, school boards must be major champions of more liberal provision for education. Even though this makes the boards unpopular with some elements in their districts, or results in the defeat of some school board members at the next election, they should persist in their efforts to prove to the total community the wisdom of a greater investment in schools.

This greater investment, they should point out, will provide more adequate salaries for better prepared teachers, more efficient and modernized buildings, more abundant and up-to-the-minute teaching materials and classroom equipment, inclusion of needed elements in the school program such as guidance, special teachers for both the handicapped and the very bright pupils, summer schools, in-service education for the professional staff, and all the other things that will help to insure to each student the opportunity to attain his highest development.

Where school boards are not fiscally independent, but are subject to budget vetoes by city councils, finance committees, or other partisan governmental agencies, the boards, both directly and through their state associations, must work unremittingly for changes in the law which will give them or their successor boards independence to secure maximum financial support for the public schools (see pages 45-46, 141-42, and Chapters 11, 12, and 13).

The Educational Program. Much of the challenge to local control of education centers around what the schools are teaching. The claim that there should be a national curriculum will only be silenced when local school boards, with the advice and guidance of their professional administrators, make certain that they adopt educational programs that meet national as well as state and district needs. Chapter 10 is devoted in its entirety to this problem, and all that can be added here is urgent insistence that school boards look upon the curriculum as perhaps their number one responsibility in the years ahead.

A mandatory national curriculum for all the public schools of America would abandon the principle of local adaptation which is the cornerstone of our system. But it would appear that if local administrators and boards could be provided with curriculum standards representing national concensus in the various subject matter fields, this could be most helpful.

Such curriculum standards would indicate for each subject the recommended sequence of content, suggested grade levels, contributions of the study to individual, state, and national needs, interrelationships between the subject in question and other subjects in an educational program, and various other considerations which would aid in determining its appropriate inclusion in the curriculum of a particular school district.

Numerous suggestions along this line are constantly being offered by professional associations in subject matter areas and undoubtedly, as time goes on, these will be more fully coordinated into a set of suggested curriculum standards to be used by local school authorities as a basis for developing the best possible educational programs.

Follow-Up and Evaluation. One of the most effective answers to the challenge to local control of schools could be provided by more adequate records on how students fare after they leave school, whether by graduation or dropout.

A school board possessing records of this kind is in a better position to evaluate its educational program in terms of the product, and hence to make indicated changes and adjustments promptly. Too few districts keep such records, but it is urged that all districts do so, and that provision in the budget for this purpose will be money well spent.

True it is that a period of years must elapse before followup records become fully useful, but they will never be of use unless a start is made. The years pass swiftly and once such records become a consistent item in a board's evaluation process, their significance will soon be apparent.

Research and Experimentation. The claim is made by advocates of national control of public education that it would make possible much more research and experimentation in the educational field than exists under our local control system.

The critics point out that few school districts provide in their local budgets for any experimental research and that many districts are reluctant to get involved in such activities even when these can be financed through foundation grants. Educational research is compared disparagingly to that carried on by business, industry, and some of the professions like medicine.

There is undoubted basis for these criticisms, but the answer is to support more experimentation and research locally rather than to throw the control system overboard for the sake of getting more such activities in the schools.

School boards must recognize that research studies and experiments with new teaching methods and devices are important in a field where such rapid changes are taking place as in education today. They must help their communities to understand this need and to support items in the school budget to meet it.

Professional Relationships. Successful operation of the public schools in any district, large or small, lies in harmonious working relationships between the school board on the one hand and the administrative and teaching staff on the other.

Because the professional staff is employed by the board and is charged with carrying out board policies, it is the board which at all times must take the initiative in seeing that these working relationships are kept on a friendly and effective basis, and that no conditions are allowed to develop which will lessen the quality of the school program and open the door to those who would substitute national for local control of public education.

Much of this book is devoted to discussing these professional relationships and to presenting the principles and standards on

274

which they are based (see especially, Chapters 6, 14, and 15).

Public Relations. While school boards bear the major responsibility for proving that local control is better than national control of public education in America, they cannot do the job alone. It must be done in cooperation with all other local groups and organizations which believe in working toward the same objective.

The issues at stake must be understood and supported by the community public and by all the media of communication in each district, to the end that the strongest possible educational program is provided under our established system.

Every time there is a crisis in any school district in the nation, it lends ammunition to those who claim that if national control were to replace local control such controversies would be eliminated. Whether this is true or not, the obvious answer is to resolve controversies before they become crises (see Chapter 18).

Again, it is the school boards which must take the initiative and exercise the leadership that will bring about the desired cooperation of interest, coordination of effort, and accumulation of proof (see Chapters 16 and 17).

Concern Over School Legislation. At every session of state legislatures, numerous bills seeking changes in school law are introduced for consideration. Many of these are minor or are based on special interests, but some are of statewide importance and necessity.

Local school boards must share in making certain that desirable legislation is pressed to passage, and that needless and harmful legislation is defeated in its early stages. State school boards associations usually keep member boards advised on bills before the state legislatures. Having this information, local boards can keep in active and constructive contact with members of the legislature and so demonstrate their freedom from provincialism and their concern for the general advancement of public education (see Chapter 25).

In the same spirit, school boards, individually and through their state associations, should make known to members of Congress their considered views with respect to proposed legislation on the national level dealing with any phase of public education.

WHAT PRICE EDUCATION?

"The whole people must take upon themselves the education of the whole people and be willing to bear the expense of it."

— JOHN ADAMS

In the words above, the second President of these United States set forth a principle underlying the new democratic republic, which was less generally accepted in his day than it is in ours, but which still needs to be constantly emphasized. Why must we all be willing to pay the cost of educating ourselves —the whole people, young and old—to a continually higher level of character, culture, and capacity? Because only men so educated can successfully continue to govern themselves. And because only through self-government can men retain their freedom. And because only free men can eventually build a world of brotherhood and peace—a world where the integrity and worth of each individual is recognized and respected by all others. This is our goal, our hope, our faith. Universal public education is the road to its attainment. That road must be made straight and strong by all for all. — E. M. T.

CHAPTER 33

Democracy and Education

American democracy is dedicated to the development of the individual.

Education is the instrument for this development.

But education can be a two-edged sword, depending upon its character and quality.

If we simply teach the individual to be smarter, without at the same time teaching him ethical concepts, social values, and a civic sense, he will use his education solely for his own selfish ends and work harm rather than benefit to our democratic pattern.

But if, on the other hand, we give the individual a balanced education so that

in addition to knowledge, he will acquire wisdom;
in addition to skills, he will develop vision; and
in addition to ambition, he will cherish ideals;

then the best interests of the individual will be found to coincide with the best interests of our democratic heritage, and both will grow together.

What a balanced education should do for the individual can be stated in very simple terms. It should

1. Help him to live more happily with himself.

2. Help him to live more harmoniously with others.

3. Help him, in the long run, to earn a better living.

4. Help him to be a better citizen of his community, state, nation, and the world.

On this basis, public school teachers have a far more critical and valuable function in a democratic society than have most other types of public employees.

School Board Leadership in America

Teaching in a democracy, when it is of such a quality as to stimulate growth in personal resourcefulness, in social adaptability, in economic capability, and in civic responsibility, has a significance beyond estimate or reward in advancing mankind toward the goal of the "high calling of God."

The most important question before our nation today is much easier to state than it is to solve. How are we going to provide adequate education for our rapidly growing population, education which will develop each individual to his fullest capacity for successful living, education which will assure a citizenry capable of courageously discharging its responsibilities in a democratic republic of free men seriously challenged by the Communist doctrine of a dictator state?

The American people cherish their schools, in the abstract. Were the existence of the public school system seriously threatened, we would fight to preserve it.

How long will it take us to see that, because of past apathy and short-sightedness, we have starved and crippled the thing we cherish?

In so doing, we have made it impossible for many of our children—America's future—to grow into the capable, healthy, intelligent, devoted, moral, and courageous citizens that potentially they might become.

Can we continue to excuse ourselves for such neglect in the face of present day problems and responsibilities for the building of a better world for our children and our children's children?

Increasing numbers of our people must become aware that an effective answer cannot be longer delayed or further halfway measures condoned.

Many forces are at work to stimulate this awareness and to provide opportunities for widespread discussion based on the facts of the situation.

Once the American people really understand this problem they can be trusted to find the right solution.

Democracy must undergird public education in order that public education may perpetuate democracy.

278

REDEMPTION

"Were half the power that fills the human world with terror,
Were half the wealth bestowed on camps and courts,
Given to redeem the human mind from error,
There were no need of arsenals and forts."

— HENRY WADSWORTH LONGFELLOW

The poet dreamed of a millenium, but all men of intelligence and good will know that he was right. The "error" in question would involve such human failings as arrogance, brutality, covetousness, cowardice, demagoguery, dishonesty, hate, immorality, impiety, injustice, intemperance, selfishness, vanity, vulgarity, and all the other ugly and degrading traits that plague mankind and keep the world an armed camp. Could such vices be "redeemed" and turned into the virtues which are their opposites, the world might be a lovely and a peaceful place in very truth. We shall not live to see it, but it is equally unthinkable that we should give up working toward that goal with all the power we can command. And in proportion as we increase the tiny fraction of our resources now devoted to this constructive process, as compared to the uncounted treasure we pour into the forces of destruction, we shall make progress toward the brotherhood of man. — E. M. T.

"Ideals are like stars.
You will not succeed in touching them
with your hands;
but, like the seafaring man,
you choose them as your guides,
and following them,
you will reach your destiny."

— CARL SCHURZ

"Technical knowledge is a good thing in its way;
but a knowledge of life, in whatever form,
is a far better thing. . . .
The technical, indeed, cannot by itself be appreciated.
It must be appreciated as an expression of life,
as an expression of the plastic spirit
of thought and feeling."

— HIRAM CORSON

"It is a shining day in any educated man's growth
when he comes to see and to know
and freely to admit
that it is just as important to the world
that the ragamuffin child of his worthless neighbor
should be trained
as it is that his own child should be.
Until a man sees this he cannot become a worthy democrat
nor get a patriotic conception of education;
for no man has known the deep meaning of democracy
or felt either its obligation or its lift
until he has seen this truth clearly."

— WALTER HINES PAGE

APPENDICES

CITIZENSHIP

*"Exercise your own judgment and do
right for the public interest."*

— ABRAHAM LINCOLN

To be a citizen of the United States is one of the
most priceless possessions a human being can have
in the world today. One has only to watch the
solemn joy with which qualified men and women
from foreign lands become naturalized American
citizens to realize that those of us who inherit this
distinction by birth commonly hold it in too little
esteem. Millions elsewhere would gladly change
places with us if we would give up our citizenship
for theirs. This we would never consider, but neither
do many of us consider what we should be doing
to deserve our citizenship and to discharge the responsibilities which its privileges entail. First and
most important of these is the exercise of the ballot
upon every occasion which arises in primary, general, and special elections—local, state, and national. Abraham Lincoln's admonition comes to us
as free men in a representative democracy. Heed
it, and vote! — E. M. T.

APPENDIX A

Bibliography of Background
Materials for Board Members

Board members are busy laymen. Time for adding to their understanding of educational affairs outside of board meetings is limited.
Nevertheless, a certain amount of reading is desirable and helpful. The
question is, What to read? Here are a few suggestions of most useful
materials for a School Board Reference Library.

Magazines

The American School Board Journal, 400 North Broadway, Milwaukee 1, Wisc.

The Nation's Schools, 919 North Michigan Ave., Chicago 11, Ill.

Overview, 470 Fourth Avenue, New York 16, N. Y.

School Management Magazine, 22 West Putnam Ave., Greenwich,
Conn.

Pamphlets

American Association of School Administrators (Series), 1201
Sixteenth Street, N. W., Washington, D. C. 20036

What to Pay Your Superintendent (1952) (Joint N.S.B.A.)

Managing the School District Insurance Program (1953)

Written Policies for School Boards (1955) (Joint N.S.B.A.)

*Shoring Up Legal and Policy Provisions for the Superintend-
ent* (1957)

*Something to Steer By—35 Proposals for Better Preparation
of School Administrators* (1958)

ABC's of School Public Relations (1959)

Safety Sanity and the Schools (1959)

The Year-Round School (1960)

Commitment to Excellence (1961)

On Selecting a Superintendent of Schools (1962) (Joint
N.S.B.A.)

Hints to the Beginning Superintendent of Schools (1962)

Private Philanthropy and Public Purposes (1963)

*Roles, Responsibilities, Relationships of the School Board,
Superintendent, and Staff* (1963)

283

Bibliography of Background Materials

Pamphlets (cont.)

Educational Policies Commission, 1201 Sixteenth Street, N.W., Washington, D. C. 20036

Moral and Spiritual Values in the Public Schools (1951)

The Contemporary Challenge to American Education (1958)

An Essay on Quality in Public Education (1959)

National Policy and the Financing of Public Schools (1959)

The Central Purpose of American Education (1961)

National School Boards Association, Inc., 1940 Sheridan Road, Evanston, Illinois (Write for complete list of publications)

New Approaches (1955) (see page 243)

School Boards Plan for Disaster Problems (1958) (see page 256)

Seven Studies (1958)

Improving Education—A Free People's Responsibility (Convention Proceedings 1959)

Judging Schools with Wisdom (1959) (Joint A.A.S.A.)

What Price Double Sessions? (1959)

Education for World Leadership (Convention Proceedings 1960)

Policy Manual Reference Notebook (1960) (Joint N.E.A.)

Quest for Quality—A series of 14 pamphlets describing local district efforts to evaluate public schools (1960) (Joint A.A.S.A.)

This We Believe (1963) (Joint A.A.S.A.)

Working Guides of the National Citizens Council for Better Schools, including

How Can We Discuss School Problems?

How Can We Conduct a Winning Campaign?

How Can Citizens Work with the Press?

How Have Our Schools Developed?

How Can We Get Enough Good Teachers?

How Can We Help Our School Boards?

How Good Are Our Teaching Materials?

What Are Our School Building Needs?

How Do We Pay for Our Schools?

How Should Our Schools Be Organized?

Bibliography of Background Materials

Pamphlets (cont.)

American Standard Guide for School Lighting, New York: Published by the Illuminating Engineering Society, 345 East 47th Street, New York 17 (1962)

Economies in School Construction, Nashville: Published by Interstate School Building Service, George Peabody College for Teachers, Nashville, Tenn. (1962)

Guidelines for Professional Negotiation, by the National Education Association of the United States, 1201 Sixteenth Street, N.W., Washington, D. C. 20036 (1963)

Guidelines for Textbook Selection, by Joint Committee of the NEA and the American Textbook Publishers Institute, 432 Park Avenue, So., New York 16 (1963)

Merit Salary Programs: In Six Selected Systems, by James P. Steffensen, Specialist, U. S. Office of Education, Washington: Superintendent of Documents, Government Printing Office, Washington 25, D. C. (1963)

Our Public Schools, by Willard E. Givens and Belmont M. Farley, The Supreme Council, 33°, Ancient and Accepted Rite of Freemasonry, Southern Jurisdiction, United States of America, 1733 Sixteenth Street, N.W., Washington 9, D. C. (1959)

Paying for Better Public Schools, A Statement on National Policy, by the Research and Policy Committee of the Committee for Economic Development, 711 Fifth Avenue, New York 22 (1959)

The Pursuit of Excellence: Education and the Future of America, the "Rockefeller Report" on Education, published by Doubleday & Company, Inc., Garden City, L.I., N. Y. (1958)

Rankings of the States, Research Division, National Education Association, 1201 Sixteenth Street, N.W., Washington 36, D. C. (latest edition)

The School Business Administrator, by Frederick W. Hill, published by the Association of School Business Officials of the United States and Canada, 1010 Church Street, Evanston, Illinois (Joint A.A.S.A. 1960)

The Story of Our Schools, by Robert A. Marshall, Washington: National Council for the Social Studies, 1201 Sixteenth Street, N. W., Washington 36, D. C. (1962)

Winning Ways: How to Conduct Successful Election Campaigns for Public School Tax and Bond Proposals, Washington: National School Public Relations Association, 1201 Sixteenth Street, N. W., Washington 36, D. C. (Joint A.A.S.A. 1960)

Bibliography of Background Materials

Books

The American High School Today, A First Report to Interested Citizens, by James B. Conant, New York: McGraw-Hill Book Company, Inc., 330 West 42nd St., New York 36 (1959)

American Public School Finance, by W. Monfort Barr, New York: American Book Company, 55 Fifth Avenue, New York 3 (1960)

The Ax-Grinders: Critics of Our Public Schools, by Mary Anne Raywid, New York: The Macmillan Company, 60 Fifth Avenue, New York 11 (1962)

Changing Demands on Education and Their Fiscal Implications, by John K. Norton, Washington: National Committee for Support of the Public Schools, 1424 Sixteenth Street, N.W., Washington 36, D. C. (1963)

The Child, the Parent, and the State, by James B. Conant, Cambridge, Mass.: Harvard University Press (1959)

County School Administration, by Shirley Cooper and Charles O. Fitzwater, New York: Harper & Row, Publishers, 49 East 33rd Street, New York 16 (1954)

Education and the Foundations of Human Freedom, by George S. Counts, Pittsburgh: University of Pittsburgh Press, Pittsburgh 13, Pa. (1962)

Education and Public Understanding, by Gordon E. McCloskey, New York: Harper & Row, Publishers, 49 East 33rd Street, New York 16 (1959)

The Effective Board, by Cyril O. Houle, New York: Association Press, 219 Broadway, New York 7 (1960)

An Evaluation of Existing Forms of School Laws, by Madaline Kinter Remmlein and Martha L. Ware, Cincinnati: The W. H. Anderson Company, 646 Main Street, Cincinnati 1, Ohio (1959)

Handbook of Financial Accounting for Local and State School Systems, and others. (Cooperative Project of the U. S. Office of Education with the N.S.B.A. and other national organizations, see page 90), Washington: Superintendent of Documents, Government Printing Office, Washington 25, D. C.

How to Get Better Schools, A Tested Program, by David B. Dreiman, New York: Harper & Row, Publishers, 49 East 33rd Street, New York 16 (1956)

Local School Boards—Organization and Practices, by Alpheus L. White, Specialist, U. S. Office of Education, Washington: Bulletin 1962, No. 8, Superintendent of Documents, Government Printing Office, Washington 25, D. C.

286

Bibliography of Background Materials

Books (cont.)

The Public and Its Education, by Herbert M. Hamlin, Danville: The Interstate Printers & Publishers, Inc., 19-27 North Jackson Street, Danville, Ill. (1955)

School Board-Superintendent Relationships, 34th Yearbook, American Association of School Administrators, 1201 Sixteenth Street, N.W., Washington 36, D. C. (1956)

School Budget Policies for Fiscal Control, by Herbert S. Mitchell, Danville: The Interstate Printers & Publishers, Inc., 19-27 North Jackson Street, Danville, Ill. (1963)

School District Organization, A Report of the A.A.S.A. Commission on School District Reorganization, Washington: American Association of School Administrators (1958)

Schoolhouse, edited by Walter McQuade, New York: Simon & Schuster, 630 Fifth Avenue, New York 20 (1958)

Schools and the Law, by E. Edmund Reutter, Jr., Dobbs Ferry: Oceana Publications, Inc., 40 Cedar Street, Dobbs Ferry, N. Y. (1962)

Secondary Education in the United States, by Lindley Stiles, Lloyd E. McCleary, and Ray C. Turnbaugh, New York: Harcourt, Brace and World, Inc., 757 Third Avenue, New York 17 (1962)

Slums and Suburbs: A Commentary on Schools in Metropolitan Areas, by James B. Conant, New York: McGraw-Hill Book Company, Inc., 330 West 42nd Street, New York 36 (1961)

Staff Personnel in the Public Schools, by Willard S. Elsbree and E. Edmund Reutter, Jr., Englewood Cliffs: Prentice-Hall, Inc., Englewood Cliffs, N. J. (1954)

Step by Step in Better Board and Committee Work, by Roy Sorenson and William C. Tuck, New York: Association Press, 219 Broadway, New York 7 (1962)

Studies in School Administration, A Report of the CPEA, Washington: American Association of School Administrators, 1201 Sixteenth Street, N.W., Washington 36, D. C. (1957)

Toward Better School Design, by Willian W. Caudill, New York: F. W. Dodge Corporation, 119 West 40th Street, New York 18 (1955)

The Yearbook of School Law (Published Annually), by Lee O. Garber, Danville: The Interstate Printers & Publishers, Inc., 19-27 North Jackson Street, Danville, Ill.

APPENDIX B

Boards of Education

— American Plan*

WHY?

Public education of all children and youth, without discrimination, lies at the heart of the American plan.

The success of our republican form of government, of our democratic way of life, and of our business and technological development depends upon a literate and alert citizenry.

One of the major duties of government is to provide an adequate system of tax-supported schools.

Chief responsibility for public education is vested in the several states but a large measure of local control through Boards of Education is everywhere deemed desirable, even essential.

Governors and state legislatures, without exception, are bound by state constitutions, by court decisions, and by tradition to establish and maintain public schools free from political entanglements and the domination of any special-interest or selfish-interest group.

Today, all states have set up standards for a minimum of twelve years of schooling at public expense.

WHAT?

Boards of Education are the responsible governing bodies of the public schools.

They are designed as the policy-making groups in education and should be responsive to the needs and wishes of the citizens of their respective communities.

Boards are everywhere invested with far-reaching authority for a great variety of important decisions concerning the public schools.

They are the connecting link between the public which supports the schools and the professional personnel which administers the schools, and they are in a position to interpret each to the other.

*Originally written by Edward M. Tuttle for publication in the April 1949 issue of *Chicago Schools*, the organ of the Citizens Schools Committee of Chicago. Later, September 1, 1951, it was approved as an official pronouncement of the National School Boards Association.

Boards of Education—American Plan

Almost universally, members of Boards of Education serve without remuneration, except expenses; they are voluntary servants of the people—a striking example of democracy in action.

WHO?

Other things being equal, the caliber of individual board members largely determines the adequacy and quality of the educational service they provide as a group.

High standards of personal integrity and successful accomplishment as American citizens are essential in the men and women who serve on Boards of Education, but it is also desirable that, severally, they should be the products of varying backgrounds and experience in human affairs.

Each should be chosen to represent impartially all the people of the community rather than any political, social, religious, economic or other vested interest or special area.

Board members should possess abounding physical health, sound mental balance, and great social poise, and should be willing to devote their time freely to a study of the problems of the schools.

Their views should be tolerant, their cooperation generous, their minds open, their judgments considered.

They should evidence a profound interest in the children of the community as a whole, and not in one particular segment or faction.

They should develop a sympathetic understanding of the teaching and learning process as it involves the human relationships between those who would teach and those who would learn.

Above all, members of Boards of Education should be men and women who hold universal public education in greatest esteem; who believe that America's future rests primarily on the superior development —physical, mental, moral, spiritual—of our children and youth for personal, social, economic, and civic competence; and who will work unremittingly to provide, defend, and support the highest degree of public education which their respective communities can be persuaded to demand.

> *"No one knows where the influence*
> *of a good teacher ends."*
> —HERBERT SPENCER

APPENDIX C

Thirty Critical Requirements
for School Board Membership*

by Dr. Richard E. Barnhart

Note: Dr. Barnhart completed his doctorate at Indiana University in 1951. The following list of critical requirements, taken from his thesis, was derived from a study of 741 incidents reported by school board members and superintendents in 12 midwestern states.

For effective results, a school board member should:

Area 1. Board Unity
1. Subordinate personal interests.
2. Adhere to the policy-making and legislative functions of the board.
3. Accept and support majority decisions of the board.
4. Identify self with board policies and actions.
5. Refuse to speak or act on school matters independent of board.

Area 2. Leadership
6. Suspend judgment until the facts are available.
7. Make use of pertinent experience.
8. Help to identify problems.
9. Have the ability to determine satisfactorily solutions to problems.
10. Devote time outside of board meetings as board business requires.
11. Be willing to accept ideas from others.
12. Have enthusiastic interest in the welfare of the children.

Area 3. Executive Function
13. Understand the desirability of delegating administrative responsibility to the chief executive officer.
14. Support the executive officer in his authorized functions.
15. Encourage teamwork between the executive officer and the board.
16. Recognize problems and conditions that are of executive concern.

Requirements for School Board Membership

Area 4. *Staff and Group Relationships*

17. Have ability to speak effectively in public.
18. Believe firmly in democratic processes and in the right of all groups to be heard.
19. Work tactfully and sympathetically with teacher groups.
20. Understand how groups think and act.
21. Assist others in working effectively.
22. Have mature social poise.

Area 5. *Personal Relationships*

23. Be willing to work with fellow board members in spite of personality differences.
24. Display both tact and firmness in relationships with individuals.
25. Treat patrons and teachers fairly and ethically.
26. Foster harmonious relationships.

Area 6. *Courageous Action*

27. Be able to weather criticism.
28. Maintain firm convictions.
29. Be willing to take sides in controversies.
30. Share responsibilities for board decisions.

*From the *Hoosier School Board Journal*, September, 1955

Men Are Four

He who knows, and knows he knows;
　He is wise, follow him.

He who knows, and knows not he knows;
　He is asleep, wake him.

He who knows not, and knows not he knows not;
　He is a fool, shun him.

He who knows not, and knows he knows not;
　He is a child, teach him.

— ARABIAN PROVERB

APPENDIX D

A Code of Ethics
for School Board Members

(Developed by a Special Committee and Adopted by the Board of
Directors of the National School Boards Association, Inc.,
May 2, 1961)

I.   As a member of my local Board of Education, representing all
the citizens of my school district, I recognize

1.   That my fellow citizens have entrusted me with the educational development of the children and youth of this community.

2.   That the public expects my first and greatest concern to be
in the best interest of each and every one of these young
people without distinction as to who they are or what their
background may be.

3.   That the future welfare of this community, of this State, and
of the Nation depends in the largest measure upon the quality of education we provide in the public schools to fit the
needs of every learner.

4.   That my fellow board members and I must take the initiative
in helping all the people of this community to have all the
facts all the time about their schools, to the end that they
will readily provide the finest possible school program, school
staff, and school facilities.

5.   That legally the authority of the Board is derived from the
State which ultimately controls the organization and operation of the school district and which determines the degree
of discretionary power left with the Board and the people
of this community for the exercise of local autonomy.

6.   That I must never neglect my personal obligation to the community and my legal obligation to the State, nor surrender
these responsibilities to any other person, group, or organization; but that, beyond these, I have a moral and civic obligation to the Nation which can remain strong and free only so
long as public schools in the United States of America are
kept free and strong.

A Code of Ethics for School Board Members

II. In view of the foregoing considerations, it shall be my constant endeavor

1. To devote time, thought, and study to the duties and responsibilities of a school board member so that I may render effective and creditable service.

2. To work with my fellow board members in a spirit of harmony and cooperation in spite of differences of opinion that arise during vigorous debate of points at issue.

3. To base my personal decision upon all available facts in each situation; to vote my honest conviction in every case, unswayed by partisan bias of any kind; thereafter, to abide by and uphold the final majority decision of the Board.

4. To remember at all times that as an individual I have no legal authority outside the meetings of the Board, and to conduct my relationships with the school staff, the local citizenry, and all media of communication on the basis of this fact.

5. To resist every temptation and outside pressure to use my position as a school board member to benefit either myself or any other individual or agency apart from the total interest of the school district.

6. To recognize that it is as important for the Board to understand and evaluate the educational program of the schools as it is to plan for the business of school operation.

7. To bear in mind under all circumstances that the primary function of the Board is to establish the policies by which the schools are to be administered, but that the administration of the educational program and the conduct of school business shall be left to the employed superintendent of schools and his professional and non-professional staff.

8. To welcome and encourage active cooperation by citizens, organizations, and the media of communication in the district with respect to establishing policy on current school operation and proposed future developments.

9. To support my State and National School Boards Associations.

10. Finally, to strive step by step toward ideal conditions for most effective school board service to my community, in a spirit of teamwork and devotion to public education as the greatest instrument for the preservation and perpetuation of our representative democracy.

APPENDIX E

Outline for a Ten-Session Workshop Study of School Board Functions and Relationships

This outline is offered to provide suggestions for leaders of groups desiring to study and discuss school board functions, responsibilites, and relationships in a systematic way. It should serve as a starting point in planning, and may be modified, expanded, or condensed so as to be best adapted to the needs and desires of any particular group.

Such a study program may be undertaken by a single board in a series of special monthly meetings devoted to its own "schooling." Or it may be the basis for a series of weekly evening sessions in connection with adult education courses in a high school or junior college, in which case board members from the surrounding area could be invited to enroll for a moderate fee. Or it may be used in planning regional or statewide workshops for new board members, meeting for two or three days of intensive study.

The success of any of these study groups will depend on (1) careful advance planning, (2) competent leadership for the course as a whole and for each session where some expertness of knowledge and experience is desirable, and (3) provision of adequate study and reference materials for the members of the group.

Some General Observations on the Outline

1. In the final selection of subjects under a given topic, and in the formulation of questions to be discussed, it is recommended that selectivity rather than all-inclusiveness be the guiding principle. Obviously, in a single two- to three-hour session, only the most pertinent and fundamental phases of a topic can be covered.

2. Even with the selectivity suggested above, care will have to be taken to keep the sessions from going off on tangents which, although they may be of undoubted interest and importance, would prevent the achievement of a good overall view of the board member's job by the end of the workshop sessions. Some such tangents might be federal support, teacher tenure, "merit" rating, strikes and sanctions, religious education, insurance problems, etc., etc. Further, if a participant brings up what seems to be a purely local or personal problem without a general lesson of interest to all, he should not be allowed to take up the group's time, but some way should be found to help him privately after the session.

3. In connection with assembling and using study and reference materials, it should be borne in mind that the literature on all of these topics is rather extensive and in great variety as to quality, availability, and usability. Care must be taken not to overwhelm the workshop participant. Session leaders should carefully review the literature on their respective topics and should select for use or reference only the most timely, direct, and helpful materials.

4. It is recommended that at the close of the first session, and of each subsequent session, an agenda sheet of the topic, scope, questions, and references for the following session be handed to each participant. Also a sheet of reproductions of a small number of selected excerpts from the literature, which will give the participant quickly some basic principles and viewpoints on the topic in question, so that he will at least have that much in mind when he comes to the session. Few participants will do any more self-preparation no matter how much it may be urged or desired.

Outline for the First Session

Topics: Introduction to the Workshop
What It Means To Be a School Board Member

Scope: Some or all of the following:

Public Education in America, Yesterday and Today—very brief background of historical development, goals, and theory of control. (*Note:* Probably better if woven in throughout the session than in one large dose.)

Unique Role of Lay Citizens in Control of Schools

Who School Board Members Are—what we know about the composition of boards

Qualifications for Effective Service (Main emphasis of the session should center here)

Outline for a Ten-Session Workshop

Board Members as Educational Statesmen—As Community Leaders

The School Board Member's Code of Ethics (See Appendix D) (*Note:* Many of the elements covered in the Code will point the way to topics at following sessions of the Workshop.)

Questions: (A few suggestions. Session leader to formulate final choices)

What is the relation between tax-supported education for all our people and the strength of our form of government and way of life?

Why do we in America believe in state and local control of public education, rather than in national control and administration?

Why is it essential that a school board member should possess as many as possible of the following qualifications? (Discuss each)

Personal qualities of leadership such as integrity, initiative, even temper, courage, perserverance, etc.

Belief in public education without reservation

Subordination of personal ambition to the public welfare

Wise judgment and sound discretion

Foresight and breadth of view that relates the educational program to local, state, national, and world needs

Ability to work cooperatively with others

Faith in the people as the sovereign authority in a democracy like ours

Outline for the Second Session

Topic: The Status of School Board Authority and Jurisdiction—with special reference to your own state

Scope: Some or all of the following:

School Board Status—An Instrument of the State, Selected and Functioning Locally

Essential State Law Respecting School Boards—Size of Boards; Terms of Office; Rotation; etc., etc.

School District Organization and Reorganization

Various Types of School Boards in the State—County, Village, Township, Community Unit, Consolidated, Elementary, Secondary, Junior College, etc.

Study of School Board Functions and Relationships

Relationships of School Boards to Other Governmental Agencies
—Municipal Boards, Park Boards, Library Boards, Political
Parties, etc.

School Board Independence, Fiscally and Otherwise

School Board Elections—When Held; How Conducted; etc.

The Caucus Plan for School Board Nominations (*Note:* Relate
to the Ninth Session)

School Board Responsibilities—Legal, Civic, Social, Economic,
Moral, and Ethical

Questions: (A few suggestions. Session Leader to formulate final
choices)

What authority has a school board member as an individual?

What authority has the school board as a whole? How is it
exercised?

What legal limitations are there on school board authority?

What are the discretionary powers of school boards?

How long should a school board member serve?

What are optimum conditions as to board size, terms, rotation
of members, etc.?

Should school board members be paid?

Why should a school board be fiscally independent?

What should a local board be doing to offset the threat of national control of public schools?

Outline for the Third Session

Topic: The School Board in Action (*Note:* Relate to the Fourth
Session)

Scope: Some or all of the following:

Organization of the Board—Chairman or President; Secretary or
Clerk; Committees (if any); etc.

School Board Meetings, Regular and Special—Time and Place;
Open to Public and Press; Preparation of Agenda; Procedures at Meetings; Minutes; etc.

The Policy-Making Function—How Identified and Exercised

Distinctions Between Policy Making and Administration of Policy (*Note:* Relate to the Seventh Session)

The Use of Legal Counsel

Orientation of New Board Members (Extensive treatment)

Outline for a Ten-Session Workshop

Questions: (A few suggestions. Session Leader to formulate final choices)

What are the specific responsibilities of the Chairman (President) of the Board?

Why are the functions of the Secretary (Clerk) of such importance?

What are the distinctions between policies and rules and regulations?

What are the advantages of written school board policies, annually reviewed and revised?

What steps should be followed in the formulation of policy?

What disposition should be made of the minutes of school board meetings?

How can a new school board member best prepare himself for effective service?

Outline for the Fourth Session

Topic: Stumbling Blocks to School Board Effectiveness

Scope: Some or all of the following:

Lack of Confidence and Frank Discussion
Among Individual Members of the Board
Between the Board and the Administrator
Between the Board and the Community—Citizens, Organizations, Media of Communication, etc.

Partisanship of Any Kind (Kinds to be identified)

Lack of Clearly Formulated Policies

Disproportionate Attention to Business Details to the Neglect of the Educational Program

Abuse of Executive Sessions

The Use of Standing Committees

Dual Administration Within the School System

Fiscal Dependence of the Board on Other Agencies of Government (*Note:* Relate to the Second Session)

Questions: (A few suggestions. Session Leader to formulate final choices)

What can be done to promote maximum school board effectiveness: By the individual board member? By the board chairman? By the superintendent?

Study of School Board Functions and Relationships

What are the dangers of any form of partisanship in relation to public education?

Why does a lack of written policies often lead to confusion and controversy?

How can a school board maintain a proper balance of attention between school business and the educational program?

What has experience shown to be the disadvantages of standing committees? How can their use be avoided?

When is an executive session of the board justifiable?

Why is a dual administration system a source of danger?

Why should a school board be fiscally independent?

Outline for the Fifth Session

Topic: School Board Responsibility for the Curriculum (*Note:* Relate to the Eighth Session to avoid overlapping)

Scope: Some or all of the following:

The Goals of Public Education: Local—State—National

How Curriculums Have Developed
The Fundamentals—State Requirements
The Supplementaries—Community Desires
The Growing Importance of the National Interest

How a School Board Should Exercise Its Responsibility for the School Program

Methods of Teaching in Relation to Various Subjects

The Need for Ample Instructional Materials

Modern Aids to Teaching—TV, Recordings, Teaching Machines and Programed Instruction, etc.

Provisions for Pupil Guidance (*Note:* Relate to the Seventh Session)

Questions: (A few suggestions. Session Leader to formulate final choices)

What should we be aiming for in public education today?

How can the local curriculum be adapted to state and national needs?

What interest should the school board take in the school program (curriculum)?

What is meant by a comprehensive high school?

Are we preparing our youth for life in a changing world?

How closely are we meeting the needs of individual children: the gifted? the average? the retarded? the handicapped?

What is a good counseling program?

Should the schools teach moral and ethical values? Religion?

What is the place in the curriculum of Physical Education? of Vocational Education? of Driver Education? etc.

Outline for the Sixth Session

Topic: School Board Responsibility for School Plant and Finance

Scope: Some or all of the following:

The Annual Budget—based on the needs of the School Program. Preparation; Review; Hearings; Adoption

School Plant Planning, Construction, and Maintenance
Short Range and Long Range Planning
Capital Outlay Procedures—Architects; Bids; Contracts; etc.
Bond Issues and Tax Referendums (*Note:* Relate to the Ninth Session)
Insurance: What kinds and how much?

Assessments and Tax Rates

Accounting System and Annual Report

Balance of School Support among Local, State, and National Sources of Revenue

Questions: (A few suggestions. Session Leader to formulate final choices)

How much should education cost?

How far ahead should a school board be in making long-range plans?

Who is responsible for preparing the school budget?

What steps are desirable in securing community support for the budget?

Are assessment and taxing procedures equitable?

How can a bond issue be floated successfully?

How is State support received and administered?

What is standard practice in school accounting to conform to state and national statistical requirements?

How can Federal money be provided for public education without undue Federal control?

Study of School Board Functions and Relationships

Outline for the Seventh Session

Topic: School Board Responsibility for Personnel

Scope: Some or all of the following:

Selecting the Superintendent of Schools

School Board—Administrator Relationships—Re-emphasis on Policy Making vs. Administration (*Note:* Relate to the Third Session)

School Board Relationships with the Staff—Professional—Non-Professional

Procedures re Employment, Transfers, Promotions, Terminations, etc.

Reward for Superior Teaching (*Note:* Relate to the Sixth Session)

Dealing with Professional Organizations, Unions, etc.

Tenure—Pros and Cons—Legal Status in Your State

School Board Pupil and Parent Relationships—Provisions for Counseling and Guidance (*Note:* Relate to the Fifth Session)

Questions: (A few suggestions. Session Leader to formulate final choices)

What are the qualifications of a good school administrator?

What procedures should be followed in selecting the superintendent of schools?

What should the school board expect of its superintendent?

What should the superintendent expect of his school board?

How can we recruit an adequate supply of competent teachers?

What can the school board do to promote the prestige, well-being, and growth of the teaching staff?

What are desirable tenure and retirement policies?

Should the board enter into collective bargaining with organizations of school personnel?

Outline for the Eighth Session

Topic: School Board Responsibility for Evaluation and Adaptation to Change (*Note:* Relate to the Fifth Session)

Scope: Some or all of the following:

What Makes a Good School

Needs of Today in Education. Are They being Met in Local Districts?

Outline for a Ten-Session Workshop

Methods of Evaluation

Use of Outsiders—Consultants and Surveys

Experimentation in Education

Questions: (A few suggestions. Session Leader to formulate final choices)

What changes have occurred in recent years that require us to take a closer look at what our schools are accomplishing?

By what means can a school board find out how effective the local school program is in relation to current needs in education?

What sources of help are available to a local board in evaluating the schools of its district?

When is a survey of the schools by an outside agency justifiable?

How complete should student cumulative records be?

Why is it worth while to keep track of students after graduation or drop out?

How rapidly should new materials and new methods of instruction be introduced into the school system?

What can be done to encourage some experimentation each year and to report its outcome most helpfully to all concerned?

Outline for the Ninth Session

Topic: School Board—Community Relationships

Scope: Some or all of the following:

Role of the School Board in Leading the Community

Role of the School Board in Following the Community

The Public Relations Role of the School Administrator—Of Teachers

Importance of the School Secretary as a Public Relations Person

School Board Relations with the Media of Communication—Press; Radio; TV; etc.

Criticisms of the Schools—Local; Nationwide

Pressures on the School Board

Parent-Teacher Associations—Their Function and Value

Other Community Organizations That Affect the Schools

Citizens Advisory Committees—Their Use and Abuse

Study of School Board Functions and Relationships

Questions: (A few suggestions. Session Leader to formulate final choices)

Should all the people have all the facts all the time about their schools? If so, in what ways can this goal best be accomplished?

What responsibility has each of the following for maintaining cooperative relationships between the schools and the community: The Board? The Superintendent? The Teachers? The Parents? The Taxpayers? The Press? Community Organizations? etc.

How should the school board meet criticisms of the schools?

How can the school board deal effectively with pressure groups?

From what sources may crises in school affairs arise?

How can crises best be anticipated and avoided?

What principles should be followed in the organization and functioning of citizens committees on school affairs?

What principles should govern the use of the caucus plan for school board nominations? (*Note:* Relate to the Second Session)

Outline for the Tenth Session

Topics: School Boards Association—Their Scope and Functions
Summary of the Ten-Weeks Workshop

Scope: As much as desired concerning:

Reasons for Associations of School Boards

Your State Association of School Boards
History and Ranking Among State Associations
Organization, Financing, and Services
Regional and Statewide Meetings
Relations with the State Legislature
Cooperation with Other Statewide Organizations

The National School Boards Association, Inc.
History, Growth, and Importance to American Education
Organization, Membership, and Services
The National School Board Convention
Affiliation with Other Nationwide Groups Concerned with
Public Education—Professional and Lay

How State and National Associations Recruit Their Leadership

Outline for a Ten-Session Workshop

Questions: (A few suggestions. Session Leader to formulate final choices)

Why should a local school board hold membership in its State Association? In the National Association?

What should a local school board expect to contribute to and receive from its Association memberships?

What qualities in a local board member may determine his selection for leadership in a regional division of his State School Boards Association, and later, perhaps, in the State Association itself, or even in the National Association?

Beatitudes of a Leader

BLESSED *is the leader who has not sought the high places, but who has been drafted into service because of his ability and willingness to serve.*

BLESSED *is the leader who knows where he is going, why he is going, and how to get there.*

BLESSED *is the leader who knows no discouragement, who presents no alibi.*

BLESSED *is the leader who knows how to lead without being dictatorial; true leaders are humble.*

BLESSED *is the leader who seeks for the best for those he serves.*

BLESSED *is the leader who leads for the good of the most concerned, and not for the personal gratification of his own ideas.*

BLESSED *is the leader who develops leaders while leading.*

BLESSED *is the leader who marches with the group, interprets correctly the signs on the pathway that leads to success.*

BLESSED *is the leader who has his head in the clouds but his feet on the ground.*

BLESSED *is the leader who considers leadership an opportunity for service.*

AUTHOR UNKNOWN

APPENDIX F

Procedures for Selecting
the Superintendent of Schools

Note: The material for these pages has been adapted, by special permission, from the February, 1956 issue of *Administrator's Notebook,* published by the Midwest Administration Center of the University of Chicago. This issue, entitled "Selecting the Superintendent" by Thomas R. Bowman and William W. Savage was, in turn, a condensed summary of an extensive study by John E. Baker, 1952, reported in an unpublished Ph.D. dissertation on "The Selection of Superintendents of Schools by Boards of Education."

No list of suggested procedures is necessarily appropriate in its entirety for every school board. However, there are at least three broad principles which should guide a board's action:

1. It should develop and follow a definite policy.

2. It should define clearly the position it has to fill and the requirements necessary for the job.

3. It should act as a board rather than as a disjointed collection of assorted individuals.

On the basis of his study, Dr. Baker developed a tentative guide for use by school boards that contains the following fourteen steps which seem important in selecting an administrator:

1. Announce the vacancy publicly.

2. Name the person to whom application should be made.

3. Make it clear that applicants will be interviewed only by the board as a whole.

4. Develop a list of qualifications for the position (see page 306).

5. Ask the directors of several placement bureaus to furnish, without the knowledge of the candidates, the credentials for three or four candidates who meet the qualifications established by the board.

6. Ask several successful school leaders who are not likely to be interested in the job themselves to nominate qualified candidates.

7. Invite applications from qualified local staff members, but emphasize that selection will be made upon the basis of the candidate's qualifications for the position.
8. Obtain the credentials of all persons who apply and any others the board wishes to consider.
9. Screen the candidates to identify the ten or twelve who are best qualified.
10. Invite each of the best qualified candidates to an extended interview with the whole board and pay their expenses. (Invite only one candidate for any single interview period.)
11. Plan the interview to obtain evidence concerning the degree to which the candidate possesses the qualifications desired by the board (see opposite page). Record should be kept of each interview.
12. After all the best qualified candidates have been interviewed, select three or four for final consideration. (In this process, the board may obtain each candidate's written reactions to school policies and problems, visit the candidate's school and community, check carefully all of his references, etc.)
13. Recall the most promising candidates for a second interview.
14. Make a final, unanimous selection and agree on the terms of employment. (The contract should be for more than one year.)

*Dr. Baker's Suggested List of Qualifications (see Step 4, page 305)

The following are suggested qualities which board members may wish to consider. Other qualities may be needed in your particular community.

1. Ability to make decisions.
2. Knowledge, skills, and understandings of the purposes and processes of education.
3. Ability to assume and delegate responsibility.
4. Ability to organize and to give directions.
5. Ability to take initiative and to stimulate others to drive toward educational goals.
6. Ability to select and to improve personnel.
7. Ability to communicate well with others.
8. Disposition to cooperate.
9. Good health and high energy output.
10. Professional preparation.
11. Demonstration of effective leadership.

*Dr. Baker's Suggested List of Questions (see Step 11, opposite)

The candidate's response to the following questions, among others, may assist the board to judge whether he has the qualifications desired.

1. What do you consider to be the most important purposes of a public school system?
2. If you were to inherit a staff of traditionally-minded teachers who are smug and satisfied with what they are doing, what would you do?
3. How would you prepare a school budget?
4. How have you kept people informed about the schools?
5. What improvements have been made in education as a result of your work? How did you assist in bringing these changes about?
6. What factors have kept you from accomplishing what you feel should have been done?
7. How would you distinguish between the functions of the board, the superintendent, and the principals?

---

*The lists of qualifications and questions developed by Dr. Baker in his doctorate study were supplied by the Midwest Administration Center of the University of Chicago, with the personal permission of Dr. Baker himself, to supplement the procedures taken from the *Administrator's Notebook.*

APPENDIX G

Barriers and Break-Throughs
of School Architecture*

by WILLIAM CAUDILL, Research Architect

School people and architects have reason to be proud of their progress in school construction. But there are still barriers to break through before we achieve the best in school architecture.

Some of the Barriers:

1. *Architectural Prejudice:* Preconceived ideas as to what a school should look like, unwillingness to accept a new architecture, and the lack of understanding of a dynamic society which must have a dynamic architecture, hold back rapid progress toward better school plants.

---

*Prepared by the author in connection with the N.S.B.A. Kansas City Symposium (see Chapter 29) and included here by special permission.

Barriers of School Architecture

2. *Educational Prejudice:* That "what's good enough for me is good enough for junior" attitude of people responsible for the education of the community, together with the demands of these same people who insist that their school buildings be as obsolete as their educational programs, create great barriers to school building progress.

3. *Obsolete Codes:* Old codes, even some new ones, and misinterpretations of both, often dictate excessive construction expenses.

4. *Sound Technology:* The use of movable partitions, light wall panel construction, open planning techniques, and higher sound level teaching activities make sound problems more difficult to solve.

5. *Building Complexity:* Too many trades stepping on one another's toes, involved in too many building processes, slows down construction.

6. *Too Small Building Units:* Thousands of small pieces of material go into an ordinary school building, necessitating high labor costs to put them together. What the architects need are fewer and larger units with which to formulate economical, beautiful school building solutions. We are not talking about prefabricated schools or classrooms, but about low cost, low maintenance prefab building units for walls, floors, ceilings, roofs, windows and doors, and for plumbing, heating, and lighting.

7. *Static Thinking:* Use of stock plans and the static thinking behind them is one of the greatest barriers of all. The people who build these barriers must be made to realize that good design pays off and actually costs less than poor design.

Some of the Break-Throughs:

1. *Group Dynamics of Planning:* At last the architects, the engineers, the educators, the patrons, and in some cases the children are beginning to find that teamwork pays off in better school design.

2. *Research Approach:* A few, but influential, creative architects, working together with creative educators, have made substantial progress through a research attitude approach in solving school building problems. They are never satisfied with just answers, but continually search for a *better* answer to problems of educational feasibility, lighting, sound, heating, ventilation, and structures.

3. *Plan Types:* School planners are beginning to realize that in order to solve their problems they must have at their disposal all kinds of plan types—finger plans, quadruplexes, campus plans, back-to-back arrangements, single loaded corridors, double loaded corridors, com-

308

binations of the two, spokewheels, or any other combination of geometric arrangement—and that the traditional, code-dictated double loaded corridor arrangement is just one of the many.

4. *Learning Walls:* Thinking school planners no longer consider the classroom wall as a mere wall, but as a vertical teaching surface.

5. *Outdoor Learning:* The concept that learning does not stop at the door threshold or the window sill—is opening up new opportunities for effective and economical educational facilities.

6. *Teaching Space Dividers:* One of the major break-throughs of recent years is the use of the teaching space dividers which are in essence pieces of educational furniture used to subdivide a large loft space into teaching stations—an economical and effective solution to the cry for flexible classroom wings.

7. *Student Center:* The slow but final recognition that every school should be designed to be the nicest place in town for youth to work and live has given school architecture and the children the so-called student center or commons—the living room of the school plant.

8. *New Materials:* The plastic bubble skylight, transparent and low brightness glass, sandwiched insulated wall panels, and other items have given impetus to school building progress.

9. *Low Ceilings:* Research in lighting and ventilation has led the way to the use of lower and more economical ceilings over better lighted and better ventilated spaces.

10. *Renaissance of Top Lighting:* Improved lighting techniques, materials, and flashing methods allow school buildings to be more compact, better lighted, and better adapted for maximum flexibility.

11. *Landscaping:* The acceptance that a successful school plant is more than a building situated in the middle of a city block with Christmas-tree-like planting on each side of a main entrance has given us beautiful, functional sites with terraces, screens, and outdoor teaching spaces, as well as green lawns.

12. *Movable Equipment:* Another break-through for education has been the development of movable furniture and equipment to facilitate the activity concept of learning.

13. *Humanistic Architecture:* More and more school planners have accepted the premise that achitecture can help the child to grow and develop mentally, physically, emotionally, and socially, and have made great effort to produce a more humanistic architecture—healthful, functional, non-confining, colorful, warm, friendly environment for children.

INDEX

310

Index

Index

314

Index

Index

Index

"We know that we ought to pass on to our children
the best and noblest in our heritage;
surely never the worst and the meanest.
We know also that these children, in their maturity,
will have to face new problems in life,
new ways of living, working, and governing themselves,
and that we must seek to develop in them
those qualities which constitute strength for life —
thoughtfulness, application, consideration for others,
and willingness to face strange situations squarely."

— CHARLES A. BEARD

320

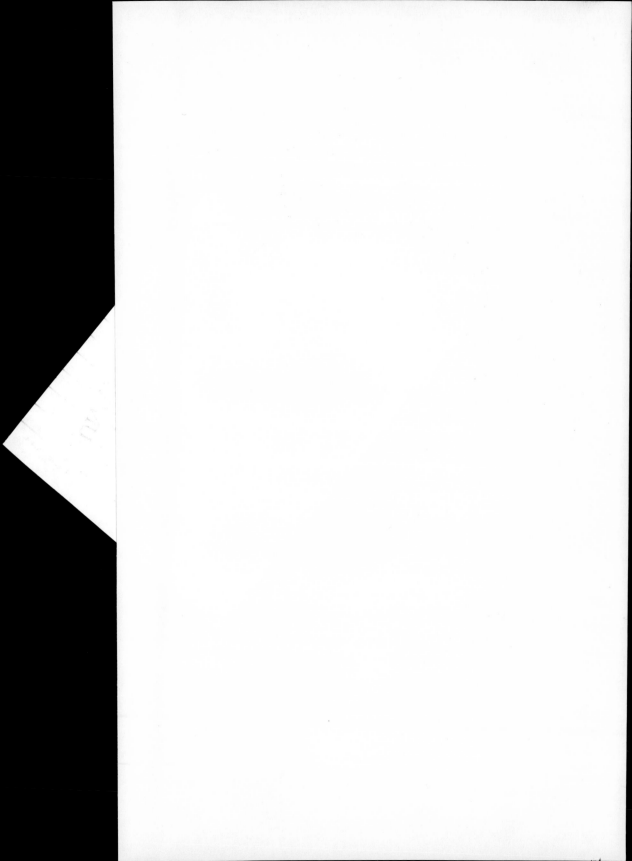

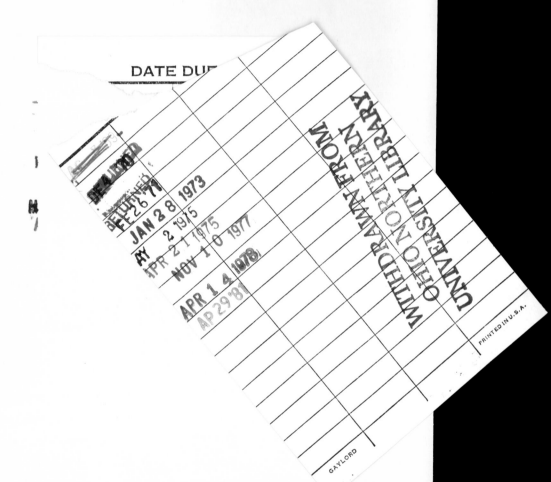